LEARNING A SECOND LANGUAGE
THROUGH INTERACTION

STUDIES IN BILINGUALISM (SiBil)

Volume 17

Rod Ellis

Learning a Second Language through Interaction

LEARNING A SECOND LANGUAGE THROUGH INTERACTION

ROD ELLIS
University of Auckland

With contributions from
Sandra Fotos, Qien He, Rick Heimbach, Hide Takashima,
Yoshihiro Tanaka, Atsuko Yamazaki and Hoda Zaki

JOHN BENJAMINS PUBLISHING COMPANY
AMSTERDAM/PHILADELPHIA

The paper used in this publication meets the minimum requirements of American National Standard for Information Sciences — Permanence of Paper for Printed Library Materials, ANSI Z39.48-1984.

Library of Congress Cataloging-in-Publication Data

Ellis, Rod.
  Learning a second language through interaction / Rod Ellis ; with contributions from Sandra Fotos ... [et al.].
    p.   cm. -- (Studies in Bilingualism, ISSN 0928-1533 ; v. 17)
  Includes bibliographical references (p.) and index.
  1. Second language acquisition. 2. Interaction analysis in education. I. Fotos, Sandra. II. Title III. Series.
P118.2.E38   1999
401'.93--dc21   99-40612
ISBN 90 272 4124 4 (Eur.) / 1 55619 736 5 (US) (Hb; alk. paper)   CIP
ISBN 90 272 4125 2 (Eur.) / 1 55619 737 3 (US) (Pb; alk. paper)

John Benjamins Publishing Co. • P.O.Box 75577 • 1070 AN Amsterdam • The Netherlands
John Benjamins North America • P.O.Box 27519 • Philadelphia PA 19118-0519 • USA

Table of Contents

Acknowledgments   vii

Preface   ix

SECTION 1
Introduction   1

1.   Theoretical Perspectives on Interaction and Language Learning 3
     Rod Ellis

SECTION 2
Input, Interaction and Vocabulary Learning   33

2.   Factors in the Incidental Acquisition of Second Language
     Vocabulary from Oral Input   35
     Rod Ellis

3.   Modified Input and the Acquisition of Word meanings by
     Children and Adults   63
     Rod Ellis, Rick Heimbach, Yoshihiro Tanaka and Atsuko Yamazaki

4.   Modified Output and the Acquisition of Word Meanings   115
     Xien He and Rod Ellis

5.   Modified Input, Language Aptitude and the Acquisition of Word
     Meanings   133
     Hirota Nagata, David Aline and Rod Ellis

6.   Learning Vocabulary Through Interacting With a Written Text   151
     Hoda Zaki and Rod Ellis

SECTION 3
Interaction and Grammar Learning   171

7. Output Enhancement and the Acquisition of the Past Tense   173
    Hide Takashima and Rod Ellis

8. Communicating About Grammar   189
    Sandra Fotos and Rod Ellis

SECTION 4
Pedagogical Perspectives   209

9. Making the Classroom Acquisition Rich   211
    Rod Ellis

SECTION 5
Conclusion   231

10. Retrospect and Prospect   233
    Rod Ellis

References   259

Index   281

Acknowledgments

We gratefully acknowledge the following permissions to reprint material from previously published work: Cambridge University Press for R. Ellis and X. He 'The Roles of Modified Output and Input in the Incidental Acquisition of Word Meanings', *Studies in Second Language Acquisition* 21: 285–301; Defense Language Institute Foreign Language Center for R. Ellis 'Factors in the Incidental Acquisition of Second Language Vocabulary from Oral Input: A Review Essay, *Applied Language Learning* 5: 1–32; Language Learning for R. Ellis, Y. Tanaka and A. Yamazaki, 'Classroom Interaction, Comprehension, and the Acquisition of L2 Word Meanings', *Language Learning* 44: 449–491; Oxford University Press for R. Ellis, 'Modified Oral Input and the Acquisition of Word Meanings', *Applied Linguistics* 16: 409–441; Pergamon Press for 'Bugs and Birds: Children's Acquisition of Second Language Vocabulary through Interaction', *System* 25: 247–259; SEAMEO Regional Language Centre for R. Ellis 'Discourse Control and the Acquisition-Rich Classroom' in W. Renandya and G. Jacobs (eds.). *Learners and Language Learning* pp. 145–171. Teachers of English to Speakers of Other Languages for S. Fotos and R. Ellis, 'Communicating About Grammar: A Task-Based Approach', *TESOL Quarterly* 25: 605–628.

Preface

This book has two purposes. First, it is intended to contribute to the growing body of theory and research that has addressed the role of interaction in second language (L2) learning. Second, on a more personal note, it serves as a testimony to the years I spent at Temple University, first in Japan and then in Philadelphia, representing the work undertaken by myself and a number of students during this period.

The role of interaction in L2 learning is not an uncontroversial matter. On the one hand there are theories of L2 learning that minimize the contribution that interaction makes, emphasizing instead the centrality of learner internal mechanisms. Theories based on Universal Grammar view interaction as neither necessary nor especially important for acquisition. At best, interaction is seen as just one way in which learners can obtain the input needed to trigger parameter setting and resetting. On the other hand there are theories that view interaction as quite central in the process of L2 acquisition. Starting with the seminal work of Evelyn Hatch in the 1970s, 'interactionists' such as Long, Pica and Gass have gradually accumulated a range of theoretical arguments in support of the general claim that, while not strictly speaking necessary, interaction nevertheless constitutes the primary means by which language learners obtain data for language learning, both in the sense that interaction is how most learners obtain input and in the sense that the input obtained through interaction works better for acquisition than input obtained in other ways. Starting from Hatch's axiom that learners learn the grammar of the language *through* interaction rather than learn grammar *in order* to interact, second language acquisition (SLA) researchers have developed and tested theories relating to how interaction assists acquisition. Much of this work has taken place from the guiding perspective of an input-output model of L2 learning but, more recently, researchers have begun to pay attention to other theoretical perspectives, in particular those that view interaction as a sociocultural phenomenon in which learning actually takes place. This book is firmly interactionist in outlook and no attempt is made to debate the merits of such an outlook in relation to innatist outlooks. In general, the input-output model frames the approach to interaction that is adopted. However, recognition is given to the need for alternative theoretical perspectives. While I see no need for a paradigm shift from an input-output model to these alternative perspectives, I can see great advantage in widening the scope of interactionist research in SLA by adopting a pluralistic stance.

Although most of the chapters in this book were written after I left Temple University, it remains true that Temple University is where the work on which these chapters are based took place. Temple University afforded me the time to develop my own thinking on the role of interaction. It also gave me the opportunity to work with some remarkably able students on a number of classroom studies of interaction. I am indebted, therefore, to both the university itself and to the individual students, whose names appear on the title page of this book. Without the support of the university and the perspicacity and industry of the students this book would not have been possible.

Rod Ellis
University of Auckland
April 1999

Section 1

Introduction

This book explores the relationship between interaction and second language (L2) acquisition. It addresses three general questions:

1. In what ways does interaction/input contribute to L2 acquisition?
2. Which types of interaction/input promote L2 acquisition?
3. What kind of language pedagogy is needed to ensure that classroom learners experience acquisition-rich interaction?

These questions are addressed both in chapters that review interactionist theories of L2 acquisition and in those that report specific research studies. The chapter in this introductory section provides a general review of interactionist theories.

It is useful to distinguish two different but related meanings of 'interaction'. First, interaction can be viewed as the social behaviour that occurs when one person communicates with another. Interaction in this sense is *interpersonal*. It can occur face-to-face, in which case it usually takes place through the oral medium, or it can occur as displaced activity, in which case it generally involves the written medium. In some sense, oral interpersonal interaction is basic to human communication, as all communities, whether literate or not, engage in it. Also, it constitutes the primary purpose for our species-specific language capacity and the means by which it has developed both phylogenetically and ontogenetically. This book will concern itself mainly with oral interaction of the interpersonal kind.

Second, interaction can occur inside our minds, both when we engage in the kind of 'private speech' discussed by Vygotsky (1978), and, more covertly, when different modules of the mind interact to construct an understanding of or a response to some phenomenon. In reading, for example, we draw interactively on our ability to decode print, our stored knowledge of the language we are reading and the content schemata through which our knowledge of the world is organised. Interaction of this kind, then, is *intrapersonal*. This book will also consider intrapersonal interaction and its relation to second language (L2) learning.

The purpose of the following chapter is to outline the theories of interpersonal and intrapersonal interaction that inform the rest of the book. There are, of

course, a large number of such theories. However, three in particular have
figured in L2 research and we will restrict the discussion to these. They are
Long's Interaction Hypothesis (Long 1983a, 1996), socio-cultural theory, as this
has been applied to L2 learning (e.g. Lantolf and Appel 1994; Lantolf 2000), and
depth of processing theory (Craik and Lockhart 1972; Craik and Tulving 1975).
These theories all address the relationship between interaction, in its interpersonal
and intrapersonal forms, and language learning. However, they do so in very
different ways and involve very different discourses. They will be viewed,
therefore, as incommensurable and no attempt to construct an integrative theory
will be made. However, Chapter 1 will conclude with a general discussion of the
'interactionist perspective' on L2 learning.

CHAPTER 1

Theoretical Perspectives on Interaction and Language Learning

Rod Ellis

What do we mean when we talk of 'interaction'? In fact, we can mean two quite different things. Generally, the term is used to refer to the interpersonal activity that arises during face-to-face communication. However, it can also refer to the intrapersonal activity involved in mental processing. Furthermore, interpersonal and intraspersonal interaction are closely connected with regard to both our use and our acquisition of language. That is, intrapersonal interaction is required in order to interact interpersonally and, also, interpersonal interaction serves to trigger intrapersonal operations, including those that are involved in language acquisition. This chapter is especially concerned with the relationship between interpersonal and intrapersonal interaction. It examines three theories that address this relationship, albeit in very different ways; the Interaction Hypothesis, Socio-cultural Theory and Depth of Processing Theory.

The Interaction Hypothesis

The Interaction Hypothesis (IH) draws on early work in ethnomethodology which examined how native speakers repair breakdowns in communication (e.g. Schegloff, Jefferson and Sacks 1977) and on Hatch's (1978b) key insight that learners' can learn a second language (L2) *through* the process of interacting rather than just manifesting what they have already learned *in* interaction. The IH concerns itself with one particular kind of interaction — that which has become known as the **negotiation of meaning** This concerns the conversational exchanges that arise when interlocutors seek to prevent a communicative impasse occurring or to remedy an actual impasse that has arisen. These exchanges involve what

Long (1980) has called **interactional modifications** (i.e. changes to the structure of a conversation to accommodate potential or actual problems of understanding). They contrast with the **input modifications** found in foreigner talk (i.e. changes, both grammatical and sometimes ungrammatical, in the formal properties of utterances addressed to learners). Such modifications may arise as a result of interactional modification but they can also occur in monologic discourse.

According to Varonis and Gass (1985), conversational exchanges involving communication problems have a definite structure, involving two stages, a trigger and a resolution. The latter can be further broken down into an indicator, a response and optional reaction to the response (see example (1) below). Such exchanges are accomplished by means of a variety of conversational strategies, such as comprehension checks (which can serve to head-off potential problems) and confirmation checks and requests for clarification (which are used to deal with problems that have arisen). These strategies often lead to **modified input** (i.e. input that has been adjusted to facilitate the interlocutors' comprehension). For example, in (1) student 2 uses a confirmation check to signal a communication problem and in the process modifies 'retire' by producing it in the correct form.

(1)   Student 1: And what is your mmm father's job?
        Student 2: My father is now retire.   Trigger
        Student 1: Retired?   Indicator of problem
        Student 2: Yes.   Resolution: Response
        Student 1: Oh, yes.   Reaction
        (From Varonis and Gass 1985: 74)[1]

The general claim of the IH is that engaging in interpersonal oral interaction in which communication problems arise and are negotiated *facilitates* language acquisition. That is, it creates conditions that foster the internal processes responsible for interlanguage development. Thus, the IH addresses how **incidental acquisition** (i.e. the acquisition that occurs, with of without awareness, when learners are primarily concerned with trying to communicate) takes place. It does not address **intentional acquisition** (i.e. deliberate attempts on the part of the learner to study and learn the L2). An assumption of the IH is that the acquisition of linguistic competence is primarily incidental rather than intentional.

IH researchers are at pains to emphasise that interaction involving meaning negotiation only facilitates acquisition; it does not *cause* acquisition to take place. In other words, modified interaction can only 'set the scene for potential learning' (Gass, Mackey and Pica 1998: 304). Furthermore, as Pica (1996b) has pointed out the Interaction Hypothesis does not claim that meaning negotiation is the only type of interaction in which the conditions that foster learning arise.

She acknowledges that 'uninterrupted communication' (i.e. communication where there is no problem of understanding) can also contribute to acquisition, although, like Long, she maintains that learners' data needs are best met through negotiation.

The early version of the IH was closely associated with the Input Hypothesis (Krashen 1985). This claims that learners will acquire an L2 when they have access to comprehensible input and when their 'affective filter' is low (e.g. they are motivated to learn and are not anxious) so that the comprehended input is made available to the internal acquisitional mechanisms for processing. Krashen viewed interaction as just one of three ways in which input can be made comprehensible, the other two being simplified input, such as that found in graded readers, and learners' use of context to help decode messages in the L2. Krashen has consistently argued that, although interaction can serve as a good source of comprehensible input, it is neither necessary nor especially privileged (see Krashen 1982 and 1998). Long (1980, 1983a) agreed with Krashen that comprehensible input was necessary for acquisition but differed from him with regard to the importance of interactionally modified input, which he claimed was especially beneficial in that it supplied learners with information relating to linguistic forms that were problematic to them. However, the early version of the IH (like the later) did not claim that such input was necessary or sufficient for acquisition.

To facilitate empirical research based on the IH Long (1985) suggested that researchers follow three steps. First, they need to show that conversational adjustments that arise when meaning is negotiated promote the comprehension of input. Second, they need to show that comprehensible input promotes acquisition. Third, they can then deduce that conversational adjustments assist acquisition. The research that ensued focused on the first of these steps. It demonstrated that when learners had the opportunity to negotiate meaning they were better able to comprehend input (e.g. Pica, Young and Doughty 1987; Loschky 1994). Other studies focused on identifying the participatory, task and learner variables that influenced whether and to what extent meaning negotiation took place (e.g. Pica and Doughty 1985; Duff 1984; Gass and Varonis 1984). However, until very recently, there have been few studies that have investigated directly whether comprehension results in acquisition or indeed whether interactionally modified input assists acquisition. Instead, researchers relied on indirect evidence for the necessity of comprehension for language acquisition (e.g. studies of the hearing children of deaf parents which showed acquisition was delayed because of an absence of comprehensible input — see Long 1983a).[2]

This early version of the IH was challenged on a number of fronts. First, Long's second hypothesis, that comprehension promotes acquisition, was questioned. A number of theorists (e.g. Sharwood Smith 1986; Faerch and

Kasper 1986) have argued that it is necessary to distinguish input processing for comprehension and input processing for language learning. Learners can comprehend input by drawing on context and their schematic knowledge of the world in such a way that they do not have to attend to the actual linguistic forms in the input. They can infer the meanings of messages. This results in successful comprehension but not in acquisition. For acquisition to take place, learners need to attend to the linguistic forms in the input and the meanings they realise and to compare what they notice with their own output. In these ways they can obtain the data they need to restructure their interlanguages. In such cases, acquisition may take place with or without message comprehension. In other words, according to this position, it is 'processing input' rather than 'comprehending input' that is crucial for acquisition. In many cases, of course, the two may co-occur but clearly occasions can arise where they do not.

Second, Long's claim that interactionally modified input was especially beneficial for acquisition was challenged. We have already noted that Krashen disputed this claim, arguing that simplified input that was not interactionally derived (i.e. **premodified input**) served equally well. There is, in fact, substantial support for the claim that premodified input is highly effective in promoting comprehension (see Chaudron 1988 for a review of this research), although, again, until recently there has been no research that has investigated whether premodified input facilitates acquisition. A question of some interest is whether interactionally modified input is more effective in promoting comprehension than premodified input. Pica, Young and Doughty (1987) investigated this question in a study that compared learners' comprehension of directions under three conditions; a baseline condition (which involved listening to directions of the kind native speakers address to other native speakers), a premodified condition (where baseline directions were simplified in accordance with the kinds of modifications native speakers make when they address non-native speakers) and an interactionally modified condition (where the learners were given the opportunity to negotiate the directions if they did not understand them). Pica, Young and Doughty found that learners comprehended the directions best in the interactionally modified condition and worst in the baseline condition, with comprehension in the premodified condition intermediate. It should be noted, however, that the interactionally modified input condition took considerably longer than the premodified condition. To address the role of time, Pica (1989) carried out a study where the length of time taken up by the premodified input and interactionally modified input was controlled. In this study, the comprehension scores of the two groups were not statistically different. Other studies have not controlled for time. Gass and Varonis (1994) report that interactionally modified input was more effective than premodified input for both learners' comprehension and their subsequent production of directives in communicative tasks. Loschky (1994), in a similarly designed study to Pica, Young and Doughty's, also found that interactionally modified input led to better overall comprehension than premodified input. Loschky also investigated the relative effects of the two types of modified input on the acquisition of Japanese locative expressions, but found no difference. This research, therefore, provides only limited evidence in support of the IH. First, it is not clear, whether the beneficial effects of interactionally modified input on comprehension are the result of more input and longer processing time or of the kinds of qualitative differences Long and others have claimed to be important. Second, it has failed to show that interactionally modified input works better than premodified input in supporting acquisition.

There are other criticisms of the research based on the early version of the IH (see Ellis 1991). First, as Hawkins (1985) has shown, learners often fake comprehension. That is, they frequently pretend they have understood as a result of negotiating a comprehension problem when, in fact, they have not. Clearly, there are social constraints that influence the extent to which learners are prepared to negotiate to achieve understanding. Second, Aston (1986) has pointed out that the forms used to realize the topic management functions associated with meaning negotiation can also be used to realize entirely different functions. For example, modified repetitions of learner utterances (such as that in (1) above) need not be confirmation checks; they might serve to show that the addressee is in fact following what the speaker has said (i.e. they can function as conversational continuants). The identification of negotiation sequences, therefore, is problematic, although this is rarely acknowledged by IH researchers. Two other criticisms are potentially even more serious for the hypothesis. In general, researchers have sought to evaluate the quality of interaction for acquisition by simply counting instances of conversational modifications. However, it does not follow that more negotiation leads to more and better comprehension. Ehrlich, Avery and Yorio (1989) report a study showing that, on occasions, native speakers over-elaborated in the attempt to remedy learners' problems and that this had an overall detrimental effect on their comprehension. In other words, it would seem to be the *quality* of negotiation that is as much if not more important than the sheer quantity. Finally, Satos's research (1986) has led researchers to recognize that there may be some aspects of the L2, in particular inflectional morphology, that do not get negotiated. Sato found that the two Vietnamese children she investigated longitudinally failed to show any progress in acquiring past tense markers over a ten month period and suggests that one reason for this was that the interactional support they were given obviated the need for them to attend to these features.

The later version of the IH has gone some way to address these criticisms. Long's (1996) updated IH emphasizes that the role of negotiation is to facilitate the kinds of conscious 'noticing' that Schmidt (1990, 1994, 1996) has argued is required in order for learners to process input for 'intake'. Long writes:

> ... it is proposed that environmental contributions to acquisition are mediated by selective attention and the learner's developing L2 processing capacity, and that these resources are brought together more usefully, although not exclusively, during 'negotiation for meaning'. (p. 414)

In contrast to the early version of the IH, which simply postulated an effect for comprehensible input, this later version seeks to account for *how* interactionally modified input contributes to acquisition by specifying the learner internal mechanisms that are involved. Interactionally modified input works for acquisition when (1) it assists learners to notice linguistic forms in the input and (2) the forms that are noticed lie within the learner's 'processing capacity'. In effect, then, the updated version of the IH incorporates both an interpersonal and an intrapersonal view of interaction. Interpersonal interaction helps learners to notice features in the input; intrapersonal activity, involving different kinds of processing operations, is required for learners to process and acquire from the negotiated input.

Learners are credited with a limited processing capacity which makes it difficult for them to focus simultaneously on both meaning and form. Robinson (1995), in a review of **information processing models**, discusses capacity models[3] which credit learners with the ability to attend simultaneously to both message and code. However, dual processing of this kind only becomes possible when learners are able to draw on automatized knowledge of the L2. VanPatten (1988) has shown that learners, particularly beginning learners, have great difficulty in attending to form when they are focused on meaning and, conversely, of extracting meaning when they are focused on form. It is not difficult to see the connection between the IH and an information processing model of this type; the opportunity to negotiate meaning provides learners with the time they need to attend to form while processing the message content. Furthermore, as discussed below, it can also show learners how these forms are constructed and how they map onto meaning.

The new version of the IH also affords a much richer view of how negotiation can assist language learning. As in the early version, negotiation is seen as enabling learners to obtain comprehensible input, thereby supplying them with **positive evidence** (i.e. 'models of what is grammatical and acceptable' — Long 1996: 413). The exchange in (1) above illustrates this; student (2) receives a model of the past tense form, 'retired'. Pica's detailed analyses of negotiation sequences (see, for example, Pica 1992, 1996a) have shown how negotiation can give salience to both form-function relationships and also how it helps learners to segment message data into linguistic units. In (2), for example, the native speaker's modification helps the learner to segment a constituent ('above') in the input. Such external segmentation processes can be expected to assist 'noticing' because they help learners to analyze chunks of input into their parts.

(2)   NS: with a small pat of butter on it and
       above the plate
                        NNS hm hmm
                        what is buvdaplate?
       NS: above
                        NNS: above the plate
       NS: yeah
       (Pica 1992: 225)

Pica (1992) distinguishes between three kinds of modification that can occur in negotiated input; semantic, segmentation (as in (2) above) and movement of constituents. She reports that out of the 569 negotiation sequences she investigated 346 involved one or more of these types of modification, a remarkably high percentage. However, she also reports that there were no instances of morphological modifications, a finding that bears out Sato's claim that interaction may contribute little to the acquisition of morphosyntax. It should be noted, however, that although there is now a rich body of descriptive research documenting how negotiation leads to input that has been modified in ways that can potentially promote acquisition there is still no research demonstrating a link between such input and acquisition. Linnell (1995), for example, failed to show that learners who engaged in interaction with negotiation outperformed learners who experienced interaction with no negotiation or learners with no opportunity to interact at all. He found that 'syntactization appeared to continue regardless of the type of discourse learners engaged in' (p. 96). It remains to be shown, therefore, that Pica's and Long's claims regarding the positive evidence learners obtain from negotiated input actually works for acquisition.

The later version of the IH also posits two other ways in which interaction can contribute to acquisition; through the provision of **negative evidence** and through opportunities for **modified output.** Long (1996: 413) defines negative evidence as input that provides 'direct or indirect evidence of what is grammatical'. It arises when learners receive feedback on their own attempts to use the L2. One of the major ways in which this takes place is through 'recasts' (i.e. utterances that rephrase a learner's utterance 'by changing one or more sentence components (subject, verb or object) while still referring to its central meanings' (Long op cit; 435). (3) provides an example. Here the learner produces an erroneous utterance ('I don't have a telephones picture') which the native speaker immediately recasts by modifying the direct object to 'a picture of a telephone'.

(3)   NS: and right next to her a phone rings?
                            NNS: forring?
        NS: a phone? Telephone? Is there a
        telephone next to her?
                            NNS: yeah ... I don't have a telephones picture.
        NS: you don't have a picture of a telephone?
        (Pica 1996a: 8)

Long argues that recasts provide the opportunity for 'cognitive comparison' (i.e. for learners to compare their own deviant productions with grammatically correct input). Gass (1997) suggests that the negative evidence learners obtain through negotiation serves only to *initiate* interlanguage change but that permanent restructuring may only take place after an 'incubation period' during which the learner has access to input that provides further evidence of the need for the change.

A number of studies have investigated recasts in conversations involving L2 learners (see Long 1996 for a review). Richardson (1993) found that in adult NS-NNS conversations the NSs were more likely to recast ungrammatical utterances that were easy to remedy and very rarely provided multiple corrections. Richardson also found that learners were more likely to imitate corrective than non-corrective recasts. Oliver (1995) distinguished moves relating to the negotiation of meaning (e.g. requests for clarification and confirmation checks) and recasts. She found that in conversations involving NS and NNS children aged between 8 and 13 meaning negotiation arose as a response to utterances containing errors involving auxiliary verbs, copula, pronouns, word order and word choice whereas recasts were more likely to occur after utterances with singular/plural and subject-verb agreement errors. An experimental study by Mito (1993) compared the relative effects of recasts and models[4] targeted at two Japanese grammatical constructions. The results showed that whereas no learning occurred in any of the learners in the modeling condition, the recasts led to small but statistically significant gains by 6 of the 19 learners in this condition. Long, Inagaki and Ortega (1998) report a similar study involving adult learners of L2 Japanese and Spanish. In the case of the Japanese learners, recasts did not prove more effective than models in promoting acquisition of the same two grammatical structures that Mito investigated. However, recasts did prove more effective than models where one Spanish construction (adverb placement) was concerned, although not for two other constructions. Mackey and Philps (1998) compared two groups of adult learners, one of which received interactionally modified input through negotiation and the other intensive recasts. They found that the recasts had a stronger developmental effect on advanced learners' use of question forms than interactionally modified input without recasts. However, recasts did not prove beneficial for the less advanced learners. Interestingly, in this study, the positive effect for recasts was evident even though the advanced learners rarely incorporated the corrections into their own utterances.

Clearly, research investigating negative feedback through recasts in interaction involving L2 learners is still in its infancy. There are some obvious problems. First, there is a theoretical difficulty. Acquisition can only take place if learners pay attention to the *form* of the recast and it is not clear that this is what they typically do. In general, utterances are not stored verbatim, in the form they were produced, but semantically (Clark and Clark 1977). It would seem, then, that for recasts to work for acquisition a number of further conditions must be met. (1) the learner must possess the necessary proficiency to process the recast as form. Mackey and Philps' (1998) study shows, learners need to be at a developmental stage that enables them to process the negative feedback they receive. (2) the learner must be oriented towards form rather than meaning in order to undertake the necessary formal representation of the utterance. Many learners may not be so inclined or may not be able to do so in the context of making sense of on-going conversation.

Second there is a methodological problem. Long (1996) clearly views 'meaning negotiation' and 'recasts' as distinct. In fact, though, a confirmation check (a negotiation move) often cannot be distinguished formally from a recast unless intonation (rising versus falling) is used as the distinguishing feature. This problem is fully evident in example (3) above, where the NS clearly rephrases the learner's utterance but, in fact, appears to be doing so in the context of negotiating meaning by means of a confirmation check. Oliver (1998) recognized this problem, admitting that she double coded such utterances as both confirmation checks and as 'other repetitions' (i.e. as recasts). This reflects a broader methodological issue which will be addressed at the end of this section.

Research based on the later version of the IH has also focused on the modified output that learners produce as a result of meaning negotiation and recasts. Theoretical interest in output as a source of language acquisition was stimulated by Swain's (1985) proposal that comprehensible output as well as comprehensible input may be required in order for learners to achieve high levels of grammatical and sociolinguistic competence in an L2. Swain argued that what she called 'pushed output' obligated learners to engage in syntactic processing, as opposed to the kind of semantic processing involved in comprehension, and that this fostered acquisition. Swain (1995) discusses three functions of output where accuracy is concerned. First, it serves a consciousness-raising function by triggering 'noticing'. That is, producing language helps learners to notice their problems. Second, producing language enables learners to test out hypotheses about the L2. One way in which this occurs is through the modified output that learners produce following negative feedback. Third, output allows learners to reflect consciously about L2 forms. This can occur in the context of communicative tasks where the content is grammar (i.e. when learners negotiate for meaning as they grapple with a grammar problem). In addition, to these three functions, output can also help learners to achieve greater fluency by increasing control over forms they have already partially acquired. De Bot (1996) views this function as the most likely way output aids acquisition. He points out that production helps learners to increase automaticity of processing and, as a result, enables them to devote more attentional resources to the higher-level processes involved in message generation.

This theoretical framework has led researchers to address a number of questions. One is whether learners do in fact modify their output as a result of meaning negotiation. The answer to this question depends to a considerable extent on the nature of the indicating move. In (4) the indicating move consists of a confirmation check (which, in effect, functions as a recast). Here the learner responds simply by saying 'yes'; thus, no modified output occurs. In contrast, in (5) the indicating move is performed by means of a request for clarification, which results in the learner modifying his initial utterance. Pica's research (see Pica (1988) and Pica, Holliday, Lewis and Morganthaler (1989)) has shown that this constitutes a general response pattern. Learners generally do not modify their output when confronted with a confirmation check or a recast, a finding borne out by other studies. For example, Oliver (1998) found that children incorporated only 10% of all recasts into their following utterances. Lyster and Ranta (1997), in a study of immersion classrooms, report that learners 'uptook' 31% of the teachers' recasts. In contrast, learners are likely to modify their output when confronted by a request for clarification (e.g. Lyster and Ranta report that clarification requests resulted in a 88% uptake rate). However, as Pica (1992) documents, learners are overall less likely to modify their output than native speakers responding to a learner comprehension problem. Also, the scope of learners' modifications is more restricted.

(4)   NNS: I think on the front is a small store
         NS: on the front?
                                       NNS: yeah oh doors
         NS: in the front of the door?
                                       NNS: yeah
         NS: there is a small step, yes
                                       NNS: oh yes
(5)   NNS: they are think about the fun thing so they
                                       are change the position each other
         NS: what?
                                       NNS: they change up the position so they think
                                       father went to pre-school and son went to the
                                       company OK

A second question of obvious interest is whether modified output assists
language acquisition. In this respect, it should be noted that Krashen's Input
Hypothesis and the revised Interaction Hypothesis make very different claims.
As we have already seen, Krashen argues that acquisition is input driven. He
specifically rejects the output hypothesis on the grounds that output (and
especially modified output) is too scarce to make a real contribution to the
development of linguistic competence, high levels of linguistic competence are
possible without output and there is no direct evidence that modified output leads
to acquisition (Krashen 1998). However, in part, Krashen misses the point, as,
even if pushed output is scarce, it may afford qualitative opportunities to notice
specific features that are problematic to learners. Long and Pica have both argued
that modified output contributes significantly to acquisition. Long (1996) sees
spoken production as 'useful ... because it elicits negative input and encourages
analysis and grammaticization' ; it is 'facilitative, but not necessary' (p. 448).
Pica (1996b) argues that modified output helps learners to analyze and break a
message into its constituent parts and also to produce forms that may lie at the
cutting edge of their linguistic ability. These conflicting positions can only be
resolved through empirical studies of the effects of output modification on
acquisition. There have, however, been very few such studies.

    In a small scale study involving just three learners, Nobuyoshi and Ellis
(1993) found that two of the learners were able to improve the accuracy of their
use of past tense forms in oral narratives as a result of being 'pushed' by means
of requests for clarification. Furthermore, their improvement was sustained in
narratives produced one week later when they were not pushed. The other learner
neither modified his output initially nor showed any later gains in accuracy.

Krashen (1998) dimisses this study on the grounds that the sample size was very small and that the learners who improved may have been monitoring using explicit knowledge.[5] Stronger evidence comes from Mackey's (1995) study of questions forms. Mackey compared the effects of three environmental conditions on learners' development of English question forms; (1) participation in interaction focused on the question forms, (2) observation without the opportunity to produce, and (3) exposure to premodified input with no opportunity to interact. Mackey found that only active participation resulted in development (i.e. (1) was effective but (2) and (3) were not). Furthermore, those learners who modified their responses during interaction were the ones who benefited most in condition (1). Van den Branden (1997) found that 11–12 year old children who had been pushed to modify their output in the context of a two-way communicative task produced significantly more output, more essential information and a greater range of vocabulary in a similar communicative task performed later than did children who had not been initially pushed. Van den Branden argues that the post-test results provide a clear indication of the potential effects of pushed output on acquisition.

The updated version of the IH, with its emphasis on the contributions of negative feedback and modified output as well as comprehensible input and its recognition that interaction works by connecting input, internal learner capacities and output via selective attention, is obviously a major advance on the early version. There are, however, a number of caveats. The first has already been hinted at; there are obvious problems in distinguishing the separate components of meaning negotiation for study. The second is that a theory of language acquisition based on a single type of interaction (negotiation sequences) which constitutes only a small part of the total interaction a learner experiences would seem to be unnecessarily restrictive. The third concerns the problem of individual differences.

Earlier we noted the difficulties in distinguishing 'meaning negotiation' and 'recasts'. This reflects the more general problem in isolating specific negotiating moves for study. Consider the negotiation sequence in (2) above. Here the learner requests clarification and as a result obtains input that is comprehensible and also, perhaps, clues about how to parse the phrase 'buvdaplate'. But in this sequence the learner also produces a 'response to the response', repeating 'above the plate'. This constitutes modification of her own output. This sequence then incorporates both comprehensible input and modified output. Such exchanges are not rare. Also, in exchanges between learners, one learner's modified output is another learner's comprehensible input. Clearly, it is not an easy matter to devise experimental studies to examine the acquisitional effects of specific interactional moves. Nor is this purely a methodological problem because, as Van Lier (1996) has pointed out, counting individual units of negotiation may result in important qualitative aspects of the discourse being missed. Van Lier rejects the atomistic approach that the IH has given rise to, arguing that discourse needs to be treated as holistic, collaborative and dynamic, a position that resonates closely with sociolcultural theory (see below).

As we have already noted, IH researchers are careful not to overstate their case. Long (1996) explicitly points out that the updated version of the IH is not a complete theory. Pica (1996b) points out that interaction, even when it is rich in meaning negotiation, may not be sufficient to ensure full linguistic competence and that some kind of focus on form may also be required to provide additional support. She also suggests that negotiation may work best with intermediate learners; beginner learners lack the resources to negotiate effectively while advanced learners tend to focus on opinion and interpretation rather than comprehension or linguistic clarity. Further, negotiation centres on lexical problems and larger syntactic units and, as we have already noticed, rarely involves inflectional morphology. The IH, then, is clearly limited in its scope in these respects. But perhaps its greatest limitation lies in the restricted focus on interactional sequences involving some kind of communication problem. This limitation has two sides to it. First, as Pica (1996b) acknowledges, the processes presumed beneficial to acquisition that occur in negotiation sequences can also occur in uninterrupted communication. Second, and perhaps, most important, there must be surely much else going on in uninterrupted communication that is facilitative of acquisition. These limitations do not warrant a dismissal of the IH, for, indeed, it has prompted some revealing research (including a number of studies reported in subsequent chapters of this book). However, they do suggest the need for researchers to broaden the scope of their enquiry.

Finally, there is the question of individual differences. The IH, like many other theories in SLA, is universalistic in its frame of reference; it seeks to identify the environmental conditions that pertain to L2 acquisition in general. It would seem obvious, however, that learners vary enormously in their ability or their preparedness to negotiate. The bulk of the research has studied adolescent or adult learners. Do children negotiate in similar ways? Oliver (1998) found that children aged between 8 and 13 years negotiated in similar ways to adults but differed in their proportional use of individual strategies (e.g. they made less use of comprehension checks). Van den Branden (1997), in the study referred to above, also found that 11–12 year old children negotiated each other's output, although he noted that this negotiation was directed principally at meaning and content rather than form. As we will see in Chapter Three, younger children (under 7 years) appear to differ more radically in their ability to negotiate.

Another area of difference concerns interactants' negotiation styles. Polio and Gass (1998) found marked differences in the way native speakers engaged learners in communicative tasks, some adopting a 'leading' role by asking questions to elicit the information they needed while others allowed the learners, who had control of the information to be communicated, to lead. They provide evidence to suggest that learners comprehend better when they have control over the content and form of the discourse. There are obviously a whole host of individual difference variables (see Skehan 1989) that can potentially impact on negotiation. As Gass, Mackey and Pica (1998) have pointed out, individual differences need to be looked at carefully in future research.

Sociocultural theory, interaction and L2 acquisition

The view of interaction, and its relationship to L2 acquisition, embodied in the IH has been challenged on a number of fronts, in particular from a perspective that can be broadly characterized as social or socio-pyschological in orientation. Firth and Wagner (1996), for example, suggest that there exists a tension in SLA research between acknowledgement of the social and contextual dimensions of language use and acquisition on the one hand and of the internal, cognitive processes of the individual on the other. They argue that the two perspectives have not been in balance, with researchers favouring the psycholinguistic over the social, and that, overall, SLA as a field of enquiry has become distorted and blinkered. They point specifically to the work on meaning negotiation and input modification, criticizing it for treating learners as 'defective communicators', for assuming that NSs can provide a 'baseline' against which to measure NNSs, for implicitly constructing the NNS as a subordinate of the NS, and for failing to recognize the diversity that exists within NS and NNS groups — in short, for an uncritical acceptance of the prevailing monolingual orientation in SLA that ignores the complexity of multilingual societies. They argue that SLA should give more attention to language acquisition as a social phenomenon by examining how L2s are used interactively in a variety of contexts and for myriad purposes.

To adopt the kind of social perspective Firth and Wagner advocate is, in effect, to challenge the predominant metaphor of SLA — that of the learner as a computer that processes input in accordance with the mechanisms wired into the 'black box' of the mind and that subsequently produces output on demand. As Lantolf (1996) has shown SLA has borrowed this metaphor from Chomskyan linguistics. It situates SLA as a process that takes place in the mind of the individual rather than in people-embedded activity. The IH fits neatly into this picture; the role of interaction is to supply the black box with the right kind of data for the internal mechanisms to set to work on. Pica (1996a), for example, specifically talks of the learner's 'data needs'. Like Firth and Wagner, Lantolf sees the need for SLA to take on board alternate metaphors that attribute greater agency to learners and that situate acquisition outside in the social world rather than inside the head of the learner. In particular, a social view of language learning favours the metaphor of 'participation' with its entailment of active involvement rather than the traditional metaphor of 'acquisition' with its entailment of possession (see Sfard 1998).

The critique of the computational metaphor in SLA extends beyond the way learners have been constructed to the way they have been studied; it is a methodological as well as conceptual critique. As we have seen, the IH, typical of theory derived from the computational metaphor, has been tested by means of research that is nomothetic in style. That is, it has adopted an atomistic approach to learner discourse, samples of which are generally collected in laboratory settings, quantified, and subjected to analysis by means of inferential statistics. In contrast, a social view of language acquisition calls for research that is idiographic in style, that adopts a more holistic approach to discourse involving learners and their settings, and which, therefore, employs qualitative methods that are more sensitive to the ways in which interactions are constructed by participants as they dynamically negotiate not just meaning but also their role relationships and their cultural and social identities. Such an approach is evident in the work of ethnomethodologists and ethnographers. However, as Donato (2000) points out this approach can also be criticized for focusing exclusively on the social, communicative aspects of interaction and ignoring its cognitive function. In this respect, the methodology developed by socio-cultural researchers, such as Frawley and Lantolf (1985), which examines the microgenesis of cognitive behaviours through the detailed study of interactional sequences over time, may be more compatible with the overall goals of SLA (i.e. the description and explanation of the process of L2 acquisition).

There are, of course, a number of theories (and accompanying metaphors) that view acquisition as essentially a social or socio-psychological process that is best studied hermeneutically. We will focus on one of these — the socio-cultural theory that orginated in the work of Vygotsky and which has been applied to the study of L2 acquisition by researchers such as Lantolf. As Lantolf and Appel (1994) and Lantolf (2000a) make clear, the key construct in this theory is **mediation**. Learning, including language learning, occurs when biologically determined mental functions evolve into more complex 'higher order' functions through social interaction. This transformation results in 'consciousness', which involves both awareness of cognitive abilities and also the self-regulatory mechanisms employed in problem-solving. It is brought about through the creation of 'tools' which serve as the means by which individuals achieve their goals. These tools reflect the particular cultural and historical conditions in which they have developed. They can exist in a variety of forms; mechanical (e.g. a pencil), technical (e.g. a computer) or psychological (i.e. words). It is these tools, then, that mediate between individuals and the world. Development entails identifying and learning to use the culturally defined tools required to achieve higher order functions.

One type of mediation of particular importance for learning is interpersonal interaction. Talk serves as a tool that enables parents to pass their particular culture to their children. According to socio-cultural theory, functions are initially performed in collaboration with others, typically through interacting with some other person, and then are subsequently performed independently. As Vygotsky (1981: 163) puts it:

> Any function in the child's development appears twice or on two planes, first it appears on the social plane, and then on the psychological plane, first it appears between people as an interpsychological category, and then within the child as an intrapsychological category.

One way in which this occurs in L2 acquisition is through the 'vertical construct-ion' of syntactical structures, as illustrated in (6). Here, a teacher is showing the learner a What's Wrong Card depicting a bicycle without a pedal and is trying to get him to say what is wrong, a task that is linguistically beyond him. The sequence ends with the learner producing the two-word utterance 'black taes/', (i.e. 'black tyres'). He achieves this by first saying 'black' in one turn and then adding 'taes' in a second turn, in response to the teacher's question, 'Black what?'. Structurally simple as this utterance appears, it represents the first occasion that this beginner learner produced a two-word constituent of this kind. Subsequently, however, this learner began to produce such two word constituents on this own. Here, then, we see how interaction has the potential to enable a learner to advance linguistically (see Hatch 1978b and Wagner Gough 1975 for further examples).

(6)   T: I want you to tell me what you can see in the picture
              or what's wrong with the picture.
                                   L: a /paik/ (= bike)
        T: A cycle, yes. But what's wrong?
                                   L: /ret/ (= red)
        T: It's red, yes. What's wrong with it?

                              L: Black.
    T: Black. Good. Black what?
                              L: Black /taes/ (= tyres)
    (From Ellis 1985)

Interaction of the kind illustrated in (6) provides **scaffolding**; that is, it serves as the means by which one person assists another to perform a function that he/she could not perform alone. At one level this refers to the collaborative process by which interactants construct their conversation in such a way that language learners are able to produce linguistic forms that lie outside their existing competence. But at another level it refers more broadly to the social, cognitive and affective support that interactants afford each other. Wood, Bruner and Ross (1976) identify the following features of scaffolding:

1. recruiting interest in the task
2. simplifying the task
3. maintaining pursuit of the goal
4. marking critical features and discrepancies between what has been produced and the ideal solution
5. controlling frustration during problem solving and
6. demonstrating an idealized version of the act to be performed.

One way in which such scaffolding can occur is in the context of an 'instructional conversation' (Tharp and Gallimore 1988). These are formal, classroom versions of the non-formal conversations that take place between a child and a parent. They are conversational in nature (e.g. they involve distributed turn-taking, spontaneity and unpredictability) but they have an instructional focus (i.e. are oriented towards a particular curricular goal) and are directed at helping learners reshape and extend their use of language. As Donato (2000) points out 'instructional conversations' constitute a potentially insightful target for analysis by SLA researchers because they involve a far wider range of communicative and cognitive functions than negotiation sequences. The study of scaffolding, then, provides a way of demonstrating how an 'expert' assists a 'novice' to perform a difficult task through interaction and, also, how learners, interacting among themselves, can collaboratively manage a task that would be beyond any of them acting as individuals.[6]

    Like mainstream models of L2 acquisition that draw on the computational metaphor, socio-cultural theory acknowledges that the mediating power of interaction is constrained by learner-internal factors — that there is a psychological as well as social dimension to learning. Vygotsky (1978) evoked the metaphor of the **zone of proximal development** to refer to the psychological dimension. Let us envisage three types of goals; (1) goals that the learner can meet without assistance, (2) goals that are completely beyond the learner even if given assistance and (3) goals that the learner can perform if he/she has access to mediational assistance. The ZPD consists of (3); it constitutes an area of potential development, lying between (1), the learner's actual development, and (3) an area of non-development. Mediation, in the form of social interaction, enables learners to transform skills that lie in the ZPD. Superficially, the notion of the ZPD and Krashen's notion of 'i + 1', on which the IH draws, resemble each other. However, there are essential differences. As Dunn and Lantolf (1998) have pointed out, Krashen views acquisition as involving a movement from one stage to the next in a fixed and, therefore predictable order, Vygotsky saw development as a ripening process along a path that was in part at least uncertain, dependent on the interactional experiences of the individual. In socio-cultural theory, then, interaction is not just a device that facilitates learners movement along the interlanguage continuum, but a social event which helps learners participate in their own development, including shaping the path it follows.

In broad terms, however, sociocultural theory does provide an account of how development proceeds universally. Vygotsky proposes that children are initially subject to 'object-regulation' (i.e. they are influenced by whatever object catches their attention), then pass through a stage of 'other-regulation' (i.e. they allow a parent to dialogically influence the locus of their attention) and finally achieve 'self-regulation' (i.e. they are able to regulate their own attention). Interesting, Foley (1991) has suggested that the topic-incorporation devices employed in the negotiation of meaning, can be viewed as devices for achieving self-regulation in conversation. As we noted, above, children below the age of seven are not typically able to make use of these devices. They do, however, make use of what Vygotsky has called **private speech** (i.e. speech that is addressed to themselves). This can be thought of as a proxy for social speech, assisting them to regulate their own behaviour in problem solving. Later this private speech transforms into **inner speech**, the semantically dense language (and gestures) that we use to talk silently to ourselves. Inner speech reflects the achievement of self-regulation. This general pattern of development, however, does not refer to how language itself develops but rather to how children develop cognitively by learning to control the use of language as a tool for mediating activity. Frawley and Lantolf (1985) have advanced the 'principle of continuous access', according to which adults do not forget the knowing strategies they practised as children and reactivate early strategies (such as private speech) when faced with a task that is cognitively challenging. In accordance with socio-cultural theory, then, we can expect to observe two different kinds of 'interaction' involving L2 learners; social interaction, where they converse with other learners or native speakers, and private speech, where they interact with themselves. As Frawley and Lantolf (1985) show the linguistic properties of these two types of talk are notably different.[7]

From this brief and rather simplified account of socio-cultural theory, it is clear that the view of interaction, and its relation to language learning, that it espouses is radically different from that found in the IH. The IH concerns itself only with social interaction; socio-cultural theory views 'interaction' as something that can be both social and private. The IH concerns itself narrowly with one type of interaction (the negotiation of meaning); socio-cultural theory, while suggesting particular forms of interaction (such as instructional conversations) which can be profitably analyzed, is concerned with interaction in general. Whereas the IH views interaction as assisting acquisition by helping to meet learners' data needs, socio-cultural theory treats interaction as a social practice that shapes and constructs learning. In the case of the IH, interaction only facilitates learning and is neither necessary nor sufficient; in socio-cultural theory, interaction is the actual site of learning and while not strictly necessary (there are mediational artifacts a learner can draw on) it is clearly viewed as primary and certainly as sufficient. In short, socio-cultural theory provides a much broader and richer account of the role of interaction in language acquisition. As we will see, this constitutes both a strength and a weakness. First, though, we will consider some of the SLA research based on the theory, focussing on studies that have addressed the role of interaction in L2 learning.

As we have seen, interaction is seen as both social and external and private and internal. SLA researchers in the socio-cultural tradition have examined both types. Where social interaction is concerned a number of studies have looked at how scaffolding takes place in conversations involving L2 learners. Aljaafreh and Lantolf (1994) examined the one-on-one interactions arising between three L2 learners and a tutor who provided corrective feedback on essays they had written. They developed a 'regulatory scale' to reflect the extent to which the help provided by the tutor was implicit or explicit. In detailed analyses of selected protocols, they show how the degree of scaffolding provided by the tutor for a particular learner diminishes in the sense that the help provided becomes more implicit over time. This becomes possible because the learners assumed increased control over the L2 and, therefore, needed less assistance. Aljaafreh and Lantolf's subjects were relatively advanced learners. An interesting question is whether scaffolding in the L2 is possible with beginner learners and, if so, how it is accomplished. The sequence taken from Ellis (1985), (6) above, demonstrates that scaffolding with beginner learners does occur in one-on-one interactions between a learner and a teacher and can promote acquisition. Donato (2000) refers to a study by Todhunter of 'instructional conversations' in a beginner French classroom that also shows scaffolding is possible even in lockstep teaching. Interestingly, however, he reports that it arose only when the teacher departed from the exercises provided in the textbook.

All of these studies examined scaffolding in the context of interactions between an 'expert' (the tutor) and 'novices' (the learners). Other studies, however, have shown that scaffolding also takes place between learners when they are working in pairs or groups. DiCamilla and Anton (1996) studied five dyads discussing how to write a composition. They illustrate how the learners made use of repetition to provide scaffolded help for each other. For example, it served as a kind of platform on which the learners rested while they struggled to find the next word and it was also used to finalize a collaborative solution. Ohta (1995) demonstrates how learners' scaffold each other's contributions in a role playing task, making the point that even a less proficient learner can assist a more proficient learner. She also notes that in learner-learner interactions the notions of novice and expert are 'fluid conceptions' (p. 109); the same learner can function as both expert and novice at different times in a conversation. Kowal and Swain (1994) used a dictogloss task (Wajnryb 1990), which required learners to first listen to take notes as their teacher read a short text containing specific grammatical features and then to work in pairs to reconstruct the text from their joint notes. In this study, the learners talked about language form and were often able to decide collectively what forms to use to reconstruct a text. However, Kowal and Swain report that heterogeneous learners worked less effectively together, possibly because 'neither student's needs were within the zone of proximal development of the other' (p. 86) and because they failed to respect each other's perspective.

It is, of course, one thing to demonstrate that scaffolding occurs and quite another to show that it assists L2 acquisition. There are now a number of studies, however, that provide evidence of acquisitional effects. Ellis (1985), in the study from which extract (6) was taken, draws on longitudinal evidence to suggest that scaffolding helped learners to produce 'new' grammatical structures in the context of a particular interaction which then began to appear with regularity in their unassisted speech. This study was not located within the framework of socio-cultural theory but is clearly highly supportive of its major claims. Donato (1994) describes the collective scaffolding employed by groups of university students of French performing an oral activity based on a scenario from Di Pietro (1987). In a detailed analysis of an exchange involving the negotiation of the form 'tu t'es souvenu', Donato shows how they jointly managed components of the problem, distinguished between what they had produced and what they perceived as the ideal solution, and used their collective resources to minimize frustration and risk. This scaffolding enabled the learners to hit on the correct form of the verb even though no single learner knew this prior to the task. Donato was also able to show that learners' joint performance of new structures on one occasion was frequently followed (75% of the time) by their independent use of them on later occasions. LaPierre (1994; cited in Swain 1995) provides evidence to show that the solutions to linguistic problems that learners jointly negotiated in 'language-related episodes' occurring within the context of performing a communicative task were reflected in their subsequent performance on tailor-made tests; correct and incorrect solutions matched correct and incorrect responses in the test. Swain and Lapkin (1998) report a similar study showing how collaborative activity between learners fostered both the ability to solve problems and to acquire new linguistic resources in the process. Ohta (2000) also shows how the scaffolding that two learners provided each other while performing a demanding translation task enabled one of the learners to produce a complex grammatical Japanese structure that was initially beyond her competence. In one respect at least, then, research based on socio-cultural theory is in advance of research based on the IH; it has provided evidence in support of the acquisitional affects of one of its prime constructs (i.e. scaffolding). However, this research does raise the important question of what constitutes adequate evidence of 'acquisition'. We will return to this question later.

Private speech serves as the other principal means of development. As we noted earlier, socio-cultural theory predicts that private speech occurs when learners are required to perform tasks that cause them cognitive stress, making total self-regulation difficult. In other words, private speech functions strategically to enable learners to gain control over language forms, the use of which are problematic in the context of a challenging task. Researchers working in the socio-cultural tradition emphasize that when learners perform a task they are likely to spend as much time in the effort to self-regulate through the use of private speech as in actually communicating. However, as learners become more proficient they rely less overall on private speech.

The bulk of the research that has investigated L2 learners' private speech has made use of oral narrative tasks (see McCafferty (1994a) for a survey). The nature of the task is one of several factors that have been found to impact on learners' use of private speech. Narrative tasks where the subjects are shown the pictures one at a time are more cognitively stressful and result in greater use of private speech than tasks where they see all the pictures together. In Appel and Lantolf's (1994) text recall study, the expository text led to more private speech than the narrative text, again because of the difficulty the subjects (both native speakers and learners) experienced in achieving control in recalling the former. Other factors that impact on the use of private speech according to McCafferty (1994a) are the proficiency of the learners, their cultural background and how they relate to the task and to each other. McCafferty (1998) also shows that learners' private speech is closely related to their use of nonverbal forms of expressions (e.g. gestures) with the two working together to produce strategic solutions to verbal problems encountered in producing oral narratives.

Private speech is also evident, albeit to a lesser extent, in interactive tasks. Donato (1994), for example, finds examples in his study. He suggests that the scaffolded help his learners provided each other triggered the use of private talk as a means of organizing, rehearsing and gaining control over new verbal behaviour. McCafferty (1994a) refers to research by Ahmed (1988) which found differential levels and types of private speech in two kinds of communicative tasks. Both tasks were simulation games but one type involved imaginary situations the other a real situation (i.e. the subjects sought solutions to maths problems for an upcoming examination which they all had to take). The first type produced relatively little private speech. Also, the native speakers tended to dominate with the L2 learners showing little real interest in the outcome. In contrast, the second type led to greater and more varied use of private talk and a genuine commitment to finding solutions, with the L2 learners as likely to take on the role of 'expert' as the native speakers. Donato (2000) refers to a study by Smith which also claimed to have found instances of private speech in a teacher-led grammar lesson. In this case, the learner's private speech served to external-ize the learner's thinking about a grammar problem and thus provided a basis for teacher and student to work towards a co-constructed understanding. However, in contrast to the research on scaffolding, studies of private speech have not yet been able to provide any clear evidence that it constitutes an opportunity for acquisition to occur.

Socio-cultural studies of interaction and L2 acquisition clearly constitute a growing line of research in SLA. The strengths of the socio-cultural paradigm have already been described. It is appropriate, however, to also consider their limitations. One problem is that, with a few notable exceptions, the research to date has examined L2 *use* rather than L2 *acquisition*. This is an inevitable outcome of a method that relies on the study of the microgenesis of language abilities. In fact, the distinction between 'use' and 'acquisition' is not altogether clear from the perspective of sociocultural theory. As Sfard (1998: 7) has pointed out 'belonging, participating and communicating is evidence of knowing'. Thus, if it can be shown in the context of a single task that learners progress from not being able to perform a linguistic structure to being able to do so, this might be taken as evidence that they now 'know' the structure and, thus, have acquired it. This is the position that Ohta (1996, 2000) implicitly adopts in her research. However, such a position is not convincing. For most researchers 'acquisition' entails some kind of change to long-term memory. Thus, it is necessary to demonstrate that 'new' behaviours that arise in the course of interaction (social or private) are available for non-mediated use at a later date. In socio-cultural terms, it is necessary to show that learners have achieved self-regulation. Precisely how this is to be done, however, remains a quandary, not least because of the difficulty of providing testing tasks that adequately tap what has been acquired in learning tasks.[8] There has clearly been inadequate discussion among socio-cultural researchers of how 'use' and 'acquisition' should be distinguished both conceptually and operationally.

Socio-cultural SLA research could also benefit from tighter operational definitions of other key constructs in the theory. For instance, there need to be explicit procedures for identifying the ZPD in learners. To claim that a cognitive operation lies within a learner's ZPD, two things must be demonstrated; (1) that the learner *cannot* perform the operation independently (2) that he/she *can* perform it with scaffolded assistance. Quite often the demonstration of (2) by itself seems to be taken as evidence of the ZPD but this is clearly unsatisfactory as scaffolded assistance may sometimes be provided where it is not needed (see Lantolf and Aljaafreh 1996). Nor is it easy it see how private and social speech can be operationally distinguished. For example, Frawley and Lantolf (1986) suggest that both native speakers and intermediate level learners use the past tense in their narratives as a form of object regulation but McCafferty (1994b) takes the more obvious line that the past tense is used communicatively to signal temporal relationships cohesively. Clearly, formal criteria arc needed to determine what type of speech learners are producing on particular occasions.

Finally, there are two other methodological limitations. Socio-cultural SLA research, like research based on the IH, has typically been cross-sectional, in accordance with the microgenetic method. Too many of the studies have involved 'rich' and unsupported interpretations of data collected at a single point in time (e.g. in the activity that arises from a single task). There has been a conspicuous absence of longitudinal studies. However, it is such studies that are arguably needed to demonstrate that behavioural changes within a given interaction are representative of long-lasting cognitive changes. Also, researchers have typically eschewed quantification, although, as McCafferty (1994a) rightly points out there is nothing wrong with counting observables. Some of the more persuasive studies (e.g. Donato 1994; Swain and Lapkin 1998) have been prepared to back up discursive comment with descriptive statistics. Despite these limitations, the socio-cultural paradigm clearly has much to offer SLA researchers interested in how interaction shapes and constructs acquisition.

Depth of processing model

The final theory we will consider is entirely cognitive in orientation drawing on a traditional model of information processing. It is included here because it can also incorporate an interactionist perspective on learning; interaction serves as a means of achieving the kind of mental activity required for new material to be stored in long-term memory. This theory has been only minimally exploited in SLA but offers considerable potential.

Traditional information processing models are premised on the existence of three types of memory store. Sensory registers allow for a literal copy of input without attention and are subject to rapid and large decay. The short-term store requires conscious attention and allows for recycling of information. Decay takes place but less rapidly. The long-term store requires information to be organized meaningfully and can maintain information over a long period of time with minimal loss. Another feature of such models is that they propose a limited capacity, either in terms of the size of the memory stores or in terms of limitations in people's ability to process new information in the input or in terms of an interaction of these two.

In a widely cited paper, Craik and Lockhart (1972) propose a revision of this traditional model. They suggest that memory is less a function of different types of store and more a function of the nature of the processing in which people engage when faced with new material in the input. They argue that stimuli can be processed at different levels. Preliminary stages involve the analysis of purely formal features such as lines, angles, brightness, pitch and loudness. Later, or 'deeper' stages involve matching input against existing schemata in order to extract patterns and meaning. They propose that 'trace persistence is a function of depth of analysis, with deeper levels of analysis associated with more elaborate, longer lasting, and stronger traces' (p. 676). They refer to two types of processing; Type 1 processing involves the 'repetition of analyses that have already been carried out' while Type 2 processing requires 'deeper analysis of the stimulus'. However, they view processing depth as continuous rather than dichotomous. In their 'levels of processing' model, then, there is a single memory space which is activated differently depending on the depth of processing. The degree of retention is a product of the amount of attention given to a stimulus, the extent to which it matches existing mental structures and the processing time available.

The obvious question posed by this model is 'What influences the level of processing that an individual engages in?' In part, this will depend on a person's motivation (i.e. his or her assessment of the usefulness of the information). It is also influenced externally by the nature of the task a subject is asked to perform. In this respect, then, 'memory performance is a positive function of the level of processing required by the orienting task' (op cit; p. 678). However, one of the weaknesses of Craik and Lockart's model, is that 'depth of processing' is underspecified — one reason why they claim that the model represents 'a conceptual framework' rather than a 'theory'. In part, this problem has been addressed by Wittrock's generative model of learning (Wittrock 1974). This focuses on differentiating aspects of what Craik and Lockart referred to as Type 2 processing (i.e. processing that occurs at the semantic level). Wittrock proposed that improved retention occurs when subjects engage in 'generative processing' (i.e. processing that involves the generation or elaboration of material based on the input stimulus). Learning, then, is seen as a function of the associations, concrete and abstract, which subjects generate between the stimulus and prior experience. When such associations are developed long-term memory occurs and, also, subjects are able to transfer information to new contexts and problems.

Two types of tasks encourage such processing. First, tasks that require subjects to recall or summarize materials they have read result in deeper cognitive processing, as they have to integrate textual and schematic knowledge. In contrast, tasks that require reading without recall make no such demand. Second, tasks that require subjects to read a text, formulate a set of questions about the text and then answer them also promote elaboration of the input stimulus. This type of task is of particular interest because it allows for inter-ventional training; subjects can be taught what kinds of questions to ask. A number of studies involving subjects reading or listening to texts in their L1 provide evidence that both types of tasks are effective in promoting learning. Wittrock (1974), for example, reported a study involving 366 fifth and sixth grade children. The control group was asked to simply read a text. One experimental group was given one or two word organizers at the top of each paragraph. A second experimental group was required to generate a sentence summarizing each paragraph. The second experimental group comprehended best and remembered more of the content of the text; the first experimental group also outperformed the control group. Subsequent studies (e.g. Doctorow, Wittrock and Marks 1978) investigated a variety of other type of generative instructions involving summarizing and recall, with similar results. The second type of task is based on Pressley et al's (1987) notion of 'elaborative interrogation' of a text. This calls for subjects to generate their own elaborations of a text. The method most commonly used to achieve this is self-questioning. Students are trained to generate their own questions, especially think-type questions, during or after reading. Answering such questions involves such cognitive activities as focusing attention, organizing new material, and integrating new information with old; it also constitutes a metacognitive activity because it provides subjects with the means for testing themselves. A number of studies (e.g. Davey and McBride 1986; King 1989) have found that training is effective in enabling subjects to pose inferential type questions, in promoting higher levels of comprehension, and in enhancing recall of factual content.

Somewhat surprisingly, given the interest shown in the levels of processing and generative processing models in L1 based research, there have been very few L2 based studies. Brown and Perry (1991), in a study that drew directly on levels of processing theory, examined the effects of three different 'orienting tasks' on Arabic-speaking learners' memory for new vocabulary. One group was presented with a new word, its definition, and a keyword in Arabic; it was then given practice in making interactive images linking the target word and the keyword. A second group was given the new word, its definition, two examples of senten-ces containing the word and a question that the subjects had to answer using the word. A third group was given a task that combined the operations of the tasks for the other two groups. Brown and Perry reasoned that all three tasks would enhance memory but that the combined keyword-semantic task involved a greater depth of processing and thus would result in higher levels of vocabulary learning than either the keyword or semantic methods on their own. The results supported this prediction. The keyword-semantic group outperformed the keyword group, with the semantic group intermediate. In this study, then, information processed at the semantic level led to better memory than information processed purely at the acoustic/visual level, while information that was elaborated both semantically and visually/acoustically was remembered best of all.

Joe (1998) also investigated vocabulary learning. In this study adult ESL learners were placed in three matched groups and asked to perform a read and recall task. The text contained lexical items that a pre-test had shown the learners did not know. One experimental group received explicit instruction on using generative learning strategies but did not have access to the text during recall. The other received no explicit instruction but had access to the text. As they read, both groups were asked to retell key concepts by using phrases like 'I'm not sure but I think ..." as they thought-aloud. Both of the experimental groups outperformed the control group on measures of vocabulary learning. There was no difference between the two experimental groups; that is, giving students explicit training in generative processing did not result in more vocabulary learning. However, generation of words while the learners performed the task did effect vocabulary learning; the more generation, the greater the gains and also the deeper the knowledge of the new words. Joe concludes; 'Tasks which encourage learners to retrieve the target form during recall and to provide an original sentence using the target word will give learners extra opportunities to practice using the word to-be-learned' (p. 374).

The levels of processing and generative processing models constitute a potentially rich seam that remains largely untapped by L2 researchers. There are, however, some obvious limitations. One has already been mentioned — the models do not provide a clear theoretical basis for distinguishing different mental and behavioural activities in terms of the depth of processing they involve. More attention also needs to be paid to individual learner differences; it does not follow that a specific procedure will be universally optimal for promoting depth of processing. From the perspective of this book, however, the major limitation of the models is that they do not explicitly address the role of interaction in cognitive processing. The techniques used in the studies based on these models have not involved interaction. Nevertheless, it is clear that interaction, in various guises, can function as one means of stimulating Type 2 processing. The negotiation of meaning, for example, can be seen as a device for inducing deep processing, both because it provides more processing time and because it creates the conditions under which learners can establish links between unfamiliar items in the input and their existing knowledge. From the perspective of socio-cultural theory, tasks that encourage the use of private speech might also promote deep processing of the input. The self-questioning strategy discussed above can be seen as a form of mediation that enables learners to use private speech to achieve self-regulation. More broadly, discussion is likely to stimulate cognitive involvement and, thereby, learning. One of the more obvious ways in which these models can be exploited in SLA is by examining how interaction of both the interpersonal and intrapersonal kinds helps learners to process deeply and, thereby, to acquire the L2. Chapter 6 makes a start in this direction.

Conclusion

This chapter has been far ranging. It has explained three theories that directly or potentially address the role of interaction in L2 acquisition. It has reviewed some of the research based on these theories. It remains to be considered to what extent these theories can be unified into a comprehensive account of how interaction contributes to acquisition.

There are some obvious links between the three theories. For example, both the IH and the levels of processing model view L2 learning in terms of information-processing They emphasize the limited processing and memory capacity of the learner and the role of attention in learning. Nor is it difficult to see points of connection between socio-cultural theory and the levels of processing model. As noted above, the notion of 'deep processing' is resonant with that of 'private speech' used as tool for self-regulation. However, it would be a mistake to overstate the commonalities in these theories. As de Bot (1996) has pointed out, 'trying to falsify hypotheses from one paradigm in terms of the other paradigm is a futile exercise' (p. 554). Ultimately, too, the similarities and differences among the three theories are not important if one adopts the perspective on theory development proposed by Lantolf (1997); different theories afford different insights and thereby contribute to our understanding of the complex and multi-faceted phenomenon of L2 learning. Evaluation should be directed at the quality and usefulness of the insights that different theories provide.

It is, however, possible to identify a general interactionist perspective and it is with this that I would like to conclude the chapter. The essence of an interactionist perspective is that interaction, interpersonal and intrapersonal, plays a major part in creating the conditions in which language acquisition (first and second) can take place. In the case of L1 acquisition, interpersonal interaction may be *necessary* for acquisition. In the case of L2 acquisition, social interaction may not be necessary but it is almost certainly *beneficial*. In both primary and secondary language acquisition intrapersonal interaction is *necessary*. Furthermore, in both, certain types of interpersonal and intrapersonal interaction are likely to be more useful for acquisition than others. One of the purposes of the theories discussed in this chapter has been to try to cast light on what these facilitative types might be.

An interactionist perspective contrasts with a mentalist perspective. According to this, the primary driving force behind language acquisition is not the learners' linguistic environment but the linguistic knowledge with which they are innately endowed — in terms of the Chomskian paradigm, **universal grammar**. In this paradigm, the role of interaction is restricted to the provision of input which, in turn, is viewed only as supplying 'triggers' that activate principles and set parameters (see Braidi (1995) for a detailed exposition of this paradigm).

Again, my purpose is not to suggest that an interactionist perspective is more valid than a mentalist perspective. My position is that theories do not have inherent validity but only relative validity (see Ellis 1997). My own preference for an interactionist perspective is motivated by my conviction that for the particular purpose I have in mind, the development of an effective second language pedagogy, such a perspective is more valid than a mentalist one because it provides insights that are translatable into pedagogic proposals. This book draws an a broad interactionist perspective with a view to contributing to this purpose. The chapters in Sections 2 and 3 explore the interactionist perspective in a series of empirical studies, all of which took place in real-life classrooms. The chapter in Section 4 considers pedagogical issues. The concluding chapter in Section 5 examines a number of general issues relating to the study of the interactionist perspective and its application to language pedagogy.

Notes

1. I have made one small change to Varonis and Gass's example of meaning negotiation. In the original, the indicating move consisted of a repetition of 'retire', not the reformulation ('retired') I include. This change reflects what often happens when learners negotiate meaning and serves to illustrate a point made later in the chapter.

2. Kees de Bot (personal correspondence) questions the strength of the indirect evidence Long cites in his 1983a paper. He refers to Long's citation of Snow et al. (1981), given in support of the claim that children acquiring their first language need comprehensible input. In fact, all that Snow et al. provide in the way of evidence is a footnote reporting a remark someone had made to them. De Bot suggests that Long's 'evidence' needs to be carefully checked.

3. Robinson (1995) also discusses another type of information processing model — filter models. These view information as being processed serially and attention as selective. Robinson, like other SLA researchers, favours capacity models.

4. 'Models' consisted of utterances containing the target structures which were provided by the researcher in the context of performing a communicative activity. The group receiving the models was not allowed to negotiate.

5. I consider this unlikely. There was no evidence of any monitoring (e.g. pauses immediately before the production of a past tense form). The learners appeared to be focused on telling the story.

6. Wells (1998) suggests that 'scaffolding' is not the best term to refer to the assistance students provide each other with and, instead, proposes 'collaborative problem solving'.

7. Frawley and Lantolf suggest that many of the features of learner-language that have been traditionally characterized as 'interlingual' may, in fact, reflect learners' use of private speech as they grapple to achieve the self-regulation needed to complete a complex task.

8. A prediction of socio-cultural theory is that changes in the kind of task learners' are asked to perform, or more precisely changes in learners perception of the activity they are performing, can influence their language use. Thus, failure to use a particular structure on a testing task does not preclude the possibility of it being used correctly on the kind of learning task in which it was initially experienced.

SECTION 2

Input, Interaction and Vocabulary Learning

The chapters in this section are all concerned with how input of one kind or another contributes to the acquisition of second language (L2) vocabulary. They draw on all the theoretical perspectives outlined in Chapter 1, in particular the Input and Interactional Hypotheses. All the chapters are concerned with *incidental* acquisition (i.e. the acquisition that occurs when learners are not making a special, focussed effort to learn).

There are two good reasons for focussing on vocabulary acquisition. The first is that vocabulary development is now recognized by researchers, as well as learners, as a major aspect of learning a new language. Learners have long recognized the importance of vocabulary learning (see, for example, the comments of 'good language learners', as in Naiman et al. (1978)). Applied linguists, particularly SLA researchers, have traditionally been more concerned with grammar than with lexis but in the last decade have increasingly paid attention to vocabulary learning (see, for example, Huckin, Haynes and Coady 1993; Hatch and Brown 1995; Coady and Huckin 1997; Schmitt and McCarthy 1997). Clearly, any comprehensive theory of L2 acquisition must account for how learners develop a knowledge of vocabulary. The second reason is that vocabulary acquisition is in one important respect easier to investigate than the acquisition of grammatical or pragmatic knowledge. Where incidental L2 acquisition is concerned, learners generally need considerable exposure to L2 input in order to manifest measurable gains in specific grammatical or pragmatic features, as acquisition in these areas is typically slow with learners shifting gradually from one stage to the next. In contrast, the incidental acquisition of L2 vocabulary that arises from quite small amounts of exposure can be measured relatively easily. Of course, vocabulary acquisition is also gradual, especially where 'depth' of knowledge is involved, but exposure to a unknown word on just a few occasions is sufficient for some measurable learning to occur.

However, although vocabulary acquisition research has increased greatly over the decade, most of it has investigated the learning that occurs from *written* input (i.e. through reading); there has been relatively little attention to vocabulary acquisition from *oral* input (i.e. through listening). In this respect, then, it is hoped that the research reported in this section helps to fill a gap in the current literature as it deals predominantly with oral input.

All the chapters in this section involve *modified* input, as this has been defined in Chapter 1. They help address key issues related to the role of modified input in L2 acquisition:

- the relationship between comprehension and acquisition;
- the relative effects of different kinds of modified input on comprehension and acquisition;
- the relative effects of modified input and modified output on comprehension and acquisition;
- individual differences in learners' ability to comprehend and learn from modified input.

Most of the studies reported involve interaction of one kind or another. However, input in language learning need not be interactionally derived so the extent to which learners can benefit from non-interactionally modified input is also addressed.

Chapter 2 provides a review of the factors that can be hypothesized to influence acquisition from oral input. Chapters 3, 4 and 5 all report actual studies of vocabulary acquisition from oral input. Chapter 3 describes two studies that investigated the effects of interactionally and premodified input on the vocabulary acquisition of adolescent and child learners and a third study that sought to identify the specific factors relating to modified input that facilitate vocabulary acquisition. Chapter 4 reports a further study of adult learners with a similar research design but extends the enquiry to the effects of modified output on acquisition. Chapter 5 is a study of how one aspect of individual difference — language aptitude — affects learners' ability to process modified input for comprehension and for acquisition. Chapter 6 examines how the 'generative processing' of written text affects learners' ability to comprehend and to acquire.

CHAPTER 2

Factors in the Incidental Acquisition of Second Language Vocabulary from Oral Input

Rod Ellis

Introduction

In Chapter One we considered a number of general theories that explain the role of the linguistic environment, in particular interactionally created enivironments, in second language (L2) acquisition. In this Chapter we will focus specifically on how learners acquire L2 vocabulary from input. We will be primarily concerned with oral input but also draw extensively on literature that has examined vocabulary acquisition through reading. This Chapter, then, provides a foundation for the empirical studies reported in Chapter Three.

Second language acquisition (SLA) research makes a traditional distinction between **incidental** and **intentional acquisition**. This distinction is reflected in (although not equivalent to) a variety of terms, e.g., 'acquisition' vs. 'learning' (Krashen 1981) and 'implicit' vs' 'explicit' learning (Bialystok 1978; Ellis 1990). On the one hand learners are credited with the ability to 'pick up' L2 items and rules while their attention is focussed primarily on trying to understand and convey messages and without any conscious intention of so doing. On the other hand many learners also have the ability to focus their primary attention on the language code itself in order to deliberately learn new L2 items and rules. The two types of learning cannot be distinguished solely in terms of 'attention', though, for, as Schmidt (1990) has convincingly argued, incidental learning necessarily involves a degree of consciousness when learners 'notice' new items and rules in the input. The distinction rests, somewhat uncomfortably, on a secondary distinction between 'focal' and 'peripheral' attention; whereas intentional learning requires focal attention to be placed deliberately on the linguistic code (i.e. on form or form-meaning connections), incidental learning requires focal attention to be placed on meaning (i.e. message content) but allows peripheral attention to be directed at form.[1]

The distinction between incidental and intentional learning is of particular significance to the acquisition of vocabulary and there is a considerable literature on the relative effectiveness of the two types of learning. In general, it appears that intentional learning that utilizes contextual inferencing strategies and mnemonic strategies such as the keyword method results in better recall of word meanings than incidental learning (see Pressley, Levin and McDaniel 1987; Hulstijn 1992; N. Ellis 1997).[2] However, it is also generally recognized — although not universally (see, for example, Goulden, Nation and Read 1990) — that learners, even the most conscientious, can never acquire a native-like vocabulary through intentional learning. The argument is that no matter how much effort they put into deliberately attending to new words they encounter and no matter how effective their memoriziation or practice strategies are, they simply do not have the time to learn the amount of vocabulary at stake intentionally (see Nagy 1997). Therefore, they must learn a large portion of it incidentally. As Sternberg (1987: 89) uncompromisingly states: 'Most vocabulary is learned from context'.

A number of studies have shown that incidental vocabulary acquisition can take place through extensive reading. For example, Pitts, White and Krashen (1989) report that intermediate level students were able to acquire a measurable amount of invented 'nasdat' words after reading Burgess' *A Clockwork Orange* for 60 minutes. Other studies by Day, Omura and Hiramatsu (1991), Dupuy and Krashen (1993) and Paribakht and Wesche (1997) also report successful vocabulary learning from reading when no instruction was provided. However, some studies have failed to find evidence of learning (e.g. Tudor and Hafiz 1989). Also, as Hulstijn (1992) points out, 'the retention of word meanings in a true incidental learning task is very low' (p. 122). Horst, Cobb and Meara (1998) have pointed out that these studies are methodologically limited in that the amount of text the learners were exposed to was small (e.g. only 907 words in the case of Hulstijn's study) with the result that the frequency of exposure to the target items was very low. Their own study, which involved exposure to a complete graded reader over six days, resulted in a much higher level of incidental acquisition (i.e. about 22% of the targeted words). This study is of particular relevance here as it involved oral as well as written input (i.e. the subjects followed in their books as the story was read aloud to them).

How does this incidental learning take place? The general assumption (see Nagy and Herman 1987; Sternberg 1987; Nation 1990; Stoller and Grabe 1993; N. Ellis 1997) is that the learning of word meanings involves the utilization of various cues that enable learners to infer the meanings of new items from context. But there is a problem here, for, as Coady (1993) points out, no study has yet been designed that shows how contextual learning really occurs. Furthermore, there is a logical problem, again succinctly described by Coady:

> ... it is striking that the very redundancy or richness of information in a given context which, on the one hand, enables a reader to successfully guess an unknown word also predicts, on the other hand, that the same reader is less likely to learn the word-form because he or she was able to comprehend the text without needing to know it. (p. 18)   — Interesting

As we saw in Chapter One, if learners can successfully decode meaning without attending to the form/meaning of a new item, they may not notice the item and, if they do not notice it, they will not learn it. Inferencing from context, therefore, can obviously aid understanding, but may do nothing for learning. Nevertheless, it is likely that inferencing will lead to noticing and, therefore, potentially to acquisition at least on some occasions. Obviously, though, learners need to have built up a sufficient L2 vocabulary to enable them to make use of the contextual clues available in the linguistic input. For this reason, Coady (1997) suggests that learners probably require a working vocabulary of some 5,000 words in order to learn new vocabulary through inferencing from written texts.

In fact, inferencing may be a more effective mechanism of acquisition when the input is oral than when it is written. In the case of written text the only cues available to learners for inferencing the meanings of new words are those contained in the text itself (although there may also be extralinguistic cues in the form of pictures and diagrams). Often enough these cues are inadequate (see Stein 1993). As Hulstijn (1992) has shown, many of the inferences that learners make from written context are incorrect. Oral text, particularly that which derives from face-to-face interaction is different, however. In addition to the cues provided by the verbal text itself, there are other cues available from the intonation and gestures used by the speaker and from the situational context. Furthermore, as we saw in Chapter One, interaction affords opportunities for learners to indicate their non-comprehension and through the negotiation of meaning to receive input that is more finely tuned to their abilities to comprehend. What this often means where difficult words are concerned is that learners are provided with synonyms or definitions. Nagy and Herman (1987) are surely right when they claim;

> Written context will, therefore, generally not be as rich or helpful as oral context in providing information about the meanings of new words. (p. 24)

It seems reasonable to suppose that oral input can constitute an effective source of data for incidental vocabulary learning even in the beginning stages of language acquisition. Indeed, the success which children have in developing a substantial vocabulary in their first language before they come to school testifies to this.

Given the primacy of oral input in many learning contexts[5] together with its potential to facilitate vocabulary acquisition, it is surprising that so little attention has been paid to it in L2 vocabulary acquisition research. Whereas there are whole books given over to the relationship between reading and vocabulary (e.g. McKeown and Curtis 1987; Huckin, Haynes and Coady 1993), and other books that address a variety of issues relating to L2 vocabulary (e.g. Nation 1990; Arnaud and Bejoint 1992; Coady and Huckin 1997; Schmitt and McCarthy 1997), it is difficult to locate a single article on the relationship between oral input and L2 vocabulary development. A number of studies have addressed the effects of listening to stories on vocabulary acquisition (e.g. Wells 1986; Eller, Pappas and Brown 1988; Elley 1989; Feitelson, Goldstein, Iraqi and Share 1993) but most of this research has concerned L1 vocabulary acquisition. Also, it has focussed on on what might be called 'spoken written input' rather than naturally occurring oral input.

The purpose of this Chapter, therefore, is to make a start in examining how incidental L2 vocabulary acquisition can take place from oral input. To this end it addresses this question; what factors govern the learnability of L2 lexical items from oral input? The aim is to provide an initial framework that can serve as a basis for empirical research. Before embarking on this framework, however, it is necessary to give some consideration to the dependent variable — vocabulary acquisition.

The nature of the learning task — vocabulary acquisition

There is a quantitative and qualitative dimension to vocabulary acquisition. On the one hand we can ask 'How many words do learners know?' while on the other we can enquire 'What do the learners know about the words they know?' Curtis (1987) refers to this important distinction as the 'breadth' and 'depth' of a person's lexicon. The focus of much vocabulary research has been on 'breadth', possibly because this is easier to measure. Arguably, however, it is more important to investigate how learners' knowledge of words they already partly know gradually deepens.

As Nation (1990) points out there is considerable variation in the estimates of the breadth of native speakers' vocabulary. This reflects variation in the definition of a word (e.g. whether 'govern', 'governing', 'governed', 'governer' and 'government' are considered five different words or the same word) and differences in the way in which vocabulary is measured (e.g. whether recognition or recall of a word is required). Goulden, Nation and Read (1990) suggest that the average educated native speaker has a vocabulary of about 17,000 'base words', a figure that suggests a rate of acquisition of between two and three a day. A frequently cited figure, however, is Nagy and Herman's (1987) 40,000 for a senior high school student, which suggests students must add around 3,000 new words each year to their lexicon. Nagy et al. (1985) estimate that the rate of vocabulary acquisition necessary to achieve this is around .25 words per minute. Of course, there is considerable variation from one person to another.

Variation in the breadth of L2 learners' lexicons can be expected to be even greater, a reflection not just of the number of years they have been learning the L2, but also the extent and nature of their exposure to it and, also, their purposes for learning it. Learners who need to develop cognitive academic language proficiency (Cummins 1983) in order to study through the medium of the L2 at university level are likely to manifest greater breadth than learners who need only to develop the basic interpersonal skills to participate in day-to-day interactions.

A number of studies have investigated the size of L2 learners' lexicons (e.g. Barnard 1961; Quinn 1968; Jamieson 1976 (all cited in Nation 1990); Yoshida 1978; Palmberg 1987; Wode et al. 1992). More interesting, perhaps, than the absolute size of learners' vocabularies, is the rate at which they increase under specific learning conditions. Yoshida's study found that a three-year old beginner learner exposed to English for two to three hours a day at nursery school had acquired productive use of 260–300 words over seven months. Wode et al. (1992) analyzed the productive vocabulary of German children acquiring English naturally in the US and noted that the rate of acquisition tended to peak quite early and then gradually decrease. This contrasts with L1 acquisition, where growth is slow up to 50 words and then accelerates. Barnard (1961; cited in Nation 1990) found that school children in India learnt between 1000 and 2000 words over a five year period. Palmberg (1987) found evidence of a steady increase in Swedish children's vocabulary as a result of their English studies at school (two 45 minute lessons per week), with the number of words recalled almost doubling after a four and a half month period.

As we have already noted, the depth or quality of L2 learners' vocabulary knowledge is arguably of greater importance than breadth. A learner may 'know' 2000 words but this knowledge may be restricted to the recognitition of these words in specific contexts. For example, a learner may understand the reference of 'ruler' in one context:

I drew a line with my ruler.

but be incapable of recognizing the same word in a different context:

My ruler gives centimetres as well as inches.

and substitute another, incorrect word in production:

*Do you have a scale I can borrow?

Another learner may 'know' only 1000 words but may be able to recognize each word in a range of contexts and also use them accurately in production. As Twadell (1973: 73) notes 'we may "know" a very large number of words with various degrees of vagueness — words which are in a twilight zone between the darkness of entire unfamiliarity and the brightness of complete familiarity'. But how can we characterize the 'depth' of a learner's vocabulary knowledge more precisely?

It is useful to distinguish 'potential' and 'real' vocabulary (Palmberg 1987). Potential vocabulary refers to L2 words that are not yet part of the learner's lexicon but can nevertheless be recognized when they are encountered because, for example, they are cognate with L1 words. Thus, a Japanese learner of L2 English may not know the word 'icecream' but is able to recognize it because it is close to Japanese 'aisukurimu'. Real vocabulary consists of those words that have actually been 'learnt' to some extent.

It is traditional to distinguish 'receptive' and 'productive' (or 'expressive') knowledge. Receptive vocabulary consists of those words that a learner can recognize but may or may not be able to use; productive vocabulary consists of those words the learner can actually use in speech or writing. It is claimed that this distinction reflects a continuum rather than a dichotomy (Crow and Quigley 1985; Palmberg 1987; Coady 1993). Meara (1997), however, has criticized this account of vocabulary learning as 'metaphorical'. Certainly the general assumption that word knowledge is initially receptive and then, over time, through frequent encounters and practice, becomes productive need not be the case. It is perfectly possible to envisage a learner having productive knowledge of a word without receptive knowledge. For example, when speaking Spanish I can say 'cosmopolita' (thus making my potential knowledge real by 'foreignizing' a cognate English word), and yet be unable to recognize this item in oral input because I have not yet formed a phonological representation of the Spanish word.

A more useful way of representing 'depth' of word knowledge involves the distinction between 'knowledge' and 'control' (Bialystok and Sharwood Smith 1985). The application of this distinction to lexis is shown in Figure 1. 'Knowledge' of a word requires the learner to (1) form a phonological/graphological representation of a word, (2) discover what words it collocates with, (3) know

what grammatical patterns it can be used in, (4) understand its denotive reference, (5) understand its connotative meaning(s), and (6) know with what other
words it is typically associated) (see Richards 1976 for a full account of these
aspects of word knowledge). N. Ellis (1996, 1997) argues that the processes
involved in these aspects of vocabulary acquisition are in part implicit and
unconscious (as in (1), (2) and (3) above) and in part explicit and conscious (as
in (4), (5) and (6)). 'Control' concerns the ability of the learner to access a word
in reception and production.

Clearly, there can be degrees of 'knowledge' and degrees of 'control'. For
example, Dale (1965) identified the following degrees of understanding, all of
which would seem to apply to knowledge of a word's denotive meaning:

Stage 1: 'I never saw it.'
Stage 2: 'I've heard of it, but I don't know what it means'.
Stage 3: 'I recognize it in context — it has something to do with ...'
Stage 4: 'I know it'.

Drum (1983) also distinguishes degrees of word-understanding on the basis of a
person's ability to produce different kinds of definition. For example, a person
may only be able to define a word by using it in a word or phrase, reflecting only
a shallow knowledge of its reference (e.g. 'The icons in the church ...'). Alternatively, the person might be able to define the word by giving an accurate paraphrase of its meaning (e.g. 'An icon is a sacred representation of a holy person').
We can also envisage that the other aspects of word knowledge will vary in
'depth'. For example, Meara's (1982) work suggests that the types of associations

			Knowledge			
Implicit Acquisition					Explicit Acquisition	
(1)	(2)	(3)	(4)	(5)	(6)	
Form	Collocations	Gram. patterns	Denotive meaning	Connotative meaning	Associations	
Control						
Reception						
Production						

Figure 1. *A model of 'depth' of vocabulary knowledge*

found in L2 learners' lexicons differ from the types found in native speakers; clang associations such as 'clog/dog' are much more prominent in the former.

Irrespective of what learners know about a word, they are likely to vary in their ability to access their knowledge in accordance with the conditions of use. As we have already noted, they may be able to use a word receptively but not productively, or vice-versa. They may be able to access a word (for reception or production) when given time to do so, but be unable to do so instantly. We are all familiar with the tip-of-the-tongue phenomenon.

Clearly, 'depth' of word knowledge is a complex issue and the above discussion has done no more than skim the surface. It will not be possible to further our understanding until we heed Meara's (1984, 1992, 1997) call and develop adequate models of how a learner's mental lexicon is constructed by considering it as a whole — as 'a large-scale structure' — rather than focussing on a small number of individual words. We will not proceed very far in our study of how incidental vocabulary learning from oral (or written) context takes place, unless we have a clear understanding of what we mean by 'vocabulary acquisition' and, arguably, we are still a long way from this.

Factors affecting incidental vocabulary learning

We can hypothesize that a number of factors will influence incidental vocabulary learning. Inevitably given the paucity of research into acquisition from oral input, this account will have to draw on research involving written texts. It should, therefore, be seen as a programmatic statement rather than a survey. The factors are grouped under four headings; (1) intrinsic word properties, (2) input factors, (3) interactional factors and (4) learner factors.

Intrinsic word properties

It seems very likely that some words will be more difficult to learn from oral input than others, irrespective of the richness of contextual clues available to the learners. We will consider four intrinsic word properties which appear to influence acquisition.

(1) Pronounceability

The extent to which learners are able to pronounce an L2 word will fairly obviously affect their ability to actually *produce* it. It is less obvious that it affects their ability to *perceive* the word and, thereby, to acquire it. Laufer (1997), however, cites a number of sources that suggest that pronounceable words are more likely to be perceived accurately (e.g. Ellis and Beaton 1993a). Laufer suggests that learners may avoid attending to phonologically problematic words. The degree of phonological similarity between the learners' first language (L1) and the target language functions as a major determinant of difficulty.

(2)   Part of speech

There is some evidence to suggest that learners learn nouns more readily than other parts of speech, at least in the early stages. Yoshida (1978) found that his subject, a three and a half year old Japanese boy, learnt mainly nouns initially — 60% of his total words after four and a half months were nouns. In contrast, he learnt few verbs. Felix (1978) also found that his subjects (child learners of L2 German) were slow to learn verbs. Nation (1990) cites a study by Rodgers (1969) that found nouns were the easiest to learn with adjectives next. Verbs and adverbs were the most difficult. Elley (1989) in a study investigating the effects of listening to stories read aloud on the acquisition of new words by seven and eight year old native speakers of English found a tendency for the children to show higher gains on nouns than on adjectives and verbs.

There are a number of explanations for these findings. One is, as Nation suggests, the meaning of nouns can be guessed from context more easily than the meaning of verbs. Another very likely explanation is that learners initially concentrate on nouns because they are more useful for decoding and encoding messages. As Ellis (1984) has pointed out, early L2 utterances are frequently propositionally reduced because learners have limited processing capacity. Verbs are omitted more frequently than nouns because they are not so important for getting a message across. They may be attended to less in the input for the same reason. Finally, N. Ellis and Beaton (1993a) suggest that nouns may be easier to learn than other parts of speech because they are more imageable (see below).

(3)   Distinctiveness of word form

A word that has a distinct form is easier to learn than a word that is similar in form to some other word. Nation (1990) describes the problems he had distinguishing two Indonesian words, 'bintang' (star) and 'binatang' (animal). Huckin and Bloch (1993) in a qualitative study of contextual inferencing found that 'mistaken identity' accounted for most of the cases of unsuccessful guessing. The learners allowed word shape to override contextual factors. For example, one learner misread 'optimal' as 'optional'. In both of these examples, it is interesting to note that the words causing the problem begin and end with the same letters, being differentiated by letters in medial position. Where oral input is concerned, mistaken identity, where unfamiliar words are heard as familiar words, are likely to be even more common. According to Ellman and McClelland's (1982) trace model of lexical access, lexical expectations can override an auditory analysis of the input. As an example of this, Laufer (1997) gives examples of 'deceptive transparency', where words are processed wrongly because learners assume the meaning of a word is equivalent to the meanings of its parts (e.g. they process 'outline' as 'out of line').

Laufer (1997) also notes that 'there is a wealth of evidence that L2 learners confuse words that sound and/or look alike' (p. 146). He reports his own study of 'synforms'. This found that the most problematic were those that differed according to suffixes (e.g. industrial/industrious) and which shared the same consonants but differed in vowels (e.g. conceal/cancel). Laufer's study involved written tests only but it is highly likely that oral synforms can also be distinguished with regard to the degree of difficulty they pose learners.

(4)   Length of word form

It seems reasonable to suppose that learners find it easier to decode and remember monosyllabic than polysyllabic words. Meara (1984) reports that Chinese learners of L2 English were found to have 'an unexpected difficulty with long words' (p. 234). However, Meara suggests that the reason for the Chinese learners' difficulty might lie in the lack of familiarity with the Roman alphabet (i.e. be a reading problem). Another possible explanation is that more effort and time is needed to process and remember polysyllabic words than monosyllabic words.

However, it may be difficult to disentangle the effects of word length from other associated factors. Long words may be less pronounceable than short words. Also, as Laufer (1997) points out, in a language such as English, shorter words tend to be more frequent in the input. Laufer also notes that length may only become significant beyond a certain point but that it is difficult to say what this point is.

(5)   The degree of correlation between form and meaning

There is considerable evidence to suggest that learners initially store words according to their sound rather than their meaning. Henning (1973; cited in Nation 1990) found that low proficiency learners tended to connect similar sounding words such as 'horse' and 'house' whereas high proficiency learners made connections according to meaning (e.g. 'horse' and 'cow'). Similarly, Meara's (1982) word association experiments showed that low-level learners were predisposed to make clang associations, whereas high-level learners and native speakers made more paradigmatic associations. If learners are initially strongly influenced by the sound of words, then it would seem likely that they will find it easier to learn words where there is a degree of correlation between sound and meaning (e.g. onomatopeic words like 'bark' or 'sigh') and also, perhaps, words where the form clearly signals the grammatical meaning of a word (e.g. 'na*tion*'; 'lov*able*').

(6) Imageability

Ellis and Beaton (1993a) review research which indicates that imageable words are more easily learnt than non-imageable words. An imageable word is one that 'arouses a mental image' (p. 5). Concrete words like 'dog' and 'cup' may be more easily learnt than abstract words like 'love' and 'cruelty', because they are more imageable. Although the studies they report (including their own) concern intentional learning, it would seem highly likely that imageability is an important factor in incidental learning too, probably because, as Ellis and Beaton note, it results in a 'richer representation'. Elley (1989), in the study referred to above, found that 'vividness' was one of six factors that was significantly correlated with his eight year old subjects' mean vocabulary gains, although less strongly than some of the other factors he investigated. However, Laufer (1997) points out that it does not follow that because a word is concrete it will be easier to learn than a word that is abstract. He notes that English speakers of Hebrew have more difficulty learning the two Hebrew words for 'blue' (kachol/tchelet) than they do many abstract nouns. The extent to which concrete and abstract words are easy or difficult will depend partly on the lexical and conceptual equivalences of the learners' L1 and the target language.

(7) Polysemy

There is substantial evidence in SLA that learners construct their interlanguages on the principle that one form corresponds to a single meaning (see, for example, Andersen's (1984) One-to-One Principle). It seems, likely, therefore that learners will find it easier to acquire those words that have single, transparent meanings than polysemous words. This claim is supported by a study by Bensoussan and Laufer (1984) which found that learners were much more likely to experience problems in lexical guessing with polysemous words. Learners proved reluctant to abandon the meaning of a polysemous item they were familiar with even if it did not fit the particular context in which they had encountered the word.

Input factors

Input factors are formal in nature; they reflect the ways in which the speech addressed to L2 learners is simplified. They can be distinguished from interactional factors (see Chapter One). In this section we will consider only input factors.

(1) Frequency

An input factor of obvious importance is word frequency, especially where the acquisition of word form and collocations is concerned (see N. Ellis 1997). Most of the research, however, has addressed frequency in written texts. Oral input tends to have a lower lexical density than written input and to contain more lexical repetition (McCarthy and Carter 1997). Thus, it is likely that oral input exposes learners to fewer lexical items more frequently. This may constitute an advantage at least for lower proficiency learners.

There is plenty of evidence to suggest that the number of encounters learners have with a word is a major factor in whether they learn it or not. Kachru (1962–cited in Nation 1990) found that words that occurred seven or more times in the course books of Indian learners were known by most learners, but that most of the words occurring only once or twice were not known by most learners. Palmberg (1987) found that the vocabulary remembered by beginner learners of English in a classroom context in Sweden reflected the frequency of the items in the text book. Beck, McKeown and Omanson (1987) report a vocabulary training study, part of which investigated the effects of word frequency on vocabulary learning by native speaking children. They found that four encounters with new words were sufficient to produce some results, although the learning that took place was 'limited'. Elley (1989) found that frequency produced the highest correlation with vocabulary gains made by seven and eight year old children from stories read to them. Eller, Pappas and Brown (1988), in another study investigating the effects of listening to stories, also found frequency a factor. Brown (1993) found a clear, although not very strong, relationship between general word frequency (determined by reference to the Brown University corpus — Francis and Kucera 1982) and the words learnt by learners enrolled on a university intensive English language program during one semester. However, she did not find any relationship between the specific vocabulary used in a video-instructional program ('Raiders of the Lost Ark') and vocabulary learning.

A question of considerable importance is whether the relationship between frequency and word learning is a monotonic one (i.e. whether the more frequent a word is, the more learners learn it and the greater the 'depth' of their learning) or whether there is a threshold effect operating (i.e. a word has to be encountered a specific number of times for it to be learnt). N. Ellis (1997) refers to Andersen's 'power law of practice' according to which the amount of improvement decreases as a function of increasing frequency. Thus, more exposures do not necessarily result in more learning. There is also research to show that little is learnt from just one or two exposures. As we have already noted, Hulstijn (1992) found that retention of word meanings in an incidental learning task that afforded just one exposure was 'very low indeed'. Brown's failure to find any significant effect for specific vocabulary frequency may reflect the fact that the words did not occur with sufficient frequency for any measurable learning to take place. In contrast, her finding that general vocabulary frequency was related to learning can be explained by the fact that the learners in her study may have received sufficient exposures for learning to take place. All this points to a threshold effect. However, Nagy, Herman and Anderson (1985) argue that a small increment in word knowledge is possible from a single exposure to written text.

In fact, much depends on the 'depth' of knowledge being measured. It is possible that a single exposure is sufficient for some learning to take place, even in the case of oral input. Learners, for example, may be able to recognize it as a 'real' word where previously they could not. But a single encounter is unlikely to be sufficient to enable learners to give the meaning of a word let alone recall its phonological form.

If by 'knowing a word' we mean 'being able to give its meaning', then the available research suggests around 6 or 7 exposures seem to be the minimum necessary, although this is obviously likely to vary depending on various other factors, such as the intrinsic difficulty of the word.[6] Palmberg (1987) refers to research by Carpay (1975) which indicates that new words should be used in at least four different contexts when they are first introduced followed by subsequent exposure on three other occasions. The assumption underlying the 'threshold' view is that each exposure adds something to a learners' knowledge of a word, moving it 'a little bit higher on the scale of knowledge' (Nagy and Hermann 1987: 27), but that not until there have been sufficient exposures will learners 'know the meaning' of a word.

(2) Saliency through 'focus'

A word may be salient (i.e. 'noticeable') because of its intrinsic properties, or it may be made salient by the way it is used in the input. One way that words can be made salient in oral input is through repetition (i.e. its frequency), but there are other ways. A word can receive emphatic stress. A word may be a 'key' word for understanding a particular message. A word can be topicalized through left dislocation (e.g. 'The dishwashing liquid — give it me'). These devices serve to focus the learner's attention on the word and thus make learning more likely.

One way in which words can be made salient is through instructional focus. This may or may not involve making them the subject of intentional learning. For example, Hultsijn (1992), in the study referred to earlier, asked learners to read a passage containing unknown words, clues to the meaning of which were provided in the margins. Hulstijn argues that this still constituted an incidental learning task because the learners were concerned only with understanding the text, not learning the words. Hulstijn found that such focussed exposure had some, limited impact on learning. Watanabe (1997) also found that focussed exposure in the form of marginal glosses resulted in more new words being learned from a written text than when either no cues were provided or paraphrases were incorporated into the text. Brown (1993) also examined saliency through instructionally focussed exposure by investigating whether glossing words and using them in exercises based on the 'Raiders' video affected learning. It did not. However, she found that 'salience from gap' affected learning. This referred to the idea of the concept labelled by a word being introduced before the word itself (e.g. the learners might see a shovel being used in the 'Raiders' film but not hear or see the word 'shovel' until later). Brown concluded that 'words that are important in a specific context are more likely to be acquired regardless of frequency' (p. 281). Elley (1989) found that words that were helpful to the plot and characterization were more likely to be learned from listening to stories than words that were less important in these respects.

(3)   Availability of contextual cues

There is general agreement that contextual cues aid vocabulary acquisition. Elley (1989), for example, found that strength of meaning cues was strongly correlated with vocabulary gains in the learners he investigated.

Sternberg (1987) provides a useful classification of the different types of contextual cues found in reading texts. As these are also applicable to oral input they are summarized in Table 1. He points out, sensibly enough, that 'it is unrealistic to expect a given kind of cue to be equally helpful in figuring out the meanings of all kinds of words' (p. 93). Some cues will work better for some words and other cues for other words (e.g. a temporal cue for 'diurnal'; a spatial cue for 'pasture' (as in 'low lying pasture')). He also notes that the helpfulness of a cue can be determined by whether it precedes or follows the word. Studies of cue utilization in reading suggest that it is easier to make use of preceding than following cues (e.g. Huckin and Bloch 1993), although this might not be the case in oral input, as learners might benefit from first hearing the unknown word and then receiving clues as to its meaning. Finally, the proximity of the cue to the unknown word is also likely to be important. Huckin and Bloch found that in most cases of successful guessing their subjects used some word or words in 'the immediate context'.

It might be argued that input that provides learners with rich clues as to the meaning of an unknown word is more likely to facilitate acquisition of its meaning than input that provides only poor clues. This is highly likely where intentional learning is concerned. Li (1988) compared the effect of 'cue-ade-quate' and 'cue-inadequate contexts' on the inferencing and retention of unknown words from both written and oral input by 48 advanced Chinese learners of English. In this study, the learners were presented with 'sixty discrete, semantically disconnected sentences' (p. 405), so it seems highly likely that they approached it as a task calling for intentional learning of the items. The results showed that both inferencing and retention were facilitated by cue-adequate contexts. However, as we noted earlier, it is not at all clear that this will also be the case in incidental vocabulary learning. A rich context may make understanding possible without any learning taking place.

There is clearly a need for much more research on the effects of contextual cues on vocabulary learning from oral input, particularly *incidental* learning. We

Table 1. *Types of contextual cues (from Sternberg 1987)*

Type of cue	description
Temporal	Cues regarding the duration or frequency of X (the unknown word) or when X can occur.
Spatial	Cues regarding the location of X, or possible location in which X can sometimes be found.
Value	Cues regarding the worth or desirability of X, or the kinds of affects X arouses.
Stative descriptive	Cues regarding properties of X (such as size, shape, color, odor, feel etc).
Functional	Cues regarding possible purposes of X, descriptive actions X can perform, or potential uses of X.
Causal/Enablement	Cues regarding possible causes of or enabling conditions of X.
Class membership	Cues regarding one or more classes to which X belongs, or other members of one or more classes of which X is a member.
Equivalence	Cues regarding the meaning of X, or contrasts (such an antonymy) to the meaning of X.

know little about the effect of different types of cues, the proximity of the cue to the unknown word and of cue-adequate as opposed to cue-inadequate contexts. It ought to be possible to tease out these effects through careful experimentation. We also need to go beyond the micro level by examining how macrostructural properties of the context influence acquisition. For example, we might examine how learners make use of their knowledge of 'story grammar' to learn new words.

(4) Input complexity

The overall complexity of the input in which new words are embedded can also be expected to affect their learnability. There is a considerable literature on the relationship between input complexity and comprehension (see Ellis 1994). Parker and Chaudron (1987), for example, review 12 experimental studies of the effects of input modifications on comprehension. Their conclusion is that although linguistic modifications (e.g. simpler syntax and vocabulary) helped comprehension they did not do so consistently. In contrast, what they call 'elaborative modifications' (e.g. repetition, paraphrase, use of synonyms, extraposition and cleft constructions) were considered more likely to promote comprehension. However, Parker and Chaudron's own study failed to show any advantage for elaborative modifications, a result they explain by suggesting that the overall lexical and syntactic difficulty of the reading texts they used was so great as to negate the effects of the modifications. This research is premised on the assumption that if input aids comprehension it also aids learning, but, as we have already noted, this assumption may not be justified.

Two measures of input complexity that can be expected to have an impact on both the comprehension and acquisition of new words are **lexical density** and **density of unknown words**. **Lexical density** is determined by establishing the ratio of content words to total word tokens. Faerch, Haastrup and Phillips (1984: 84) comment:

> The underlying assumption is that as it is the content words which primarily convey information, a text is dense if it contains many content words relative to the number of function words.

The density of unknown words is measured by establishing the ratio of new words to total words in a text. Writers of simplified reading texts set considerable store in controlling the number of new words learners will encounter. Nation (1990) refers to a study by Holley (1973) which tried to determine the optimal level of new-word density for written texts. It indicated that 'vocabulary learning continues to increase even up to a new vocabulary density of one new word per fifteen known words' (p. 343). This is considerably denser than the 1: 50 density recommended by West (1955) for supplementary readers. Nation considers that Holley's learners may have been able to handle a fairly high density because the overall length of the text they were asked to read was fairly short (750 words). Of course, the optimal lexical density and new-word density is likely to be lower for oral texts than for written texts. There appears to be little research addressing this.[7]

Interactional factors

As we have already noted, what distinguishes oral input from written input is that the latter typically involves interaction. This allows for the input to be modified at just those points where learners experience comprehension problems. When learners hear a word that prevents them from understanding the message they can request clarification and thereby obtain further clues about its meaning. Interaction, therefore, potentially enriches input in a number of ways that can be hypothesized to facilitate word acquisition.

The literature on meaning negotiation in interactions involving L2 learners is extensive (see Chapter One) but has focussed on the nature of the modifications that take place, the structure of the modified discourse and on comprehension. There has been no attempt to examine the nature of what Gass and Varonis (1985) refer to as the 'trigger' (i.e. the source of the communication problem). However, a quick look at the protocols given as examples of meaning negotiation in the published research makes it clear that, in many instances, the trigger is lexical in nature, as in this example from Pica and Doughty (1985);

A: She's on welfare.
B: What do you mean by welfare?

Often the negotiation of meaning focuses quite explicitly on lexis.

How then does interaction help learners to acquire vocabulary? Two possible ways are (1) by increasing the overall quantity of the input and (2) through elaboration that results in greater transparency of meaning.

Interaction where meaning negotiation takes place is likely to result in more input (see Chapter Three). It seems reasonable to suppose that the more input learners get, the faster they will learn.[8] Where vocabulary is concerned, sheer quantity of input may help by giving learners more time to process new words. Perhaps they tune out the redundant input, thus creating time to focus on the items they find problematic.

Gass and Varonis (1985) define 'elaboration' as information not included in the original, problem-causing utterance but subsequently added. One of the main ways in which speakers elaborate on their initial input when the problem is lexical is by adding a definition of some kind. Through negotiation learners can obtain definitions that meet all the requirements for the 'ideal' definition set by Aristotle, as summarized by Edwards (1967: 322):

1. a definition should give the essence or nature of the thing defined, rather than its accidental properties
2. a definition should give the genus and differentia of the thing defined
3. one should not define by synonyms
4. a definition should be concise
5. one should not define by metaphors
6. one should not define by negative terms or by correlative terms.

It seems very likely that learners will obtain a very good idea of the meaning of words so defined. Meaning negotiation, therefore, may be ideally suited to the incidental learning of word meanings. Such learning, it should be noted, involves a high level of explicitness.

Elaboration through definitions is also found in non-interactive discourse (e.g. lectures). However, such elaboration does not always result in a high level of transparency. Chaudron (1982) describes some of the devices used to elaborate in 'teacher-talk'. He argues that some of them (e.g. apposition, conjunction and parallel structures) can result in ambiguity; learners cannot tell 'whether new meanings are being added or whether a particular word is being elaborated' (p. 16). Here is one of Chaudron's examples taken from a high school Grade 10 history lesson. It shows how apposition might confound rather than facilitate word acquisition:

> ... the beaver is known as a very industrious and busy, uhm, hard-working animal.

The learners will find it impossible to know whether 'busy' and 'hard-working' are synonyms of 'industrious' or new ideas. One of the advantages of negotiated inter-action, perhaps, is that ambiguous definitions of this kind are less likely to occur.[9]

So far, the research has focussed on just one aspect of interaction — the negotiation of meaning triggered by lexical problems. The role of interaction in vocabulary acquisition, however, goes way beyond meaning negotiation. We need to broaden the scope of enquiry by examining how interaction helps learners' to focus attention on specific items and to clarify their meanings, even when there are no problems. We should also recognize that 'interaction' is not a necessary condition of acquisition — learners can acquire vocabulary from non-inter-actional input, as studies like Elley (1989), referred to earlier, have shown.

Learner factors

An explanation of how incidental vocabulary acquisition takes place must take account of the learner as well as the input. Any model of vocabulary acquisition that leaves out learner factors is incomplete. From the existing literature, we can identify a number of learner factors that appear to be important.

(1) Existing knowledge of L2 vocabulary

It can be hypothesized that learners with a well-developed L2 vocabulary will find it easier to infer the meanings of unknown words from context and thus will acquire them more easily and rapidly than those with a more restricted L2 voca-bulary. Horst, Cobb and Meara (1998) report that their subjects' prior vocabulary knowledge facilitated their incidental acquisition of new vocabulary from a graded reader but that the relationship was not strong. They suggest that this is because the relationship is not a linear one. Learners with low general vocabularies will lack the lexical knowledge needed to infer the meanings of new words but learners with high general vocabularies may find themselves able to understand the text without the need to notice new words. This line of argument points to some threshold level of prior vocabulary for incidental acquisition to work effectively.

(2) Background knowledge

A crucial factor is the learner's background knowledge. It is widely acknowledged that there is a close relationship between vocabulary breadth and world knowl-edge. As Drum and Konopak (1987) put it, '... the more knowledge of the world that an individual has, the more words that person will know' Given that world knowledge is an important component of general intelligence, vocabulary can be expected to provide a good indicator of a person's overall intelligence, a hypothesis supported by psychometric IQ tests (Sternberg 1987). What, then, is the nature of the relationship between what a person knows and word acquisition? The answer is almost certainly that it is an interactive one. Learners with wide background knowledge will find it easier to infer the meanings of new words from context and thus increase their vocabulary. Conversely, learners with a wide vocabulary will find it easier to utilize contexts in the acquisition of new concepts.

Imagine an L2 learner hearing (or reading) the following:

> The earthquake was devastating. It destroyed half the buildings in the city.
> Furthermore, the resulting *tsunami* flooded the whole area.

There are clues within the context as to the meaning of 'tsunami' but these are likely to be insufficient without some background knowledge (e.g. that earthquakes disrupt the seabed, causing tidal waves). The learner who already has some knowledge of how an earthquake can cause a tidal wave is in a much better position to understand, and perhaps to learn, 'tsunami'.

So too is the learner with a wide existing L2 vocabulary. This is true on two accounts. First, without a knowledge of the meaning of 'earthquake', 'resulting' and 'flooded' the learner will not have access to the contextual cues that signal the meaning of 'tsunami'. Coady (1993) claims that words that are easily recognized serve as 'access portals to schemata' (p. 11). He suggests that for succesful inferencing from written input to take place learners need an established vocabulary of about 5,000 lexical items, although, as we noted earlier this may be less true where inferencing from oral input is involved. Second, if the new word is to be learnt, the learner has to slot it into an existing lexical network. Aitcheson (1987) has suggested that a mental lexicon consists of overlapping modules (one for semantic-syntactic information, one for phonological information and one for creating new words). Each module is characterized as a complex network and within each network 'there should be clusters of dense, multiplex mini-networks' (p. 198). Aitcheson suggests that one kind of mini-network is composed of words related to the same semantic domain. The richer the network representing a domain, the easier it is to make a new entry. Thus a learner with a tightly organized network that already includes such items as 'earthquake', 'devastating', and 'flood' is better equipped to learn 'tsunami'.

Learners also possess 'word schemas'. Nagy, Anderson and Herman (1987), Nagy and Scott (1990), and Nagy and Gentner (1990) identify various types of word knowledge that can help a learner learn new vocabulary. **Morphological knowledge** consists of knowledge of the prefixes, roots and suffixes that make up words. **Knowledge of the typical patterns of word meaning** constrain the range of hypotheses that learners have to entertain when they encounter a new word. Learners have knowledge of basic semantic relationships such as synonymy, anotonymy and hyponymy. They also have knowledge of the properties of semantic domains (e.g. they know that English verbs like 'slide' and 'wobble' say something about how an object moves but not about the shape of the object that is moving). Nagy and his co-workers suggest that learners use these different kinds of knowledge to construct and evaluate hypotheses about the meanings of new words. In Nagy and Scott (1990), for example, they show that 7th graders' ability to distinguish between plausible and implausible English word meanings was related to the size of their lexicons.

From this discussion of the role of background knowledge we can suggest the following general scale of learning difficulty:

Difficult | The learner does not have an existing concept to which the L2 item can be attached; the lexical domain to which the item belongs is underdeveloped; the learner's 'word schemas' are poorly developed.

↕

Easy | The learner has an existing concept to which the L2 item can be attached; the lexical domain to which the item belongs is well developed; the learner's 'word schemas' are well-developed.

Again though, we need to acknowledge that just because a word is easy to learn with the help of background knowledge does not guarantee that it will be learnt.

(3)   Procedural knowledge

Learners also have metacognitive and metalinguistic knowledge about how new words can be learnt. This kind of **procedural knowledge** is defined by Faerch and Kasper (1985) as 'knowing how'. It consists of the strategies and procedures employed by learners to process L2 data for acquisition and use. In the case of vocabulary acquisition we can distinguish two types of procedural knowledge; that associated with contextual inferencing and that associated with negotiating meaning in interaction.

A number of researchers have examined the procedural knowledge involved in contextual inferencing, but probably the most substantial work is that of Haastrup (1991, 1992). Haastrup's model is based on her analysis of the strategies evidenced by Danish learners of English in think-aloud tasks which required them to work in pairs to guess the meanings of unknown words from written texts. Haastrup describes a continuum of word-processing strategies, reflecting the different types of cues that learners utilize. At one end of the continuum is 'pure bottom-level processing' where learners rely exclusively on word-internal cues, while at the other end is 'top-level processing with full integration' where learners use a variety of cues taken from different levels, including 'context' and 'semantics', and integrate them. Haastrup (1991) suggests that there is a 'developmental continuum' of processing ability. Learners at the first stage of development can only process zero items (i.e. words with no available linguistic cues such as 'bouts'). At the second stage they can process 'ling' items (i.e. items like 'curative' which invite interactive processing with integration of just one linguistic element). At the third stage they can handle 'ling+' words (i.e. words that invite interactive processing with integration of several linguistic cues (e.g. 'indiscriminately'). Although Haastrup's claims about a developmental continuum are somewhat speculative, her research provides strong evidence of variation in individual learners' ability to process meaning from context and also points to the way in which this ability might develop over time. It should be noted, however, that Haastrup's work (and that of just about all other studies that have investigated inferencing strategies) examined learner behaviour in the context of activities that required them to deliberately try to understand the meanings of unknown words. As N. Ellis (1997) has pointed out, we do not know whether the same strategies are at work when learners are reading for general understanding and inferencing incidentally.

Whereas Haastrup is concerned with the processing knowledge involved in inferring meanings from written contexts, Robinson (1993) considers the procedural knowledge involved in negotiating meaning, in particular lexical meaning. He notes that negotiation involves the twin processes of 'assertion' (i.e. one participant trying to fix or explain a word meaning) and 'assimilation' (i.e. the other participant trying to break down what is said into more manageable units in order to assimilate them). He argues that 'procedural vocabulary is essential to this process' (p. 241). High frequency vocabulary — Robinson calls it 'indexical vocabulary' — serves as the means by which learners negotiate understanding of new words. Obviously, learners vary in their procedural knowledge. We can expect learners with well-developed abilities to carry out inferencing involving the integration of varied cues, linguistic and contextual/ semantic, and learners who are adept at negotiating the meanings of new words to develop their lexicons — both in terms of breadth and depth — more rapidly than learners whose skills are less developed in these respects.[10]

(4)   Immediate phonological memory

In order to learn new words it is necessary to form a stable representation of their phonological form. The extent to which individual learners are able to form phonological representations rapidly and accurately, therefore, is likely to influence their ability to acquire L2 vocabulary. In the case of L1 vocabulary acquisition, Gathercole and Baddeley (1990) review research which suggests there is a close link between children's phonological memory skills and vocabulary development. They also report a study which provides results suggesting that five-year old children with poor ability to repeat non-words were slower at learning unfamiliar names for toys than children with good repetition skills. It would seem highly likely that immediate phonological memory is a significant factor in L2 vocabulary acquisition. It is also possible that phonological memory improves as a result of acquiring new words.

(5)   The learner's L1

There is ample evidence to suggest that the learners' L1 plays a major role in L2 vocabulary acquisition. One important factor is the distance between the L1 and

L2. Where the two languages are close (e.g. English and Dutch), learners will have access to a large number of cognate words. In such cases, learners are likely to find the acquisition of both the phonological and semantic representation of a 'new' word easy. Nagy et al. (1993) report a study of Spanish-English bilinguals and biliterates, which shows that they were effectively able to transfer Spanish lexical knowledge to reading in English. Even languages that are not close may contain borrowings that facilitate acquisition. Japanese, for example, contains a large number of words borrowed from English. However, because the pronunciation of these words has been adapted to the L1 phonological system (a process known as 'foreignizing') learners may have difficulty in recognizing the L2 words when they hear them.

Also, care needs to be taken not to over-emphasize the value of cognates to learners. Because an L1 word has an L2 equivalent where its basic, denotive meaning is concerned does not permit the learner to conclude that the two words are identical with respect to other aspects of use and meaning — the grammatical patterns in which they can be used, their connotation, collocation and association. Holmes and Ramos (1993) note that cognates can often prove 'false friends'. They point to the need for learners to check their initial guesses based on the recognition of cognates against other contexual cues. Nagy et al. (1993) suggest that the ability to distinguish true from false or partial cognates may require 'a high level of cognitive flexibility and metacognitive awareness' (p. 254).

The degree of similarity in the phonological features of the L1 and L2 are also likely to affect the ease of learning L2 vocabulary. Ellis and Beaton (1993b) review research which indicates 'the less overlap between the feature set of the native and the foreign word, the harder it will be for the FL learner to learn that word' (p. 3). Thus a Chinese learner of English finds words like 'pen' and 'see' easy to learn but words like 'rice' and 'eighth' difficult.

Conclusion

The purpose of this chapter has been to examine the factors that are likely to influence learners' success in learning L2 vocabulary incidentally from oral input. Unfortunately, this important aspect of second language acquisition has been largely neglected by researchers. While there is a substantial body of research relating to vocabulary acquisition from *written* context, hardly any attention has been paid to *oral* context. As a result, this Chapter is programmatic and, in places, speculative. It nevertheless seems important to ask how vocabulary acquisition from oral input takes place — if only because learners attach considerable importance to vocabulary and because many L2 learners are dependent on oral input, particularly in the initial stages of acquisition.

The following is a summary of the main conclusions:

(1) Most L2 vocabulary is learnt incidentally, much of it from oral input.
(2) Oral input may be particularly important for the incidental acquisition of vocabulary by beginners because it affords more contextual support than written input.
(3) L2 vocabulary acquisition needs to be characterized as having a quantitative and a qualitative dimension. Learning a word involves a gradual process of adding 'depth' to an initial, shallow representation.
(4) A variety of factors are likely to affect the 'learnability' of a word. These have been grouped under four general headings; the intrinsic properties of the L2 word, input factors, interactional factors and the learner factors (including knowledge of the L1). The different factors relating to these four categories are summarized for convenience in Table 2.

Table 2. *A summary of factors potentially influencing the acquisition of L2 words*

Factors	Description
Intrinsic word properties:	
Pronounceability	Learners find it easier to perceive words that they also find easy to pronounce.
Part of speech	Learners learn nouns more easily than other parts of speech.
Distinctiveness of word form	A word with a distinct word form is learned more easily than a word which is similar in form to a word the learner already knows. Words that are 'deceptively transparent' cause problems to learners.
Length of word	Monosyllabic words are easier to learn than polysyllabic words. One reason, however, might be because they are also more frequent in the input.
Correlation between form and meaning	Words where there is a degree of correlation between sound and meaning are easier to learn.
Imageability	A word that arouses a mental image (e.g. a concrete noun) is easier to learn than a word for which there is no obvious mental image (e.g. an abstract noun). However, the lexical and conceptual equivalence of the L1 and the target language is also a factor.
Polysemy	It is difficult for learners to infer the correct meaning of polysemous items from context.

Input factors:	
Frequency	Words encountered frequently are learned more readily than words encountered rarely; also frequent encounters promote depth of learning. The relationship between frequency and vocabulary learning may not be monotonic, however.
Saliency through 'focus'	Words that are made salient through some kind of focus (e.g. glossing) are more likely to be remembered.
Availability of contextual cues	Words for which there are cues in the immediate context are likely to be learned more easily than words for which there are no contextual cues, or only distant cues. But currently little is known about which cues or combinations of cues work best.
Input complexity	New words that occur in simplified input (i.e. input with low lexical density and low new-word density) are likely to be more readily learned than words that occur in more complex input.
Interactional factors:	
More input	Interaction can increase the total input available to learners, which may give increase redundancy and give more time to process problematic items.
Elaborated input	Interaction enables learners to request clarification and thereby obtain definitions of unknown words. However, not all elaborated input is beneficial for acquisition.
Learner factors:	
Existing L2 knowledge	L2 learners may require some threshold level of existing L2 lexical knowledge to be able to acquire new vocabulary from context.
Background knowledge	Background knowledge helps learners inference the meaning of new words. Possession of a richly specified lexical domain makes it easier to 'place' a new word in the domain.
Procedural knowledge	Learners vary in their ability to integrate bottom-up and top-down processing and, therefore, in their ability to inference the meanings of new words. Learners also vary in their knowledge of the procedural vocabulary needed to negotiate understanding of new words.
Immediate phonological memory	Learners vary in their ability to form accurate phonological representations of new words they hear.
The learner's L1	L2 words cognate with L1 words are easy to learn, although they may sometimes prove 'false friends'. L2 words with a similar phonological shape to L2 words may also be easier to learn.

Finally, it is necessary to reiterate one of the main points covered in Chapter One, namely that comprehending and learning an L2 word are not the same thing. Much of the above discussion has centred on what makes comprehension of new L2 items possible on the assumption that comprehension is a necessary condition for learning to take place. It is not a sufficient condition, however. This raises the question as to what else is needed for incidental vocabulary acquisition to take place. One answer is 'interest'. Elley (1989) found that the children in his study picked up almost twice as many words from listening to one story than to the other and suggests that the principal reason for this was 'lack of involvement' in the second story. Stoller and Grabe (1993: 38) argue that 'because L2 students often find themselves at a "loss for words", they are usually quite motivated to improve their vocabulary'. However, not all learners are so motivated and, more particularly, as Elley's study indicates, they are not necessarily motivated to learn every new word they come across. Ultimately, an account of incidental L2 vocabulary acquisition will have to address personal and affective factors as well as psycholinguistic issues.

Notes

I would like to thank Stephen Krashen, Leo Van lier and Lidia Woytak for their helpful comments on an earlier version of this Chapter.

1. Van Lier, in his comments on a draft version of this chapter, rightly points out that the distinction between 'incidental' and 'intentional' learning is more problematic than my discussion of it acknowledges. He notes, for example, that 'intentionality' may be considered as something external to the learner (e.g. imposed by an instructional focus) or internal (i.e. the learner's own, preferred orientation). Here, and elsewhere in this book, I am assuming that 'intentional learning' refers to intentionality on the part of the learner. He also notes that language users alternate between focal or peripheral attention in response to processing needs.

2. Krashen (1989 provides evidence to suggest that incidental learning may be more effective than intentional learning. He surveys a number of studies that have investigated the impact of silent reading on vocabulary growth and the relative effects of self-selected reading and 'regular' reading programs. He concludes that 'free readers do at least as well, and often better, than students in the regular programs on vocabulary tests, suggesting that free reading is at least as effective as traditional instruction' (p. 448). The contradiction between Krashen and Pressley et al. may be more apparent than real, however. Krashen does not consider short-term experimental studies, which do tend to find in favor of intentional learning. In long-term studies, where incidental learning has a chance to occur, the difference is less marked and, as Krashen demonstrates, such studies often find in favor of incidental learning.

3. While it is true that there is no widely accepted model that explains how learners come to understand the meaning of words they do not know from context, a number of preliminary attempts to construct a model have been made (e.g. Huckin and Bloch 1993).

4. Krashen, in comments on an earlier version of this Chapter, argues that the problem Coady identifies may not be a problem at all. He argues that a clear context can lead to acquisition even when there is no 'need' for the learners to attend to the item. He gives this example:

> If an acquirer of English has not yet acquired the word 'door', but knows the word 'close', and someone asks him to close the door in a very clear context, the acquirer's LAD will assign the correct meaning to 'door' and at least some acquisition will take place.

However, Krashen goes on to admit that when there is 'extremely rich contextual support' the learner may not notice a new item in the input. Krashen's argument suggests that we need to examine the kind of contextual support that promotes (and inhibits) acquisition. The later section on 'Availability of contextual clues' addresses this.

5. Whereas classroom learners are likely to be exposed to large quantities of written input, untutored learners such as those investigated in the European Science Foundation project on adult second language acquisition will be dependent on oral input for developing their lexicons.

6. Nation (1990) refers to a study by Saragi et al. (1978) which shows that in an incidental learning task 16 or more repetitions in a written text were necessary.

7. Rost's (1990) book, *Listening in Language Learning*, for example, has nothing on lexical density or new-word density as factors influencing input comprehension.

8. Wells' (1985) study of children learning their first language suggests that quantity of input is a major factor in accounting for differences in rate of acquisition. Those children who learned the fastest were the ones that had the most language addressed to them. However, there were also qualitative input differences that were important.

9. It is interesting to note that Drum and Konopak (1987) in a review of research that has investigated the usefulness of different types of cues to word meaning in written text report that definitions and synonyms have been found to be the most useful.

10. It may also be possible to give training to learners who lack procedural knowledge to help them overcome their limitations. A number of researchers consider the role of 'strategy training' in this respect (see, for example, Sternberg 1987; Graves 1987; O'Malley 1987).

CHAPTER 3

Modified Input and the Acquisition of Word Meanings by Children and Adults

Rod Ellis, Rick Heimbach, Yoshihiro Tanaka and Atsuko Yamazaki

Introduction

This chapter reports the results of three studies all of which examined the incidental acquisition of word meanings from modified input. The first study examined the role of interaction in assisting adolescent classroom learners to acquire L2 vocabulary. The second study focussed on young children The third study drew on some of the data collected during the first study in order to examine in detail the properties of modified input associated with the acquisition of word meanings. These studies were all carried out within the theoretical frameworks of the Input and Interaction Hypotheses described in Chapter One.

All the studies made use of a particular type of task. This is discussed in the following section. Each study is then described and the results reported and discussed. The final section of this chapter offers a number of general conclusions based on the three studies.

Non-reciprocal tasks

Tasks can be reciprocal or non-reciprocal. Reciprocal tasks are tasks that require a two-way flow of information between a speaker and a listener; they are speaking tasks. Non-reciprocal tasks require only a one-way flow of information from a speaker to a listener. When the learner is functioning as the listener non-reciprocal tasks are, in fact, listening tasks. This distinction, however, is best viewed as reflecting a continuum rather than a dichotomy as the extent to which the participants in a task are required to interact can vary. At one end of the continuum are tasks that are entirely non-reciprocal in that they do not permit learners any opportunity to interject whatsoever even if they do understand (e.g. a non-interactive lecture) while at the other end there are reciprocal tasks that can only be successfully accomplished if the participants interact to ensure mutual understanding (e.g. information-gap tasks where the information has been split among the learners). In between are tasks that provide the learners with some negotiation rights but these are restricted (e.g. an interactive lecture where students have the opportunity to interrupt the lecturer). The studies reported below made use of non-reciprocal tasks that allowed limited opportunities for the subjects to interact.

From the second language acquisition (SLA) researcher's perspective, non-reciprocal tasks have an enormous advantage; they make it possible to investigate not only the kind of language use that results from performing a task but also what learners actually acquire from the performance. There is now a very considerable literature examining the kinds of language learners produce when they undertake different kinds of tasks under different conditions (see, for example, Skehan 1998). However, this literature has not addressed directly what effect learner performance has on acquisition. There are good reasons for this. First, it is unlikely that a single task (or even a short series of tasks) will result in measurable changes in general language skill (e.g. fluency). Second, it is extremely difficult to devise tasks that make the use of some specific linguistic feature, the acquisition of which might be measurable, obligatory. Loschky and Bley-Vroman (1993) have pointed out that, while it may be possible to construct tasks that make the use of a feature 'natural' it is almost impossible to ensure that the use of the feature is 'essential'. As a result, researchers such as Skehan (1998), who are interested in the relationship between production on a task and language acquisition, have not been able to examine the relationship empirically (i.e. they have not investigated what learners actually learn from performing tasks). Instead, they have invoked theoretical arguments to make claims about the hypothesized effects that certain types of task-derived production will have on learners' interlanguage development. Non-reciprocal tasks, in contrast, do provide a means by which researchers can directly investigate the relationship between task performance and acquisition. As Loschky and Bley-Vroman have observed, comprehension tasks allow for the input to be scripted in such a way that it contains particular linguistic features, the learners' acquisition of which can be tested on completion of the task.

The tasks used in the three studies were based on the task used in Pica, Young and Doughty (1987). They all had the same essential features, consisting of:

1. structured input (i.e. input that has been specially designed to include specific linguistic features — vocabulary items).
2. a non-verbal device (i.e. a diagram).

In each task, the structured input took the form of a series of directives requesting the learners to carry out a series of actions. These actions involved them in identifying the referents referred to in the directives and shown in an array of pictures and then indicating the correct position of the referents in a matrix diagram. Such tasks are examples of what Widdowson (1978) has called information-transfer tasks, in that they require learners to transfer information from one modality (linguistic) to another (diagrammatic). The actual tasks used in the three studies are described below.

Figure 1 shows the pictorial materials for the task used in the first study. In this task, the directives consisted of instructions about where to place a series of objects in a diagram of a kitchen. Here is an example of one of the directives:

(1) Can you find the scouring pad? Take the scouring pad and put it on top of the counter by the sink — the right side of the sink.

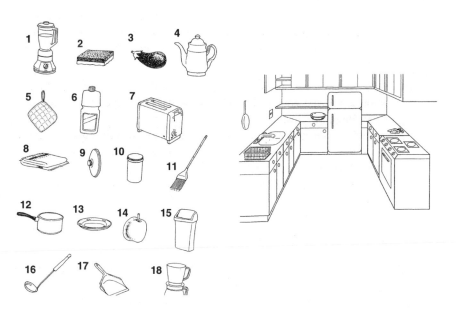

Figure 1. *Materials used in the Kitchen Task*

For this directive, the students had to identify the scouring pad in the series of small pictures and then write the number of the picture in the correct position in the matrix diagram of the kitchen.

This kind of task has a number of advantages. First, as pointed out above, it enables the research to incorporate specific linguistic features into the input (hence the term 'structured input'). In the research to be summarised below the linguistic features were lexical items (such as 'scouring pad') which prior testing had shown the learners did not know. Second, it is possible to manipulate the input in different ways in order to test what effect various input modifications have on comprehension and acquisition. The directive shown above is an example of 'baseline input' (i.e. the kind of input that native speakers provide when they talk to other native speakers). In another version of the same task, the directive consisted of 'modified input'. That is, the baseline input had been modified in accordance with how native speakers address learners. The modified directive, corresponding to (1) above), took this form:

(2)   Can you find the scouring pad? A scouring pad — *scour* means to clean a dish. A scouring pad is a small thing you hold in your hand and you clean a dish with it. Take the scouring pad and put it on top of the counter by the sink — on the right side of the sink.

In this case the directive is *premodified*. However, it also possible to cater for *interactionally modified* directives by allowing learners the opportunity to request clarification if they do not understand a baseline directive. (3) shows the directive in this form:

(3)   T: Can you find the scouring pad? Take the scouring pad and put it on top of the counter by the sink — the right side of the sink.
         S: One more time.
         T: Can you find the scouring pad? Take the scouring pad and put it on top of the counter by the sink — the right side of the sink.
         S: What is scouring pad?
         T: Scouring pad is, uh, … you hold it in your hand and you wash dishes with it. OK?
         S: Once again ………

A third advantage of this kind of task is that it contains a built-in measure of learners' comprehension. Comprehension is demonstrated if a learner can indicate the position of the correct object on the matrix picture. This obviates the need to design a separate test to ascertain whether learners have understood the directives.

The task used in study two was essentially of the same as that used in study one but differed from it in a number of ways. First, the **content** of the tasks differed. The content of the above task was 'kitchen objects', that of the task in study two was 'bugs and birds', a content deemed more suitable for young children. Another difference concerned the **response manner**. In study one the learners were adolescents who were able to respond to the directives by writing the numbers of the pictures into the matrix picture. In study two, however, the learners were young children, for whom such a response might have been problematic. In this case, therefore, the learners were provided with separate cards which they picked up and placed manually on the matrix diagram. More significantly from a theoretical point of view, the tasks differed with regard to their **interactivity** (i.e. the extent to which they catered for interactionally modified input). In study one, some of the learners were not allowed to interact when they listened to the directives even if they did not understand them while other learners were allowed (indeed, encouraged) to interact by requesting clarification; in study two, all the learners could interact if they so chose.

Study One: Classroom Interaction, Comprehension, and the Acquisition of Word meanings by Adolescent Classroom Learners[1]

In Chapter One we noted that although there is considerable evidence to suggest that L2 learners can comprehend modified input better than unmodified input there is very little evidence to show that L2 learners benefit acquisitionally from modified input. The study reported below was designed to address this gap. It examined the extent to which three types of input — unmodified (baseline) input, premodified input and interactionally modified input — resulted in the acquisition of word meanings. The study focussed on vocabulary on the grounds that the limited exposure to modified input occurring in the context of an experimental treatment might be expected to result in some measurable gains in word knowledge. Such exposure could not be expected to have much of an effect on the acquisition of a phonological, grammatical or discourse feature.

The following hypotheses were tested:

1. Input obtained from interaction will differ in quantity, redundancy, and complexity from unmodified or premodified input.
2. Learners who receive input through direct or observed interaction will achieve higher levels of L2 comprehension than those exposed to unmodified or premodified input.
3. Learners in interactive situations will learn and retain more L2 words than those receiving the other two types of input.

4. Learners in interactive situations who actively participate in negotiating meaning will achieve higher levels of L2 comprehension than those who do not.
5. Learners in interactive situations who actively participate in negotiating meaning will learn and retain more L2 words than those who do not.

Two separate studies, which we will call the Saitama Study and the Tokyo Study, were undertaken in different teaching contexts. However, the design of both was the same. This afforded a number of advantages, in particular, it enabled us to see if the results were influenced by situational factors.

Subjects

In the Saitama Study, the participants were 79 third-year students at a public high school in Saitama. They had studied English for five years. The students had been divided into three classes (28 in Group 1, 27 in Group 2, and 24 in Group 3) according to their previous English grades at the school, the aim being to create groups of equal ability. They were studying an elective course, English IIA, the goal of which was to develop listening and speaking ability.

In the Tokyo Study, the participants were 127 first-year high-school students in a Tokyo metropolitan high school, Japan. They had studied English for three years. They were in three intact classes (43 in Group 1 and 42 each in Groups 2 and 3). The classes were of equal overall academic ability, as measured by a school entrance examination, which included a test of English.[2] They all received six English classes each week, one of which was taught by a native speaker of English.

One important difference between the students in the two studies was that the students in the Tokyo Study generally had high expectations of entering a prestigious Japanese university on completion of high school whereas those in the Saitama Study did not. English is a required subject in the entrance examinations of universities in Japan.

Design

Both studies utilized the same multifactorial design with two dependent variables (listening comprehension and vocabulary acquisition) and three independent variables (baseline input, premodifed input and negotiated input). The three groups in both studies were designated Baseline Group (B), which functioned as a control group, the Premodifed Group (PM) and the Interactionally Modified Group (IM). Each group experienced the following:

1. The pretest: This was administered to all the groups one month prior to the commencement of the treatment.
2. The treatment: This took the form of the Kitchen Task shown in Figure 1. It was completed within one class period (about 45 minutes). In the Saitama Study, the teacher who gave the directives was an American male with one year's experience of teaching English. In the Tokyo Study, the teacher was a British female with several years' teaching experience.
3. The post tests: The participants in the two experimental groups (PM and IM) in both studies completed two post tests, one 2 days after the treatment and the other about a month later. The participants in the control group (B) of the Tokyo Study also completed these post tests. However, the students in the control group (B) of the Saitama Study did not, because they were inadvertently taught the target items by another teacher who was unaware that they were part of the study.
4. The follow-up test: This was administered one month after the second post test when the students returned from summer vacation, about $2^{1}/_{2}$ months after the treatment.

Instruments

The purpose of the pretest was to establish a set of lexical items unknown to the students. It consisted of 65 English words which they were asked to translate into Japanese. These words included a set of words labelling objects found in a kitchen, which were designated as potential target items, distracter items such as *fireplace* and *closet*, and a number of basic words likely to have been already acquired by the students. On the basis of the results, 18 items were chosen, all unknown by the students, as target items in the Saitama Study. 19 items, unknown by at least 88% of the students, were chosen for the Tokyo Study. The items chosen for the two studies overlapped but were not identical, as the students' previous lexical knowledge differed slightly. In the Saitama Study, the 18 items were: *sink, scouring pad, shelf, lid, garbage can, canister, broom, pot holder, stove, saucepan, faucet, dishwashing liquid, counter, eggplant, dustpan, plate, dish drainer,* and *ladle*. In the Tokyo Study, the 19 items were: *sink, dish drainer, cabinet, shelf, eggplant, lid, faucet, scouring pad, outlet, broom, dustpan, saucepan, stove, pot holder, garbage can, counter, blender, plate canister.*

The two post tests required the students to translate the target items into Japanese. In case they did not know the Japanese equivalent of an item, they were allowed to write down a circumlocution or paraphrase. Participants were awarded one mark for each correctly translated item. The order of the items in the post tests was changed to mitigate against any possible test-taking effect. In the follow-up test all the students in each study were given a picture of a kitchen and a list of the target items in English. They were asked to use all the items in the list to label the picture. One mark for each object in the picture the students labelled correctly was awarded.

Treatment

The students' performance on the Kitchen task provided a measure of comprehension; their responses to a direction were awarded one mark if they (a) chose the correct utensil and (b) also located this object in the correct position in the matrix picture. The students were familiar with the locative expressions used in the directions (e.g., *in, on top of, the right side, on*) as a result of previous instruction; failure to comprehend a direction occurred when they were unable to identify the correct object or the part of the kitchen (e.g., *sink, floor, stove*) in which to place it.

The subjects listened to either unmodified (baseline) directions, premodified directions or interactionally modified directions, as described in the previous section. There were 15 such directions in the Saitama Study and 16 in the Tokyo Study. The unmodified directions, which both the B and IM Groups heard, were read aloud at a speed of about 180 words per minute. The premodified directions were read at a speed of about 90 words per minute. The teachers paused between each direction to allow the students to write their answers on the matrix picture of the kitchen. In the case of the IM groups, the teachers wrote a number of formulas for requesting clarification (e.g. 'Will you please speak more slowly?' and 'What is a ____?') on the board to serve as prompts for negotiating meaning. No time limit on the length of the interaction resulting from a single direction was imposed. However, to ensure that comprehension of the task would be based only on spoken input, we instructed the teachers not to use any gestures. The interactions were audio-taped and transcriptions prepared.

Results

The results reported below provide data concerning (a) the redundancy and complexity of the input made available to the three groups, (b) the comprehension scores achieved by the three groups, (c) the relationship between interactional modifcations and comprehension, (d) the vocabulary acquisition scores of the three groups and, for the Tokyo Study only, (e) the relationship between individual students' active participation in meaning negotiation and their comprehension and vocabulary acquisition scores.

An Input Analysis

As might be expected, the length of the treatment given to each group varied considerably. In the case of the Saitama Study, the control group (B) received about 6 minutes of instruction, the premodified group (PM) about 10 minutes, and the interactive group (IM) about 45 minutes. The times in the Tokyo Study were approximately 10 minutes, 20 minutes, and 45 minutes, respectively, for the three groups. Clearly, then, the IM group was exposed to more input than the other two groups. The analysis shown in Table 1 confirms this difference. In both studies, the number of words per direction was substantially greater in the IM input than in the PM input, which was more than double that of the baseline input.

The input available to the three groups also differed with regard to redundancy. A redundancy score was computed by counting the number of repetitions of the target item (e.g., *pot holder*) and the location for the item (e.g., *over the stove*) in each direction and then calculating the mean number of repetitions in the input available to each group. As Table 1 shows, the difference between the interactionally modified input and the baseline/premodified input is considerable. In the Saitama Study, the interactionally modified input contained a mean of 14.73 repetitions per direction and in the Tokyo Study a mean of 13.25.

Table 1. *An analysis of the three kinds of input*

	Quantity	Redundancy	Complexity
Saitama Study:			
1. Baseline	20.07	1.27	1.00
2. Premodified	48.53	4.40	1.07
3. Interactionally Modifed	98.73	14.73	1.05
Difference Between 2 & 3	$t = 3.55$	$t = 3.79$	$t = 0.62$
	$df = 28$	$df = 28$	$df = 28$
	$p < .001$	$p < .001$	$p = .54$ n.s.
Tokyo Study:			
1. Baseline	19.19	1.13	1.02
2. Premodified	49.31	4.94	1.09
3. Interactionally Modifed	77.50	13.25	1.21
Difference Between 2 & 3	$t = 2.526$	$t = 4.104$	$t = 2.090$
	$df = 30$	$df = 30$	$df = 30$
	$p < .05$	$p < .001$	$p < .05$

Quantity = Number of words per direction; Redundancy = Number of repetitions of target items per direction; Complexity = S-nodes/T-units per direction.

Complexity of input was measured by calculating S-nodes/T-units per direction, where an S-node was indicated by the presence of a tensed or untensed verb and a T-unit was any independent clause together with any associated dependent clauses. In the Saitama Study, the differences in complexity among the three groups were negligible. In the Tokyo Study, however, the interactionally modified input was significantly more complex than the premodified input ($p < .05$).

In summary, in both studies the IM group received more input (longer directions) and also more redundant input (more repetitions of the key items) as a result of the interaction that took place. However, the IM group only experienced more complex input in the Tokyo Study.

Comprehension of the Directions

The three groups' comprehension scores were submitted to a one-way analysis of variance (ANOVA). The results are shown in Table 2. In the case of the Saitama Study, the ANOVA revealed a significant difference in the three groups. A post-hoc Scheffé test (Table 3) indicated that the students in the IM group achieved significantly higher comprehension scores than both the B group and the PM group. The IM group outscored the PM group on every single direction. However, the difference between the comprehension scores of the B group and the PM group was not significant. In the Tokyo Study, similar results were obtained. Again, the IM group obtained the highest comprehension score, with PM next and B group last. In this case, however, the difference between the PM group and the B group was sufficient to reach statistical significance ($p < .05$). In fact, on three directions the PM group outscored the IM group, indicating a

Table 2. *Comparison of comprehension scores across three groups*

Source of variance	SS	df	MS	F
Saitama Study:				
Between groups	802.44	2	401.22	48.64*
Within groups	626.90	76	8.25	
Tokyo Study:				
Between groups	1680.39	2	840.20	113.37*
Within groups	919.02	124	7.41	

*$p < .05$

Table 3. *Scheffé test of differences in comprehension across the three groups*

Group	Baseline Group	Premodified Group	Interactionally Modified Group
Saitama Study			
Mean	2.32	4.04	9.91
Baseline Group		2.13	10.28*
Premodifed Group			2.13*
Tokyo Study			
Mean	1.20	6.79	10.69
Baseline Group		8.14*	14.74*
Premodified Group			6.58*

*$p < .05$

much higher level of comprehension in this group than in the equivalent group in the Saitama Study.

Taken together, the studies demonstrate that the group receiving interactionally modified input comprehended the directions more fully than either the group receiving baseline input or the group receiving premodified input. Premodified input was also found to facilitate comprehension in the Tokyo Study.

The Relationship Between Interactional Modifications and Comprehension

Although some directions were comprehended much better by the IM group than by the PM group, there were other directions where interaction proved less effective. Given that the Interaction Hypothesis claims that it is modified interaction (not interaction *per se*) that is important for acquisition, the number of modifications (defined as requests for clarification, requests for confirmation, and comprehension checks) was calculated to see if this could account for the difference. If interactional modifications facilitated acquisition, it was to be expected that they would occur with higher frequency in those directions where the difference between the PM group's and the IM group's comprehension scores was considerable than in those directions where the difference in comprehension scores was less marked. The four directions where the difference was greatest and the four where it was smallest in each study were identified and the number of modifications occurring in the interactional sequences triggered by these directions counted. The results are shown in Table 4.

In the Saitama Study, more modifications occurred on those directions

Table 4. *Interactional modifications in relation to comprehension score differences between Premodified (PM) and Interactionally Modified (IM) groups*

Directive	Comprehension Difference (IM — PM scores)	Interactional Modifications
Saitama Study:		
01	79.3%	3
06	75.4%	7
08	65.7%	4
14	60.0%	4
Total		18
Mean		4.5
07	6.2%	9
15	12.9%	4
02	14.3%	12
12	12.9%	4
Total		29
Mean		7.25

U' (Mann Whitney Test — Small Sample Case) = 2; p = ns

Tokyo Study:		
16	50.0%	4
07	47.7%	10
04	42.8%	2
02	35.7%	7
Total		23
Mean		5.75
10	−9.5%	2
14	−9.5%	6
13	−4.7%	2
08	4.8%	3
Total		13
Mean		3.25

U' (Mann Whitney Test — Small Sample Case) = 6; p = ns

where the difference between the PM and IM group's comprehension scores was least. In the Tokyo Study, the opposite result was obtained; more modifications occurred in those directions where the IM group performed much better than the PM group. However, when the differences between the number of modifications in the two sets of directions were tested by the Mann Whitney test, they were found to be non significant in both studies. In other words, the frequency of modifications was not significantly related to comprehension scores.

Vocabulary Acquisition

In the case of the Tokyo Study, the extent to which the three groups acquired the target lexical items was measured by means of two post tests (one administered two days after the treatment and the other approximately two weeks later) and a follow-up test (administered approximately six weeks after the treatment). In the case of the Saitama Study, no post test or follow-up scores are available for the B (control) group for reasons already explained.

In the case of the Tokyo Study, the differences in the three groups' vocabulary acquisition scores in Post-test 1, Post-test 2 and the follow-up test were tested using separate ANOVAs. The results are reported in Table 5. These show significant group differences in all three tests. Post-hoc Scheffé tests were carried out to identify specific differences between the means of the three groups. The results are shown in Table 6. In the case of the Saitama Study, it was only possible to compare the vocabulary acquisition scores of the PM and IM groups. The results of the *t*-tests used to make this comparison are shown in Table 7.

In the Saitama Study, the IM group demonstrated the ability to accurately supply translation equivalents of the target items to a greater extent than the PM group in post test (1) and they also maintained this advantage in post test (2).

Table 5. *Vocabulary acquisition scores across three groups in the Tokyo study*

Source of variance	SS	df	MS	F
Post-test 1:				
Between groups	262.16	2	131.08	19.32*
Within groups	841.29	124	6.78	
Post-test 2:				
Between groups	145.92	2	72.96	11.32*
Within groups	798.89	124	6.44	
Follow-up test:				
Between groups	118.09	2	59.05	9.54*
Within groups	767.67	124	6.19	

*$p < .05$

Table 6. *Scheffé test of differences across three groups in the Tokyo study*

Group	Baseline Group	Premodified Group	Interactionally Modified Group
Post test 1			
Mean	2.02	4.02	5.55
Baseline Group		3.38*	4.90*
Premodified Group			2.93*
Post test 2			
Mean	2.53	4.29	5.10
Baseline Group		3.12*	3.93*
Premodified Group			2.18
Follow-up Test			
Mean	4.05	5.60	6.36
Baseline Group		2.89*	3.65*
Premodified Group			2.11

*$p < .05$

Table 7. *Vocabulary acquisition scores in two groups in the Saitama study*

	n	M	SD	t value	df	p
Post-test 1						
PM Group	27	2.52	2.38	4.88	49	< .001
IM Group	24	6.00	2.72			
Post-test 2						
PM Group	27	2.59	2.02	3.28	49	< .002
IM Group	24	4.75	2.66			
Follow-up Test						
PM Group	27	4.70	2.30	2.99	49	< .004
IM Group	24	7.08	3.34			

PM = Premodified; IM = Interactionally Modified

Furthermore, this group was better able to match the target items with pictures than the PM group six weeks after the instruction (i.e. in the follow-up test). However, it is not possible to say whether either the IM or PM group had performed better than the B group.

In this respect, the Tokyo Study is crucial. The PM and IM groups outperformed the B group on all three vocabulary tests, the results reaching statistical significance in each test ($p < .05$). Thus both short- and longer-term advantages in vocabulary acquisition were evident when learners had access to modified input. The comparisons between the PM and IM groups were less clear-cut, however. Whereas the IM group outscored the PM group on vocabulary learning in post test 1, this advantage was lost in post test 2 and in the follow-up test. In other words, the group receiving interactionally modified input outscored that receiving premodified input in vocabulary acquisition, but only in the short term.

A detailed examination of the results for the two post tests is revealing. In both the Saitama Study and the Tokyo Study, the vocabulary acquisition scores for the IM group reduced slightly from post test 1 to post test 2. In the Saitama Study, the vocabulary acquisition scores for the PM group stayed almost the same. However, in the Tokyo Study, the scores for the PM group increased slightly. This, together with the fact that the difference in the post test 1 vocabulary scores between the IM and PM groups was initially greater in the case of the Saitama Study than the Tokyo Study, accounts for the difference in results between the two studies.

Meaning Negotiation, Comprehension, and Vocabulary Acquisition

The relationship between learners' active participation in the classroom interaction experienced by the IM group and their comprehension of the directions and acquisition of the target items was investigated in the Tokyo Study only. Of the 42 learners in the IM group, only 7 engaged actively in meaning negotiation. The others simply listened. Table 8 gives the comprehension scores and the vocabulary acquisition scores in the three tests for these 7 learners. From this it can be seen that 3 out of the 7 learners achieved comprehension scores above the mean,

Table 8. *Comprehension and vocabulary acquisition scores of learners participating actively in meaning negotiation in the Tokyo study*

	Comprehension Score	Post Test 1	Post Test 2	Follow-up Test
Group mean	10.7	5.5	5.1	6.4
Participant 1	3	7	6	7
Participant 2	5	4	4	7
Participant 3	5	11	9	10
Participant 4	9	3	4	5
Participant 5	0	5	4	2
Participant 6	4	8	8	7
Participant 7	5	4	6	9

3 achieved vocabulary acquisition scores above the mean for post test 1, 4 achieved above the mean for post test 2, and 5 achieved above the mean for the follow-up test. It appears, then, that those learners who engaged in active meaning negotiation did not enjoy a clear advantage in either comprehension or vocabulary acquisition over those who just listened.

Discussion

The five hypotheses, all based on the Interaction Hypothesis, will now be considered in the light of the results reported above.

Research Hypothesis 1

The first hypothesis was that the interactionally modified input experienced by the IM group would differ in quantity, redundancy, and complexity from the baseline input or the premodified input experienced by the PM groups. It was important to find support for this hypothesis, for unless it could be shown that the opportunity to negotiate communication problems affected the nature of the input the learners received there was no basis for examining the relationship between negotiated input and comprehension/vocabulary acquisition. In fact, the input analysis reported in Table 1 demonstrates clearly that negotiation leads to more input and more redundant input than baseline input. Furthermore, this difference is also evident when special efforts have been made to premodify the baseline input to make it more comprehensible to learners. Contradictory results regarding complexity of input were obtained. A difference was found in the input experienced by the PM and IM groups in the Tokyo Study only, where, contrary to Hypothesis 1, the IM group received more complex input than the PM group.

It might be argued that the difference between the negotiated and premodified input reflects our failure to make the necessary adjustments to the baseline input to ensure that the premodified input was properly matched to the learners' level. However, considerable care was taken to ensure that the premodified directions were delivered at a slow speed and that the teacher provided wait time for the learners to process each one. It is simply difficult to determine what adjustments are needed in advance. The whole point of interactionally adjusted input is that it occurs in context when learners signal their comprehension difficulty.[3] It responds to problems rather than predicting them.

Research Hypothesis 2

The second hypothesis is also supported by the results of both studies. The learners in the IM group, who were given the opportunity to negotiate their comprehension problems, were more successful in carrying out the directions correctly. The opportunity to hear key target items repeated and to receive definitions of these items on demand helped them to understand the directions and thus gain higher comprehension scores.

However, maybe the advantage experienced by the interactionally modified group derived not so much from the fact that they could negotiate non-understanding as from the fact that they had more time to process the directions and were exposed to more input. Time does seem to have been a factor. The learners in the IM group enjoyed a considerable time advantage over the learners in the B and PM groups and outperformed both in comprehension. Also, the PM learners in the Tokyo Study were given considerably more time to process the directions than the PM learners in the Saitama Study (20 minutes as opposed to 10), which may have been one reason why they outscored them. More input may also help because it increases redundancy, although, as we noted above, it is not so much the overall quantity of input as the opportunity to receive more input at times when comprehension problems arise that is important. Study One, therefore, does not show whether interaction aids comprehension simply because of the additional time and input it provides or because of qualitative features in the input that it creates. This issue is addressed in Study Three. It is, of course, natural for the quantity of input to increase when interaction takes place. Trying to examine qualitative features independently of attendant quantitative features may be like trying to investigate how fish swim out of water.

Although interactionally modified input appears to facilitate comprehension, there seems to be no direct relationship between the frequency of interactional modifications and comprehension. Directions that stimulated large numbers of modifications were not necessarily the ones where the IM group learners outscored the PM learners. It is, of course, not the interactional modifications themselves that facilitate acquisition but rather the modified input they give rise to. Probably the key lies in discovering the relationship between interactional modification and input modification (see Pica 1992).

The transcripts of the negotiated directions show that comprehension is something that learners have to work at. They need to identify and address specific problems in the input and to build up comprehension of a linguistically difficult utterance in steps. This is what the opportunity to negotiate gives them, as this example from the Saitama Study illustrates:

T: We have an apple. And I'd like you to put the apple in the sink
S: What is the sink?
T: Sink is a place to wash dishes. It's a hole where you wash dishes.
S: One more time please.
T: We have an apple. And I'd like you to put the apple in the sink.
S: What is sink?
T: Sink is a hole and you wash dishes in the hole.

The mean comprehension score for this item was 90% in the IM group but only 10.7% in the PM group. The opportunity to negotiate, therefore, clearly helped. In fact, though, there were relatively few interactional modifications in this sequence. How then did the negotiation aid comprehension? The answer seems to lie in the students' ability to identify the source of their comprehension difficulty (*sink*), to make this clear to the teacher and to persist until they had elicited a definition they understood. Gass (1988) has pointed out that there is an important difference between *comprehensible* and *comprehended* input; "comprehensible input is controlled by the person providing input ... comprehended input is learner-controlled" (p. 204). As the sequence above illustrates, the opportunity to negotiate gives learners some control over the input. How they make use of this control is important.

However, premodified input can also aid comprehension. In both studies, the learners receiving premodified input achieved higher levels of comprehension than those receiving baseline input, although only in the Tokyo Study did the difference reach statistical significance. Study One suggests, however, that it does not work as well as negotiated input.

Research Hypothesis 3

We noted in Chapter One that comprehending input does not guarantee the acquisition of new word meanings, as the processes of comprehension and acquisition are not identical. However, negotiated comprehension may facilitate acquisition because it induces learners to notice unknown items in the input. If this were the case, we might expect that those learners who experienced negotiated input would acquire more new items than those who did not. The results lend some support to this argument. In the Saitama Study, the learners who experienced interactionally adjusted input achieved higher vocabulary acquisition scores in the immediate post test than those who received premodified input and, importantly, maintained this advantage over time. In the Tokyo Study we were able to show that modified input in general led to more word meanings being acquired than unmodified input. Also, in this study, the learners in the IM group outperformed those in the PM group on the immediate post-test.

We cannot know for certain what in the interactions helped learners to acquire the new items, but we can speculate that the following may have been important:

1.   Learners were able to pinpoint precisely the source of their comprehension difficulty. Because of the way the task was devised, this was almost invariably the target items.
2.   The learners were given multiple opportunities to hear the new items, which may have helped them develop auditory images of the new items.
3.   The learners had ample time to process the new items.
4.   The learners were able to identify the meanings of the new items by relating the spoken forms to their pictorial referents (Krashen 1985).
5.   The long-term storage of these items may have been facilitated by having the learners carry out an action involving the items (Asher 1977). That is, the act of responding non-verbally to a directive may help to "fix" new items associated with the action in memory.

We can further speculate that the interactionally modified input was potentially facilitative in all five ways. Premodified input is also helpful — as shown by the Tokyo Study — but less so, perhaps because it is less effective where Factors 1, 2, and 3 above are concerned.

In the Tokyo Study, we found a long-term advantage for interactionally modified input over baseline input but no such advantage over premodified input; the PM group almost caught up with the IM group by post test 2 and was not significantly different from the IM group in the follow-up test. Besides, the difference between the PM and IM groups in post test 1 was not as great in the Tokyo Study as in the Saitama Study. One possible explanation lies in the overall proficiency of the learners in the two studies. The learners in the Tokyo Study came from a prestigious Tokyo high school and were expected to do well academically, whereas those in the Saitama Study came from a less prestigious and less academically successful public high school. Therefore the learners in the Tokyo Study were probably more proficient overall in English than those in the Saitama Study.

There is, however, another reason why no long-term effect for negotiation was evident in the Tokyo Study. Informal contact with a number of the PM group learners following post test 2 revealed that several of them had made efforts to study the new vocabulary privately. This reflected their general high level of motivation to learn English and to do well in tests. If this is the reason, it merely demonstrates what is well-known: new words can be effectively acquired through study and memorization (Nation 1990). Effective as negotiation may be in promoting vocabulary acquisition, it is certainly not the only way in which new words can be learned. Learners who do not have opportunities to interact in the L2 may be able to compensate by utilizing alternative learning strategies.

Finally, obviously it cannot be claimed that the learners had fully acquired the new items. Exposure to unknown concrete nouns in premodified or interactionally adjusted input was clearly sufficient to give the learners a knowledge of their word meaning, as was demonstrated by the post- and follow-up tests. We cannot, however, say whether it also gave them a knowledge of how to use these items productively in English sentences.[4] Nor can we say whether similar exposure would enable learners to acquire a knowledge of the meaning of other parts of speech (e.g., adjectives and verbs) or of abstract nouns.

Research Hypothesis 4

Hypothesis 4 stated that learners who engaged in active negotiation would achieve higher levels of comprehension than those who merely listened. However, this hypothesis was not supported by the results obtained for the Tokyo Study. Apparently, other factors are responsible for the inter-learner variation in comprehension evident in this study.

Research Hypothesis 5

The study also failed to demonstrate that active participation in negotiating meaning was advantageous for vocabulary acquisition. In the Tokyo Study, those learners who listened to others negotiate achieved similar scores to those who engaged actively. Again, other factors must have been responsible for the inter-learner variation. Our study, then, lends some support to the claim that active participation may be less important for acquisition than is sometimes claimed. However, the study did not show that active participation had any detrimental effect on either comprehension or acquisition. Those learners who participated actively did not do any worse than those who just listened.

The finding that active participation is neither necessary nor detrimental to comprehension/acquisition is important. First, it suggests that non-reciprocal tasks of the kind used in this study can be beneficially employed in lock-step instruction, with the whole class attending to input supplied by the teacher. This has the advantage of ensuring that learners have access to well-formed input[5] (see Prabhu 1987, for arguments in favour of teacher-led task-based instruction.) Second, it suggests that teachers do not have to make efforts to ensure that opportunities for negotiating meaning are evenly distributed across all the learners in the class. It may be sufficient to allow learners to volunteer responses. The work required to comprehend difficult input may be performed publicly through interaction or covertly through mental activity. Those learners who prefer the quieter route can benefit from the interactional activity of their more public comrades.

Conclusion

The results of Study One confirm the results of earlier studies regarding the role of interaction in comprehension. Interaction may help learners work toward comprehension through the control over the input it gives them and by enabling them to systematically identify and solve comprehension problems. In this respect, it is superior to premodified input. Along with Gass (1988), we would argue that it is not comprehensible input but comprehended input that is important and that interaction provides the means by which learners can successfully strive to comprehend. The main contribution of Study One, however, lies in the support it gives to the claim that interactionally modified input facilitates acquisition. The study shows that interactionally modified input leads to the acquisition of more word order meanings than premodified input. It should be noted, however, that the studies also indicate that premodified input can be effective in promoting acquisition.

These studies have not shown (or tried to show) how interactionally modified input aids acquisition. Nor have they shown that interactionally modified input works more *efficiently* than premodified input (given that the IM group spent much longer on task than the PM group). These are important issues which are addressed in Study Three. First, though, we will consider if interactionally modified input works as effectively for young children as it appears to do for adolescents.

Study Two: Interaction, Comprehension, and the Acquisition of Word meanings by Young Children[6]

As we saw in Chapter 1 the bulk of the studies that have investigated meaning negotiation have involved adult or adolescent learners. There are reasons for questioning whether interaction is as important for child learners as it is for adults. Early descriptive work on the kinds of interactions involving child and adult L2 learners points to some notable differences. Hatch (1978b) shows that in child-learner discourse, it is the child who typically begins an exchange and the adult who responds. In a typical exchange involving children there is little need for meaning negotiation because input is tailored to the child's level of comprehension. In contrast, Hatch notes that in conversations involving adult learners, it is the native speaker who typically initiates an exchange, which is often rooted in displaced activity. As a result adult learners have difficulty in identifying the topic and frequently resort to clarification requests and confirmation checks. In other words, adults may have a greater need to engage in meaning negotiation than children.

This conclusion is borne out research involving children acquiring both their first and a second language. Andersen and Lynch (1988) refer to a number of studies (e.g. Patterson and Kirsten 1981) conducted within the 'referential communication paradigm' which found that children below the age of seven have difficulty in assessing the quality of messages directed at them and consequently are likely to fail to provide feedback. In other words, they typically do not negotiate for meaning. Scarcella and Higa (1981) compared conversations between native speakers and child and adolescent L2 learners. They found that the native speakers expected the adolescent learners to play their part in keeping a conversation going, whereas they were prepared to shoulder the brunt of the work with child learners. This again suggests that meaning negotiation may figure less prominently in conversations with children.

The study reported below was designed to examine the role of negotiation in child L2 acquisition. It addresses the following questions:

(1)   To what extent do children participate in meaning negotiation?
(2)   Do children who participate in meaning negotiation achieve higher levels of comprehension than those who do not?
(3)   Do children who participate in meaning negotiation achieve higher levels of vocabulary acquisition than those who do not?
(4)   What is the relationship between children's comprehension of utterances containing new words and their acquisition of the meanings of these words?

Vocabulary acquisition by children

How do children acquire new words? As Clark (1993) notes in her account of L1 lexical acquisition, learning words involves three essential processes; isolating word-forms in the input, creating potential meanings and mapping meanings onto forms. Clark suggests that children are capable of 'fast mapping'. That is, they are able to assign meaning to a new form after only minimal exposure to the form. Thus, although it may take several exposures before the child is ready to try to produce a word, a single exposure may be sufficient for receptive learning. Clark suggests that children are such eager language learners that they may try to map some chunk of meaning onto every new form they detect. In fact, vocabulary learning is extremely rapid once children have acquired 20 to 30 words (Harris 1992). As children build up a lexical domain, they seem able to add several new members at the same time, even on the same day. Furthermore, Clark suggests that where reception is involved children are remarkably accurate in assigning meanings to the forms they hear (i.e. over-extensions, which are common in production, are not typically evident in comprehension).

In the case of L1 lexical acquisition, this 'fast mapping' is made possible by the fact that caretakers encode the objects they see their children attending to, thus ensuring that the words they use are related to the 'here-and-now' (Harris 1992). Also, children are guided from within by certain assumptions they make about objects. Clark (1993) lists a number of these, several of which are relevant to the present study. In the early stages children pick out forms that label 'basic level catgories'. For example, they learn 'bird' rather than the superordinate 'animal' or the subordinate 'robin'. As Clark points out, basic level terms tend to be simpler in form and thus easier to learn. When children expand their lexical domains, they look for 'equal detail' in the terms they are adding, which may lead them to maximize the number of new labels. Thus, when children begin to fill out a domain such as 'birds' by learning subordinate terms such as 'robin' they are likely to acquire several such terms around the same time (e.g. 'goose' and 'woodpecker'). Another assumption that guides children is 'contrast'. That is, they assume that an unfamiliar word has a different meaning from the words they already know. Thus, if they hear a series of words labelling different birds, they assume that each word labels a different type of bird.

The study that is described below is predicated on the ability of children (who are somewhat older than the children Clark describes) to engage in 'fast mapping' in an L2 by filling out the words for two lexical domains — 'bugs' and 'birds' — when they are given the opportunity to negotiate an understanding of what the words mean.

Participants

The participants were 10 kindergarten students who were enrolled in an ESL program in an American elementary school located in a self-contained American community in Japan. The participants' ages ranged from 5 years and 2 months

Table 9. *Background information about the individual learners*

LearnerSex		Age	L1	PRE-LAS		PPVT	
				Score	Level	Raw score	Age equiv.
1	Girl	5.9	Tagalog	78.0	3	44	4.1
2	Boy	5.8	Japanese	61.5	2	23	3.0
3	Boy	5.4	Tagalog	54.0	1	37	3.9
4	Boy	5.1	Japanese	64.5	2	32	3.5
5	Boy	5.6	Tagalog	36.6	1	9	2.2
6	Boy	5.4	Japanese	21.0	1	19	2.9
7	Girl	5.2	Japanese	0.0	1	41	3.11
8	Girl	5.2	Japanese	35.0	1	23	3.0
9	Girl	6.2	Japanese	50.5	1	33	3.6
10	Boy	5.8	Thai	81.5	4	58	5.1

Key:
PRE-LAS Pre Language Assessment Scales
PPVT Peabody Picture Vocabulary Test

to 6 years and 2 months. They spoke Japanese, Tagalog and Thai as their first languages. The children varied considerably in English language proficiency, as measured by the PRE-LAS (Language Assessment Scales) (Duncan and De Avila 1985). They also varied in their knowledge of English vocabulary, as measured by the Peabody Picture Vocabulary Test (Dunn and Dunn 1981). All the learners, with the exception of Learner 10, scored below the norms for native speaking children for this test. Information about the individual learners can be found in Table 9. Each day the students attended a regular kindergarten session of 2 1/2 hours in mainstream classes and, additionally, a 45 minute ESL class, taught by a native speaking teacher.

Design

The study was of the one-group pre-test post-test design (see Hatch and Farhady 1982: 20) and was, therefore, pre-experimental in type. The group of 10 learners experienced the following:

1. The pre-test: The pre-test was a vocabulary test, administered individually to each child.
2. The treatment: This took the form of two listening tasks performed by a native-speaker of American English, who was an experienced teacher of ESL children. The first listening task was used with each child individually.

For the second listening task, the children were divided into two groups of five, so that all the children in each group were unfamiliar with the target words for their group. Each group performed the task in the same way.

3. The post-test: The post-test was a vocabulary test, administered individually to the children 7 days after completion of the treatment.

Tests

The pre-test measured both productive and receptive knowledge of words labelling colors (e.g. 'black' and 'orange'), bugs (e.g. 'ant' and 'cricket') and birds (e.g. 'canary' and 'rooster'). It was anticipated that the children would know the names of colours but not the names of the bugs and birds.[7] The purpose of the test was to establish that this was in fact the case. Productive vocabulary was measured by asking the children to verbalize the names of objects shown on flash-cards. Receptive ability was measured immediately after by asking each subject to identify the objects named from sets of six pictures.

The post-test again measured both productive and receptive knowledge. It was identical to the pre-test. The post-test provided information about what words had been retained for productive or receptive use 7 days after the treatment.

Treatment

The treatment took the form of two non-reciprocal tasks using materials of the kind illustrated in Figure 1. The tasks required the children to listen to a set of six directions and to choose a picture of a bug or a bird and place it in the correct cage on a board. Every effort was made to make the tasks appear like games to the children. Thus, the children were told that they had to pretend they were zookeepers responsible for making sure all the animals were in the right cages. The teacher, who gave the directions, also took the role of 'helper' who would answer any questions the 'zookeepers' might have.

In task one the directions used with each learner incorporated the names of 3 bugs and 3 birds which the pre-test had shown the learner did not know, either productively or receptively. Each child, therefore was exposed to slightly different target words. The directions also incorporated a number of color words, used to label the cages, which the pre-test had shown all the children already knew. They were designed so that the only likely obstacles to the children understanding them would be their lack of knowledge of the names of the bugs and birds. The directions for task two were similarly constructed. Each group was exposed to three completely new words for labelling bugs and 3 for labelling birds. The target words for each group differed to ensure that none of the children had any prior knowledge of any of them. Altogether, each learner was exposed to 6 target words in each task.

In task one, each student worked individually with the teacher. The teacher explained and demonstrated the task to the children, making it clear that if they did not understand a direction they were free to ask for help. He then said each direction and paused to allow the child time to carry it out, attempting to clarify whenever a child indicated non-understanding. When the child had responded by placing a bug/bird in one of the cages the teacher did not indicate whether the child was correct or incorrect but simply went on to the next direction.

In task two, the children worked in groups of five. Each child had his/her own board and responded individually to the teachers' directions. Barricades were erected to prevent individual children looking at the boards of other children. The principal difference between task one and task two was that in task one each learner was dependent on him/herself for signalling non-understanding, while in task two they could rely on other learners if they so chose.

Results

To investigate the extent to which individual children participated in meaning negotiation (research question one), the number of **negotiated sequences** involving each child was counted. Following Varonis and Gass (1985), a negotiated sequence was defined as an exchange consisting of a 'trigger' (i.e. an utterance containing a source of comprehension difficulty) and a 'resolution', made up of an 'indicator', where the child indicates that a comprehension problem exists, a 'response' where the teacher attempts to overcome the problem and, optionally, a 'reaction to the response', where the child who experienced the comprehension problem in the first place reacts to the response (see Chapter 1). The following is an example of a negotiated sequence from task one:

Trigger — T: please find the **crow** and put it into the yellow cage
Resolution —
indicator S9:   a bug?
response T: a **crow** is not a bug/ a **crow** is a kind of bird/ + and it's like
                 black/ it's like a black bird
reaction S9:   yeah i know now

The interactions resulting from both tasks were recorded and transcribed.[8] Negotiated sequences were then identified.

Table 10 gives the interaction scores for the 10 learners in both tasks. In Task 1, there were a total of 19 negotiation sequences out of a possible 60 (i.e. 6 target items x 10 children). Six of the 10 children failed to participate in a single negotiation sequence, while more than three quarters of the total negotiation sequences were accounted for by one child (subject 4). In Task 2, there were 28 negotiation sequences out of a possible 60. In this task six of the nine children participated in at least one negotiation sequence. Two of the children (subjects 1 and 4) accounted for more than half the total sequences. Overall the difference in interaction scores for Tasks 1 and 2 was not statistically significant (t = .77).

Research question two concerns the relationship between the children's participation in meaning negotiation and their comprehension of the directions. Comprehension scores were determined by inspecting the children's boards after each direction to see whether they had selected the right bug/bird for each direction. Table 11 gives the comprehension scores for the 10 children. There is an obvious difference in the children's comprehension scores for the two tasks. In task one, which was performed by each child interacting individually with the teacher, the children's mean comprehension score was 1.7 (representing 28% of the total possible). Three of the children failed to select a single correct object. In contrast, in task two, which was performed by the children interacting with the teacher in small groups of five, the children's mean comprehension score was

Table 10. *Negotiated sequences involving each learner*

Subject	Task 1	Task 2
S1	2	7
S2	0	2
S3	0	0
S4	15	8
S5	1	3
S6	0	0
S7	0	0
S8	0	0
S9	1	5
S10	0	3
Total	19	28
mean SD	1.90	2.80
mean %	4.65	3.01

4.1 (representing 68% of the total) and only one child failed to select at least one correct object. Overall the difference in comprehension scores in the two tasks was statistically significant (t = 2.80; $p > 0.02$).

To further investigate the relationship between negotiation and overall comprehension scores Pearson Product Moment correlation coefficients were computed. The two sets of scores were positively and significantly related in Task one (r = .642; $p < .025$) but were negatively and non-significantly related in Task two (r = -.272).

Table 11 also gives the productive and receptive vocabulary acquisition scores. It is clear and not surprising that the exposure to the new words which the children received as a result of the interaction generated by the tasks was insufficient to develop productive knowledge of the new words. In Task one only three children were able to produce any of the words in the post-test (amounting to only 6.7% of the total words), while in Task two no child was able to produce even a single word. However, the children did demonstrate gains in receptive knowledge. Nine out of the 10 children who participated in the individual task were able to label at least one of the pictures. Overall, 28.3% of the target words used in Task one were recognized. Similar results for Task two were achieved. Again, nine out of 10 children recognized at least one word and overall 25% of the target words were recognized.

Table 11. *Comprehension and vocabulary acquisition scores*

| | Subject Comprehension | | | | Vocabulary Acquisition | | | |
| | Task 1 | | Task 2 | | Task 1 words | | Task 2 words | |
	No.	%	No.	%	prod	rec.	prod.	rec.
S1	0	0	4	75	0	1	0	1
S2	2	34	6	100	1	2	0	2
S3	0	0	6	100	0	1	0	0
S4	6	100	5	84	0	2	0	1
S5	2	34	5	84	0	1	0	2
S6	1	17	5	84	0	0	0	2
S7	1	17	4	75	0	2	0	3
S8	0	0	0	0	0	1	0	1
S9	3	50	1	17	1	5	0	1
S10	2	34	5	84	2	2	0	2
Total	17	28	41	68	4	17	0	15
mean	1.7	2.8	4.1	6.8	0.4	1.7	0	1.5
SD	1.8		2.02		0.70	1.34	0	0.85

To address research question three, Pearson Product Moment Correlation coefficients were computed between the negotiation scores and receptive vocabulary scores obtained for the two tasks. In both cases the coefficients were low and non-significant ($r = .10$ in task one; $r = -.26$ in task two).

Finally to address research question four, Pearson Product Moment Correlation coefficients were computed between the comprehension scores and the receptive vocabulary scores in the two tasks. The coefficients were positive but non-significant in both cases ($r = .44$ in Task one and $.26$ in Task two).

Discussion

Research Question One

To what extent did the children in this study participate in meaning negotiation? Two main points emerge from the results reported in the previous section. The first is that there is a great deal of variance in individual children's preparedness or ability to negotiate and that this is true irrespective of whether the children are interacting individually with an adult or in a group situation. Several of the children failed to interact at all in either task. When confronted with a direction that they did not understand they simply guessed or, in the case of the group task, waited for some other child to ask for help. In contrast, other children did make an effort to address their comprehension problems. Subject 4, in particular, demonstrated a preparedness to persist in negotiating until he had obtained the information he needed to select the right bug or bird, as this example from task one illustrates:[8]

T:	okay/ next my friend please find the **hen** and put it into the brown cage/
S4:	it got big MORE BIG leg?/ ooh/
T:	well a **hen** doesn't really have big legs no/
S4:	this?
T:	actually/ i can't look/
S4:	oh now i know it now/ this big body?/
T:	a **hen** has a big body/ but a **hen** isn't actually a bug/ a **hen** is a kind of bird and it looks/ it's

like it's the name for a mom/ the
mom of chickens

S4:   a chickens/ oh / ++ aaa/ ++

The second main point to emerge is that the children found it much easier to negotiate with the teacher in a group situation than individually. More children negotiated in the group task and the total number of negotiation sequences was also greater. The following example shows how the five children comprising group one were able to benefit from the interactional skills of S4 but also how they shared out the negotiation work among them.

T: please find the **wasp**=
S5:   =**wasp**/
T: and put it in the green cage
S4:   what it's look like?
T: keep it down S5/
S2:   it's bug or it's bird?
T: um S2 it's ah a bug/ it's a kind
of bug/ and S4 it looks like it
can fly cause it has wings and it
has a stinger/ zzz/ it stings you
if you if you dis/ if you bother
it/ if you make it angry it'll
sting you/
S5:   ah ha ha ha/
T: so please find the **wasp** and put
it in the green cage/
S4:   it got a fat belly?
S5:   = i got it/=
T: =yeah it has kind of a fat belly
S4 yes=
S5:   =i got it/=
T: =it does/ + pardon me S5 what was
that?/ + you got it/ is everybody
ready?

This is typical of the interactions generated by task two. It illustrates how when the children worked in groups, most of them were able to obtain much more useful information about the meanings of the target words than when they worked individually with the teacher.

Research Question Two

Do children who participate actively in meaning negotiation show higher levels of comprehension than those who do not? The results for task one suggest a positive answer to this question. In task one, the number of times each child participated in a negotiation sequence with the teacher was significantly related to his or her comprehension of the directions. In task two, the relationship between individual learners' rates of negotiation and their comprehension was negative and non-significant. However, there is no reason to expect a strong relationship in this task, as the children did not need to personally negotiate in order to comprehend the directions; they could rely on other children to do the work for them. It should be noted, though, that overall comprehension was greater in task two than in task one, reflecting, perhaps, the more extensive negotiation that took place in the latter. The results of this study, then, support those of previous studies involving adult L2 learners. Negotiation seems to work for comprehension for children as it does for adults.

Previous studies with adults have also shown that learners can benefit from the negotiation work of others; they do not have to actively engage in negotiation themselves. The results for task two, where the children worked in small groups, show that children can also benefit from the negotiation initiated by other children. Thus, S3 and S6 produced no 'indicators' of their non-comprehension of the teacher's directions but were able to achieve 100% and 92% comprehension respectively.

Research Question Three

Do children who participate in meaning negotiation achieve higher levels of vocabulary acquisition than those who do not? In general, the level of vocabulary acquisition was very low. It is not to be expected that the children would achieve productive control of the target items from the limited exposure they experienced. However, a higher level of receptive control than that actually achieved might have been expected given children's capacity for 'fast mapping'. Only 28.3% and 25% of the total words were recognized in tasks one and two respectively. In contrast, study one found that the adolescent learners in the Tokyo study demonstrated a receptive knowledge of over 41% of the target items after participating in a whole class activity similar to the one used in this study. One possible reason for the children's relative failure to remember the words may have been the lack of any reason to do so. Children may find it easier to learn words that label objects which they have themselves elected to attend to.

Table 12. *A comparison of two learners' interaction, comprehension and vocabulary acquisition scores*

Target item	Subject 4				Subject 7			
	Int.	Comp.	Vocab.		Int.	Comp.	Vocab.	
			Prod.	Recept.			Prod.	Recept.
Task one								
grasshopper	5	+	−	−	0	+	−	−
mosquito	1	+	−	−	0	−	−	−
cardinal	1	+	−	−	0	−	−	−
pigeon	2	+	−	+				
hen	2	+	−	−				
tick	4	+	−	+				
dragonfly					0	−	−	+
rooster					0	−	−	+
canary					0	−	−	−
Totals	15	6	0	2	0	1	0	2
Task two								
wasp	2	−	−	−	0	−	−	−
robin	2	+	−	−	0	−	−	−
centipede	1	+	−	+	0	+	−	+
cricket	1	+	−	−				
peacock	1	+	−	−				
woodpecker	1	+	−	−				
praying mantis					0	+	−	−
goose					0	−	−	+
ostrich					0	−	−	+
Totals	8	5	0	1	0	2	0	3

The results of this study failed to show any relationship between active meaning negotiation and vocabulary acquisition in either task. Children who negotiated extensively in general did no better at learning the target words than those who negotiated little. S4, for example, was obviously very skilled at meaning negotiation and, yet, was not notably successful at learning the target words, doing worse than S7, who did not participate actively in any negotiation sequences whatsoever (see Table 12).

As pointed out in the introduction, studies of adult L2 acquisition have also failed to find any relationship between active negotiation and L2 acquisition.

What is now needed is a detailed analysis of interactionally modified input which particular groups of learners have experienced with a view to identifying when it works for acquisition (which on some occasions it clearly does) and when it does not. This is undertaken in Study Three below.

Research Question Four

What is the relationship between children's comprehension of utterances containing new words and their acquisition of the meanings of these words? The results that address this question (see Table 11) indicate that although the relationship was a positive one it was also very weak, failing to reach statistical significance in either task. It is particularly striking that the overall level of receptive acquisition stayed low in task two (i.e. 25%) even though the children were fairly successful in identifying the correct objects (68.3%). Comprehending a direction containing a new word is obviously no guarantee that the word will be remembered.

Krashen (1985) has argued that the necessary and sufficient conditions for acquisition to take place are (1) the availability of comprehensible input and (2) a low affective filter. In the case of task one, it might be argued that neither condition applied for many of the children. This then might explain why acquisition was low. However, in task two, it would appear that both conditions applied. The children generally did understand the input (as shown by their comprehension scores) and, judging from the transcriptions, most of them did not appear to experience any anxiety during the task. Yet, their overall level of acquisition was much the same as in task one (25% versus 28.3%). Obviously, the relationship between comprehension and acquisition of word meanings is complex. It is possible that the tasks — particularly task two — were successful in introducing the target words into the children's short term memory but much less successful in providing the conditions that ensured their long-term retention. What is needed is an explanation of what causes items to move from short-term memory to long-term memory.

Study Three: Modified Input and the Acquisition of Word Meanings

The two studies reported above are among the very few attempts to ascertain the effect of interactionally modified input on L2 acquisition. However, although these studies lend some support to the claim that interaction facilitates the acquisition of word meanings, they do not demonstrate (or, indeed, try to do so) the specific properties of interactionally modified input that are important. It is, in fact, not yet clear how interactionally modified input helps vocabulary acquisition or, indeed, whether it works more efficiently than premodified input. We know almost nothing about what properties of premodified or interactionally modified input work for acquisition. Is it mainly a matter of the frequency of the items in the input? Does interactionally modified input work well because it results in a greater quantity of input, thus allowing learners more processing time? Is it because learners are given more information about the meanings of problematic items? Or is it some other factor or combination of factors? Ideally, we should be able to predict when new items will be acquired, and when they will not, on the basis of the kind of input learners are exposed to.

As a start to adressing these issues, the third study reported in this chapter examines the relationship between specific properties of premodified and interactionally modified input and vocabulary learning, drawing on some of the classroom data provided by study one. It will seek answers to the following questions:

1. What is the relative effectiveness of premodified and interactionally modified oral input in promoting the acquisition of word meanings?
2. Given that comprehension has been hypothesized as a necessary mediating factor between modified input and acquisition, to what extent are comprehension and the acquisition of word meanings related?
3. What aspects of modified input are related to the acquisition of word meanings?
4. Is it possible to predict which word meanings will be learnt on the basis of specific input properties?

Subjects

The 51 students comprising the premodified and interactionally groups in the Saitama study, one of the two studies reported in Study One, served as the subjects for Study Three.

Design

The details of the design have already been given in the report of Study One.[9] The two groups experienced a pre-test administered one month prior to the treatment, a treatment in the form of a non-reciprocal task, and two post-tests, one administered two days after the treatment and the other about one month later. There was also a follow-up test about two and a half months after the treatment. In this study, the interactionally modified group also provided a measure of 'uptake' (i.e. the learners were asked to self-report the new words they had learnt during the lesson immediately the task was completed). Unfortunately, no such measure was made for the premodified group.

Instruments

The instruments were identical to those used in study one with the exception of the 'uptake' measure. This consisted of an 'Uptake Recall Chart' (see Slimani 1989) on which the subjects wrote down any new word they could recall from the lesson.

Treatment

The treatment was the same as in Study One. That is, Group 1 (the premodified input group) heard directions that had been premodified whereas Group 2 (the interactionally modified group) were allowed to request clarification whenever they did not understand a baseline direction.

Input/interaction variables

The input variables investigated were drawn from a review of the relevant vocabulary acquisition research (see Chapter 2). In addition, they represent features that emerged as salient in an initial scanning of the input data (i.e. the premodified and interactionally modified directions).

1. Length of word form
    Word length serves as a common measure of 'readability'. As Harrison (1980) points out, word length is a good indicator of vocabulary difficulty because it is a correlate of general word frequency. It seems reasonable to suppose that Japanese learners might experience similar difficulty to that reported for Chinese learners (Meara 1984; see Chapter Two). Length is usually measured in terms of syllables and was so in this study.

2. Word frequency
    There is plenty of evidence to suggest that word frequency is a significant factor influencing vocabulary acquisition from written input (see Chapter Two). What is not clear at the moment is whether the relationship between frequency and word acquisition is monotonic (i.e. the more frequent the word occurs, the more likely it is to be learnt) or whether there is a threshold effect operating (i.e. a word needs only to be encountered a specific

number of times to be acquired). Of course, much depends on what we mean by 'acquired'. A few exposures (research suggests 6 or 7 where written input is concerned) may be enough for the basic meaning of a word to be acquired, but many more may be needed before 'depth' of word knowledge is achieved.

3. Range
Mackey (1965) lists range as one of the factors to be considered when selecting which items to teach. He defines it 'as the number of samples or texts in which an item is to be found' and argues 'the greater the range of an item, the more important its frequency' (p. 182). This claim is supported by research which indicates that new words should be used in at least four different contexts when they are first introduced (Carpay 1975; cited in Palmberg 1987). In the present study range is operationalized as the number of separate directions that a target item occurs in.

4. Lexical density
Lexical density was determined by establishing the ratio of content words to total word tokens. It serves as a general measure of input complexity.

5. Length of direction
A second measure of input complexity is obtained by counting the number of words in the teacher's input for each direction. In the case of the premodified input this was determined in advance. In the case of the interactionally modified input, the length of each direction reflected the learners' understanding of the baseline direction and the efforts they put into negotiating understanding it.

6. Number of requests for clarification
A number of studies based on the Interaction Hypothesis (e.g. Long 1981; Pica and Doughty 1985) have assumed that tasks which give rise to plentiful negotiation of meaning will work better for language acquisition than those that do not. The extent of negotiation in these studies has been measured in terms of the numbers of interactional modifications (e.g. requests for clarification, confirmation requests and comprehension checks) which occur. In the present study, the extent of negotiation is a direct reflection of the number of clarification requests the learners make for each direction. This measure is of course, only available for the interactionally modified group.

7. Type of definition
The directions experienced by both groups of learners provide definitions of the target items. These definitions serve as a kind of 'elaboration'. In the

case of the premodified input, definitions are built into each direction. In the case of the interactionally modified input, the learners' requests for clarification invariably resulted in definitions of the problematic items (i.e. the target items). Because definitions seemed to play such a prominent role in the input to both groups, a number of measures were based exclusively on them.

Flowerdew (1992a, 1992b) reports the results of a descriptive study of definitions in lectures by native speaker biology and chemistry lecturers to non-native speaker university students in Saudi Arabia. One of the distinctions he observed, which is also widely recognized, in the literature he reviews, is that between formal and semi-formal definitions. A formal definition consists of 'term + class + characteristic', as in this example from the premodified input:

> A sink is a hole and you wash dishes inside it and you can fill it with water.

A semi-formal definition consists only of 'term + characteristic', as in this example from the premodified input:

> A canister is usually round and you put things in it.

Flowerdew (1992a) suggests that, in general, formal definitions are 'remarkably precise' and that a semi-formal definition is 'less precise'. However, he also notes that the class word in a formal definition can be a 'dummy' (e.g. a repetition of the item or a referential item like 'one'). Such formal definitions are presumably also 'less precise'. In the present study, a four point scoring system was developed, reflecting the supposed degree of precision:

0   No class word is mentioned in the definition.
1   A 'dummy' or very vague class word (e.g. 'thing') is mentioned in the definition.
2   A precise class word is mentioned (e.g. 'hole')
3   Two precise class words are mentioned (e.g. 'place' and 'hole').

8. Number of defining characteristics
    The definitions also varied considerably — particularly in the interactionally modified input — with regard to the kind and number of defining characteristics that were mentioned. The characteristics were coded in terms of the four semantic categories Flowerdew (1992a: 210) observed in his data:

> behaviour/process/function
> composition/structure
> location/occurrence
> attribute/property

Based on this analysis, a count was made of the number of characteristics mentioned in each definition.

9.   Length of definitions
Finally, the number of words in each definition of an item was counted. It should be noted that in the interactionally modified input a definition spread across more than one turn when learners requested clarification. In this case, the total number of words comprising the definition of an item was counted. This measure provided an indication of the overall complexity of each definition.

Results

The effects of modified input on vocabulary acquisition

Table 13 shows the mean scores on Post-Test 1, Post-Test 2 and the Follow-up tests for both the premodified and the interactionally modified groups and for Uptake in the case of the interactionally modified group. The time taken to complete the listening task with the premodified group was 10 minutes and with the interactionally modified group 45 minutes. Table 13 also shows the mean words acquired per minute.

Overall, the acquisition test scores for both groups were low in all three tests, varying from a low of 2.41 (13.4%) for the premodified input group in Post Test 1 to a high of 7.5 (41.7%) for the interactionally modified group in the Follow-up Test. The Uptake score for the interactionally modified group was particularly low.

Table 13. *Mean vocabulary acquisition scores for the premodified and interactionally modified groups*

	Uptake	Post Test 1	Post Test 2	Follow-up Test
Group 1 (N = 27 subjects)				
Mean score		2.41	2.91	4.70
Mean w.p.m.		0.24	0.29	0.47
Group 2 (N = 24 subjects)				
Mean score	2.04	6.08	4.75	7.5
Mean w.p.m.	0.05	0.14	0.11	0.17

The mean scores for the interactionally modified input group were higher than those for the premodified input group in all three tests. As Study One showed these differences are statistically significant. In terms of the mean number of words acquired per minute, however, the results favour the premodified input group. The rate of acquisition is, in fact, two to three times greater in the premodified group.

The relationship between comprehension and vocabulary acquisition scores

The comprehension score for each target item was calculated as the mean comprehension score achieved by the learners for that direction in which the item

Table 14. *Means, standard deviations and range (high/low) for all variables in both groups*

	Mean	SD	Range (high/low)
Group 1 (N = 18 words)			
Comprehension	28.1	18.1	57–0
Post-test 1	13.9	13.5	44–0
Post-test 2	14.6	14.9	52–0
Follow-up test	26.1	21.7	69–0
Length of word form	2.1	1.1	1–3
Word frequency	4.1	1.9	8–2
Range	1.8	1.3	1–5
Lexical density	0.48	0.07	.62–.39
Length of direction	51.2	16.2	85–33
Type of definition	1.1	0.88	0–2
No. defining characteristics	2.5	1.3	5–0
Length of definition	19.9	9.3	38–0
Group 2: (N = 18 words)			
Comprehension	66.5	21.1	93–13
Uptake	2.7	3.4	9–0
Post-test 1	33.3	27.6	83–0
Post-test 2	26.7	22.4	67–0
Follow-up test	36.0	28.3	96–0
Length of word form	2.0	0.8	1–3
Word frequency	9.7	5.6	27–4
Range	1.8	1.4	1–6
Lexical density	0.43	0.04	.51–.36
Length of direction	104.9	61.5	260–54
Type of definition	1.2	1.00	0–2
No. defining characteristics	6.1	4.7	19–2

occurred. In most cases, each direction contained one target item. However, in three of the directions there were two target items, in which case pairs of items were assigned the same comprehension score. The mean comprehension score for each word together with the standard deviation and range (high/low) are shown in Table 14.

The relationships between these comprehension scores and the vocabulary scores obtained on the two post-tests, the follow-up tests and, in the case of the interactionally modified group, from the uptake chart were examined by means of simple product moment correlations for both groups separately. The results are shown in Tables 15 and 16. It should be noted that the N size is 18, corresponding to the number of vocabulary items investigated.

The correlations between the comprehension scores and acquisition scores for uptake and the two post-tests are positive but low and non-significant in both groups of learners. The relationship between comprehension and follow-up test scores is also positive and reaches statistical significance ($p < .01$ in the case of the premodified group and $p < .05$ in the case of the interactionally modified group).

The relationship between modified input and vocabulary acquisition

Table 14 above shows means and dispersion statistics for all input variables for both groups. Simple product moment correlations between the various measures of L2 vocabulary acquisition and the input/interaction factors described above

Table 15. *Simple correlations between comprehension and vocabulary acquisition word scores (premodified input group)*

	Post test 1	Post test 2	Follow-up test
Comprehension	.33	.40	.59**

N = 18
* $p < .05$
* $p < .01$

Table 16. *Simple correlations between comprehension and vocabulary acquisition word scores (interactionally modified input group)*

	Uptake	Post test 1	Post test 2	Follow-up test
Comprehension	.24	.42	.43	.51*

N = 18
* $p < .05$
* $p < .01$

Table 17. *Simple correlations between vocabulary acquisition scores and input measures (premodified input group)*

	Post test 1	Post-test 2	Follow-up test
Length of word form	.02	.09	−.13
Word frequency	.29	.15	.38
Range	.49*	.39	.22
Lexical density	.25	.27	.06
Length of direction	.48*	.43	.59*
Type of definition	−.04	−.10	−.14
No. defining characteristics	.01	−.11	.23
Length of definition	.03	−.07	.29

N = 18
* $p < .05$
** $p < .01$

Table 18. *Simple correlations between vocabulary acquisition scores and input/interaction measures (interactionally modified group)*

	Uptake	Post test 1	Post test 2	Follow-up test
Length of word form	−.43	−.25	−.12	.46
Word frequency	.30	.31	.32	.25
Range	.40	.56*	.49*	.51*
Lexical density	.04	.18	.09	.06
Length of direction	−.41	−.03	.01	−.03
No. clarification requests	−.48*	−.12	−.11	−.02
Type of definition	.26	.20	.24	.43
No. defining characteristics	−.29	−.49*	−.56*	−.46
Length of definition	−.36	−.53*	−.50*	−.47*

N = 18
* $p < .05$
** $p < .01$

were computed separately for the premodified input and interactionally modified groups (see Tables 17 and 18). In addition, the differences between the interactionally modified groups' vocabulary acquisition scores and those of the premodified group were calculated. In general, these favored the interactionally modified group. These difference scores were correlated with the input/interaction measures obtained for the interactionally modified group (see Table 19).

Of the nine input/interaction measures investigated only two (Range and Length of Direction) were significantly related, both positively, to the vocabulary

Table 19. *Simple correlations between differences in vocabulary acquisition (interactionally modified group scores minus premodified group scores) and input/interaction measures for the interactionally modified group*

	Post test 1	Post test 2	Follow-up test
Length of word form	−.36	−.21	−.53*
Word frequency	.29	.34	.60**
Range	.51*	.40	.65**
Lexical density	.21	.09	.11
Length of direction	−.22	−.18	.05
No. clarification requests	−.29	−.25	.01
Type of definition	.08	.06	.30
No. defining characteristics	−.51*	−.49*	−.08
Length of definition	−.61**	−.47	−.05

N = 18
* $p < .05$
** $p < .01$

acquisition scores of the premodified input group. In the case of the interactionally modified group, four measures figured in statistically significant relationships with vocabulary acquisition scores, one positively (Range) and three negatively (Number of Requests for Clarification, Number of Defining Characteristics and Length of Definitions). More interesting, perhaps, are the input/interaction factors that are related to the difference vocabulary acquisition scores, as these demonstrate which items were better acquired as a result of the interactionally modified input. Word Frequency and Range were positively related to difference scores, while Length of Word Form, Number of Defining Characteristics and Length of Definitions were negatively related. We can note that two measures (Lexical Density and Type of Definition) did not figure in statistically significant correlations with any of the vocabulary acquisition scores.

The nature of the relationships also changed according to the way vocabulary acquisition was measured. Number of Requests for Clarification was only related (negatively) to Uptake and no other input/interaction factor was strongly associated with this measure of vocabulary acquisition. Range, Length of Direction, Number of Defining Characteristics (negatively) and Length of Definitions (negatively) were related to Post Test 1 and/or Post Test 2 in one or both groups. The greatest number of statistically significant relationships, however, involved the Follow-up Test. Length of Word Form (negatively), Word Frequency, Range, Length of Direction, Number of Defining Characteristics (negatively) and Length of Definitions (negatively) were all associated with this measure of vocabulary acquisition. Also, a distinct pattern of relationships emerged for the difference scores; whereas Range, Number of Defining Characteristics (negatively) and Length of Definitions were significantly correlated with differences scores for Post Test 1 and Post Test 2, Length of Word Form (negatively), Word Frequency and Range were strongly related to the difference in Follow-up Test scores.

Input variables functioning as predictors of vocabulary acquisition

To examine which input variables predicted the learning outcomes a series of stepwise regression analyses were run on the three data sets (the premodified input, the interactionally modified input, and the difference scores) with Post Test 1, Post Test 2 and the Follow-up Test as dependent variables. Given the small N size (18), these analyses must be considered exploratory and the results treated circumspectively.

In the case of the premodified input, Range (first) and Frequency (second) predicted the scores on Post Test 1, no variable predicted the scores on Post Test 2 and Comprehension (first) and Frequency (second) predicted scores on the Follow-up Test. For the interactionally modified input, Range is a fairly good predictor of scores on Post Test 1, accounting for 31% of the variance, while Frequency accounted for an additional 19% of the overall variance. Number of Defining Characteristics was a negative predictor of scores on Post Test 2, accounting for 31% of the variance. Range and Frequency again predicted scores on the Follow-up Test. The difference between the test scores obtained by the interactionally modified and premodified input groups was predicted negatively by Length of Definition in the case of Post Test 1, this variable accounting for 37% of the variance. It was predicted negatively by Number of Defining Characteristics in the case of Post Test 2 (24% of the variance) and positively by Range accounting for 42% of the variance in the Follow-up Test, with Comprehension accounting for a further 16%. By and large these results reflect the strength of the associations identified by the correlational analyses.

Discussion

The first research question concerned the relative effectiveness of premodified and interactionally modified input in promoting vocabulary acquisition. Before considering this, it should be noted that few words were learnt by all the learners — under 50% in every case and, in many of instances, a long way under.

Table 8. *Stepwise regression analyses with premodified input variables*

Dependent variable	Predictor variables	Multiple R	R Square	F	Significance F
Post-test 1	1. Range	.49	.24	5.07	.04
	2. Frequency	.69	.48	6.94	.01
Post-test 2	None				
	1. Comprehension	.59	.35	8.69	.01
Follow-up Test	2. Frequency	.77	.59	10.63	.001

N = 18

Table 9. *Stepwise regression analyses with interactionally modified input variables*

Dependent variable	Predictor variables	Multiple R	R Square	F	Significance F
Post-test 1	1. Range	.55	.31	7.24	.02
	2. Frequency	.71	.50	7.48	.01
Post-test 2	1. Number of defining characteristics	.56	.31	7.21	.02
Follow-up Test	1. Range	.51	.26	5.70	.03
	2. Frequency	.70	.49	7.25	.01

N = 18

Table 10. *Stepwise regression analyses with difference scores and interactionally modified input variables*

Dependent variable	Predictor variables	Multiple R	R Square	F	Significance F
Post-test 1	1. Length of definition	.61	.37	9.29	.01
Post-test 2	1. Number of defining characteristics	.49	.24	5.18	.04
Follow-up Test	1. Range	.65	.42	11.72	.004
	2. Comprehension	.76	.58	10.50	.001

However, this is not surprising, given that the task called for incidental rather than intentional acquisition. Nagy et al. (1985) calculated that the rate of acquisition for children reading in their first language was .25 wpm. Dupay and Krashen (1993) report that 42 undergraduate learners of L2 French who saw and read scenes from the film *Trois Hommes et Un Coffin* gained, on average, nearly six words after 80 minutes exposure, about .075 wpm. The acquisition rates found in this study compare favourably with Nagy et al's rate.

It is clear that although interaction led to more words being acquired (see study one), it also resulted in a conspicuously slower rate of acquisition. This raises questions as to whether interactionally modified input is, in fact, more *efficient* than premodified input in promoting incidental vocabulary acquisition.[10]

The second and third research questions investigated the relationship between comprehension/input variables and vocabulary acquisition, using correlational statistics. Such an analysis is only appropriate if there is sufficient dispersal in the scores for individual variables. Table 2 indicates that there was considerable variance on all the variables investigated with the exception of two — Lexical Density and Type of Definition.

The second research question concerned the relationship between comprehension and vocabulary acquisition. In the case of three of the measures of vocabulary acquisition (Uptake, Post Test 1 and Post Test 2), comprehending directions containing the target items was only weakly related to the acquisition of the items. In fact, an inspection of the scores for the individual items shows that there were many cases where comprehension was high but acquisition low (e.g. 'ladle' and 'dish drainer' in both the premodified input and interactionally modified groups) and, conversely, cases where comprehension was quite low but acquisition high (e.g. 'stove' in the premodified input group and 'counter' in the interactionally modified group). It should also be noted, however, that when comprehension was extremely low, so too was acquisition (e.g. 'canister' and 'faucet' in both groups).

In contrast, much stronger, and statistically significant, correlations were observed between comprehension and Follow-up Test scores. In other words, the comprehension of directions containing the target items was related much more powerfully to long-term retention, as measured by the Follow-up Test, than to immediate acquisition.

In Chapter One we noted that the processes of comprehension and acquisition are not necessarily the same; learners may comprehend input without necessarily learning anything from it. The results for Uptake and the two Post-tests reflect this; learners can comprehend a direction containing a new item but fail to internalize the item for later retrieval. This is not so surprising. More difficult to explain are cases where learners fail to understand a direction and yet learn the target item embedded it. Possibly, learners' comprehension of such directions is partial (e.g. they understand the meaning of the target item but fail to understand the direction as a whole). This raises the important question as to what we mean by 'comprehensible input'. To what unit of discourse should this notion be applied? Clearly, it is not necessary to understand a complete message for some vocabulary learning to take place.

What explanations are there for the much stronger relationship between comprehension and the Follow-up Test? In this test, it will be recalled, learners were given a list of the target items and asked to use them to label pictures of the kitchen objects. The scores on this test were generally higher than those for Post Test 1 or Post Test 2 (see Table 13), despite the fact that ten weeks had intervened. This suggests that the Follow-up Test was in some way easier. The learners may have found it easier because the pictures triggered memory of the original context in which the new words were encountered (i.e. the directions and the picture of the kitchen). In contrast, the Post Tests, where the learners were asked to give translation equivalents of lists of decontextualized words, were unlikely to recall the original context. This may also help to explain why comprehension is related more strongly to scores on the Follow-up Test. Comprehending the directions may have helped the learners to establish a firm memory link between the new words and the 'situation' (i.e. the kitchen) to which they were all related.[11]

To sum up, the results suggest that the relationship between comprehension and acquisition is much more complex than the Input Hypothesis (Krashen 1985) recognizes. Comprehending a message does not guarantee acquisition of new word meanings, as Krashen has recognized. Also, although comprehension of the meaning of an individual word must be necessary for word meaning acquisition to take place, it would appear that it is not necessary to comprehend the complete message in order to learn a new word embedded within it. It also appears that comprehension of the complete message helps learners to store the new word meanings in terms of the situational context in which they were encountered.

The third research question concerned the characteristics of the input and interaction that were associated with incidental acquisition of word meaning. Only one factor — Range — figured in significant correlations (four in total) with vocabulary acquisition by both premodified and interactionally modified input groups. Hearing words used in a variety of different contexts aids their acquisition. Interestingly, Range emerges as a more important factor than Word Frequency. Although the correlations between this factor and the measures of vocabulary acquisition were all positive, only one reached statistical significance.[12]

It might be expected that Length of Direction would be positively related to vocabulary acquisition scores; the longer the direction, the more time learners have to process its meaning and to attend to problematic words. The results of the correlational analyses suggest that it is not as simple as this. Where premodified input is concerned, Length of Direction is a factor, producing moderate correlations with all three acquisition measures. However, Length of Direction has almost zero correlations with the vocabulary test measures of the interactionally modified group. It approaches significance with Uptake, but the relationship is a negative one; the longer the direction, the less likely a new word is likely to be uptaken. Length of Direction is also negatively related to difference scores on Post Test 1 and Post Test 2. Why should Length of Direction work positively for the premodified input and not at all or negatively for the interactionally modified group? The answer would seem to be that up to a point learners do benefit from more elaborated input, but that once that point is exceeded length ceases to matter and can even become a negative factor, perhaps because learners with limited short-term memories experience capacity overload.

This interpretation is given support by the negative correlations between Number of Defining Characteristics and Length of Definition on the one hand and measures of vocabulary acquisition on the other in the interactionally modified group. What these correlations tell us is that the more detailed and wordy a definition becomes as a result of negotiation, the less effective it is in promoting vocabulary acquisition. The opportunity to request clarification invariably resulted in the teacher attempting to define the target items that caused the problem. In the case of a word like 'stove', this resulted in a highly succinct definition:

Student: What is a stove?
Teacher: Stove is a hot place for cooking.

and high levels of acquisition (83% in Post-test 1, 46% in Post-test 2 and 96% in the Follow-up test). In the case of a word like 'canister' the repeated requests for clarification lead to lengthy definitions where the teacher attempts to convey the meaning by mentioning numerous features:

Student: What is a canister?
Teacher: Canister is, uh, ... it's a small place to put things like salt, or jellybeans, or coffee. You put it in a canister, like a small box, or small container — usually it's round, usually a canister is round.

This is not very successful in enabling learners to identify the picture of the object. It leads to further attempts at clarification, followed by yet more information:

Student: How to use it?
Teacher: How to use it? A canister? Uh, you open the canister and you put, for example, you put coffee in it. Then you take a small, some coffee out, coffee or salt, you can put salt in it.
Student: What else do we put ...
Teacher: What else? Uh, jellybeans, candies, sugar, flour.

Given the sheer amount of information that the learners have to process in this direction, it is little wonder that the acquisition scores for 'canister' are so low (4% in Post Test 1, 8% in Post Test 2 and 0% in the Follow-up Test).

The pattern of correlations involving measures of input quantity and vocabulary acquisition help to explain why the interactionally modified input was, overall, less efficient than the premodified input in promoting vocabulary acquisition. The premodified input offered the learners relatively short defini- tions, more like that found in the protocol for 'stove' above than that for 'canister'. The interactionally modified input worked best when it too supplied short definitions involving mention of only a few salient characteristics. Indeed, in such cases, it often worked better than the premodified input. The difference scores for 'stove' were plus 50% for Post Test 1, plus 16% for Post Test 2 and plus 34% for the Follow-up Test. The longer and more elaborate the definitions were, the smaller the difference scores. These results suggest that the claims that have been advanced for 'elaborative simplification' need to be examined very carefully, at least where the acquisition of word meaning from oral input is concerned. Elaborative simplification may help acquisition but when the input becomes over-elaborated it ceases to do so, as Chaudron (1982) suggested.

In the light of these comments it is not surprising to find that the number of clarifications (a measure of the extent to which the learners attempted to negotiate meaning) is negatively related to the vocabulary acquisition measures. In the case of Uptake, the negative impact is statistically significant; the more learners negotiated around a problematic word, the less likely they were to report having learnt it, perhaps because they became swamped with information. Thus, whereas previous research has shown that learners's comprehension is impeded when negotiation results in too much information (see Chapter One), this study suggests that vocabulary acquisition can be similarly restricted. However, this study also suggests that under certain conditions opportunities to negotiate input can be beneficial. It works better than premodified input when the target word is short (one or two syllables), when it occurs relatively frequently and in a range of contexts and, crucially perhaps, when the input supplies definitional informa- tion that is clear and concise.

It is also possible that interactionally modified input works best when it is geared to the needs of individual learners. In this study, the interactionally modi- fied input was directed at the group as a whole. Individual learners may have failed to attend to clarifications that they did not specifically request. However, study one found that learners who engaged in active negotiation by requesting clarification did not achieve higher levels of comprehension than those who just listened. Clearly, though, this is an issue in need of further investigation.

Finally, it should be noted that two input factors (Lexical Density and Type of Definition), which were hypothesized to play a role in vocabulary acquisition, were found not to do so in this study. The lack of dispersal in the scores for these two variables may explain this.

The final research question asked whether it was possible to identify variables associated with modified input that could predict the vocabulary acquisition scores. The results provided by the regression analyses can be used to answer this question but given the small N-size they must be treated as suggestive only. As might be expected, Range figures as a significant predictor in a number of analyses, often, in conjunction with Frequency. The stepwise regression analysis suggests that Range and Frequency may be functioning as distinct factors, both influencing learning outcomes independently of each other. Mackey's (1965) claim that the frequency of an item assumes greater importance as its range increases is given some support. The length and complexity of the definitions (i.e. Number of Defining Characteristics and Length of Definitions) negatively predict Post Test scores in the interactionally modified data sets. Comprehension figures only as a predictor of Follow-up Test scores, strengthening the possibility that this test measures a different aspect of vocabulary knowledge from the Post Tests (see discussion above). These results suggest that it may indeed be possible to identify characteristics of modified input that can predict vocabulary learning, although further work needs be done with a much larger N size before any conclusions can be drawn.

Summary and Conclusion

The three studies reported in this chapter tested the two principal claims of the original Interaction Hypothesis — namely that interactionally modified input facilitates comprehension and that it thereby promotes second language acquisition. Whereas there have been a number of previous studies that have examined the relationship between modified input and comprehension there have been very few studies that have investigated the effects of modified input on acquisition.

The main findings of the three studies are as follows:

1. Interaction facilitates comprehension; when learners have the opportunity to signal their non-understanding the ensuing modified input results in better comprehension than when no such opportunity is available. This holds true for both adolescents and young children.
2. As might be expected, learners vary in their preparedness to negotiate.

Relatively few of the adolescent classroom learners actively negotiated. Many of the young children in study two were unable or unprepared to negotiate with the teacher.

3. Comprehension, however, does not depend on active negotiation; L2 learners who do not negotiate can benefit from the modified input obtained for them by learners who do negotiate. Of course, if *no* learners are prepared to negotiate there can be no modified input.

4. Comprehensible input is not sufficient for acquisition to take place (Long 1996). Thus, the learners in these studies were often able to understand a lexical item that was new to them without acquiring it. In general, the relationship between comprehension and acquisition proved to be a weak one.

5. Modified input clearly facilitates the acquisition of word meanings. Both premodified and interactionally modified input are effective in this respect.

6. While interactionally modified input was found to be more *effective* in promoting the acquisition of word meanings than premodified input it was also shown to be less *efficient* in the sense that it took up more time and thus led to a slower rate of acquisition (measured in new words acquired per minute of exposure).

7. The relative inefficiency of interactionally modified input was the result of overelaboration; the more learners negotiated a particular directive the more elaborate the input became and the less likely they were to benefit acquisitionally from it.

8. The most important factor contributing positively to the acquisition of word meanings was *range* (i.e. the number of different contexts in which a target word appeared).

It is clear that, overall, the three studies do not lend unequivocal support to the original Interaction Hypothesis. The first part of the hypothesis (see Long 1983a), namely that conversational adjustments promote comprehension of input, has been demonstrated. However, the second part, namely that comprehensible input promotes acquisition, has not been convincingly shown. Moreover, although the studies found that interactionally modified input promoted acquisition (the third part of the hypothesis), they also found that it worked less efficiently than input that was not interactionally derived. In short, interaction would appear to be somewhat less crucial for acquisition (at least where vocabulary is concerned) than the Interaction Hypothesis claims. The studies, therefore, point to the need to investigate a number of questions: When does comprehension work for acquisition and when not? To what extent and in what ways is 'comprehensible input' *necessary* for acquisition? How crucial is interaction for acquisition if learners can learn more efficiently from premodified input? How can the negotiation of meaning be conducted so that it does not result in overelaborated input?

In the updated version of the Interaction Hypothesis (see Chapter One), Long (1996) proposes that negotiation for meaning works for acquisition by inducing selective attention to linguistic features in the input. What is needed, therefore, are studies that examine how this takes place. What are the properties of interactionally modified input that make features salient in such a way that they can be noticed and acquired? This is perhaps the central question facing researchers working in this paradigm.

Finally, it should be noted that the updated version of the Interaction Hypothesis claims that acquisition can result from the modified output that learners produce when they engage in meaning negotiation as well as from modified input. In the next chapter we will report a study that extends the research considered in this chapter by comparing the relative effects of premodified input, interactionally modified input and modified output on acquisition.

Notes

1. This report of this study was based on research carried out by Yoshiro Tanaka and Asako Yamazaki and originally reported in Ellis, Tanaka and Yamazaki (1994).

2. We did not obtain standardized measures of the participants' proficiency in order to ensure the comparability of the three groups. To have done so would have been to interfere unduly with their instructional program. Also, we felt that comparability of the groups was best assured by demonstrating that there were no group differences with regard to knowledge of the target lexical items. This was achieved by means of the pretest. We would also like to emphasize that it was the policy of both schools to construct classes of equal ability and that in the opinion of the two researchers who carried out the empirical investigations this had been achieved.

3. In support of this claim, it should be noted that not all the premodified and negotiated directions differed with regard to length and redundancy. For example, in Study 1 there was little difference in the premodified and interactionally modified version of Direction 1.

4. It is also likely that productive use of new target items is fostered by interaction. However, it is possible that this aspect of vocabulary acquisition requires opportunities for learners to *use* items they have begun to acquire and to receive feedback from other speakers. In this study, there was little opportunity for the subjects to use the target items.

5. It is, in fact, difficult to envisage how this task could have been performed successfully other than with the teacher taking charge of the input. Given that the directions contained items that were unknown to most of the learners, it would have been very difficult for learners to supply each other with input that led to comprehension. Such tasks do not lend themselves to small group work.

6. The report of this study was based on doctoral research carried out by Rick Heimbach and originally reported in Ellis and Heimbach (1997).

7. No attempt was made to discover whether the children knew the names of the bugs and birds in their L1 as this is not relevant to the study, the purpose of which was to establish whether children could acquire new L2 words through interaction, irrespective of whether they had L1 equivalents for them.

8. The following transcription conventions were used:

+	pause (1–2 seconds)
++	longer pause (3 seconds or longer)
=	overlap
/	end of, or abandonment of/intonation contour
?	a question (i.e. an intonation contour with a questioning intonation)
CAPS	increased stress
bold	new lexical item

9. The baseline data collected as part of study one was not used in the present study which was concerned only with the relationships between properties of modified input and acquisition.

10. Although interactionally modified input may not be so efficient as premodified input where the initial acquisition of word meaning is concerned, it may still prove to be more effective in helping learners to develop 'depth' of lexical knowledge — for example, in enabling learners to progress from passive to active knowledge of words they have acquired.

11. The idea that words may be stored in relation to the 'situation' or domain in which they were initially learnt is an intriguing one. In the case of the present study, this might suggest that the learners would learn and retain words that they considered to be good exemplars of the situation/domain better than words that they considered less clearly related to it. To test this, prototypicality scores for the 18 words were obtained by asking twenty adult native speakers of American English to rate each word for 'kitchiness' on a seven point scale (cf. Rosch 1975). Mean ratings were then calculated for each word and correlated with the two groups' vocabulary test scores. In the case of the premodified input scores, significant positive correlations were obtained between the prototypicality scores and Post Test 1 ($r = .56$; $p < .05$), Post Test 2 ($r = .52$; $p < .05$) and the Follow-up Test ($r = .64$; $p < .01$). In the case of the interactionally modified group, significant positive correlations between the prototypicality scores and Post Test 2 ($r = .49$; $p < .05$) and the Follow-up Test ($r = .49$; $p < .05$) were found. This suggests that the learners found 'basic' kitchen terms such as 'stove', 'plate' and 'sink' easier to learn and remember than less basic terms such as 'lid' and 'shelf'.

12. An anonymous reviewer of the original article on which the report of Study Three is based points out that the relationship between word frequency and acquisition may not be monotonic. That is, whereas some words may need to be encountered many times before they are retained other words (for example, those that have personal significance for the learner) may need to be encountered only once. Unfortunately, there was no way of knowing which of the target words had personal significance for the learners.

CHAPTER 4

Modified Output and the Acquisition of Word Meanings

Xien He and Rod Ellis

Introduction

A pervasive and controversial issue in second language acquisition (SLA) concerns the respective roles of input and output in the acquisition of a second language (L2). As we saw in Chapter One, different theoretical positions have been advanced. According to the Input Hypothesis (Krashen 1985), learners acquire an L2 when they are exposed to comprehensible input. In the early version of the Interaction Hypothesis, Long (1983a) saw learner output as facilitating acquisition not in and of itself but through meaning negotiation that resulted in modified input. In the later version of the Interaction Hypothesis, however, Long (1996) has recognized that meaning negotiation can induce learners to modify their own output and that this, too, may promote acquisition. Swain has claimed that 'pushed output' contributes to acquisition when learners are required to move from semantic processing to syntactic processing. Drawing on Vygotskyan sociocultural theory, Lantolf and Pavlenko (1995) suggest that acquisition involves 'the dialogic interaction that arises between individuals engaged in goal-directed activities' (p. 110). This can be achieved when one interlocutor provides 'scaffolding' that helps another to perform a new language function. Such a theory sees learner production not just as facilitative of acquisition but as constitutive of it.

These various theoretical positions have been argued tenaciously in the literature. However, there has been relatively little research that has investigated the effects of modified input, modified output and dialogic exchanges on L2 acquisition. As Pica (1994) points out 'researchers have given less attention to identifying a direct impact for learners' negotiation on restructuring of their interlanguage grammar than to documenting the contributions of negotiation in bringing about conditions claimed to be helpful for SLA namely learners' comprehension of L2 input, their production of modified output, and their attention to L2 form' (p. 499–500). In fact, then, the bulk of the research has been parasitic of these theoretical notions rather than attempting to test their roles in L2 acquisition.

We have already examined the research relating to the role of modified output in L2 acquisition (see Chapter One). For convenience sake, however, we will provide a brief summary here. Pica and her co-researchers investigated whether negotiation leads to more accurate output when learners have the chance to reformulate. Pica (1988) found that when native speakers signalled a comprehension problem the learners modified their output by making it more grammatical in less than half of the cases and concluded that negotiation may work for acquisition because it supplies models of correct language and not because of the opportunities to modify output that arise. However, Pica, Holliday, Lewis and Morganthaler (1989) were able to show that learners did modify their output by making it more grammatical when one particular type of negotiation took place — that involving requests for clarification. Building on this, Nobuyoshi and Ellis (1993) conducted a small scale study which indicated that reformulations that make output more target-like may assist acquisition. They found that two learners who were 'pushed' to reformulate by means of requests for clarifications in a story-telling task responded by correcting their past-tense errors and subsequently used this feature more accurately when they repeated the task one week later. Drawing on sociocultural theory, Donato (1994) showed that when L2 learners of French had the opportunity to 'scaffold' knowledge for each other they were able to appropriate this knowledge for subsequent use in novel situations. This study lends support to the Vygotskyan claim that learning involves a progression from the inter- to the intrapersonal. Swain (1995) cites a study by LaPierre (1994) which showed that solutions to 'critical language episodes' which learners reached dialogically while performing meaning-focussed tasks were reflected in performance on tests one week later. Correct solutions resulted in test scores of approximately 80% while incorrect solutions resulted in much lower scores (approximately 30%).

As we saw in Chapter Three, a problem of the experimental studies is that of controlling for time on task. The time taken to complete a task in the interactive condition is inevitably much greater than the time taken in the non-interactive conditions, for as Loschky (1994) has pointed out, 'increased time is an inherent difference between negotiated and unnegotiated interaction' (p. 313). We cannot be certain, then, what it is about interactionally modified input or output that helps comprehension. Does it work because it enables learners to sort out misunderstandings and construct a shared mental model of the task to hand, as suggested by Brown (1995)? Or does it work simply because learners have more time to process input and output?

To sum up, SLA theories differ in which learning conditions they claim are optimal for L2 acquisition. Different theoretical arguments have been advanced on behalf of premodified input, interactionally modified input, modified output and dialogically constructed learning. As yet, however, few studies have tested the claims of these theories and the results to date have been mixed. The study reported in this chapter is an attempt to address this gap by carrying out an experimental comparison of the effects of premodified input, interactionally modified input and modified output on the incidental acquisition of L2 vocabulary. The study also seeks to control for time on task in order to examine the *qualitative* effects of the different treatments.

Research questions

The study was designed to investigate the effects of various conditions of exposure and use of new L2 words on L2 learners' comprehension of input containing the words and their acquisition of these words. The task the learners were asked to perform as part of the study did not require them to learn the new words, and therefore we consider that the type of acquisition involved was incidental rather than intentional.[1] The research questions were:

1. What are the relative effects of premodified input, interactionally modified input and modified output on L2 learners' comprehension of directions containing new L2 words?
2. What are the relative effects of premodified input, interactionally modified input and modified output on L2 learners' ability to subsequently recognize new L2 words?
3. What are the relative effects of premodified input, interactionally modified input and modified output on L2 learners' ability to subsequently produce new L2 words?

Subjects

The subjects of this study were 50 students[2] from six intermediate level classes of the Intensive English Language Program (IELP) at Temple University in

Philadelphia. 27 of the subjects were male and 23 female. A majority were Koreans (26) while 15 came from other parts of Asia (Japan, Taiwan, Hong Kong, Malaysia and Thailand) and 12 from other parts of the world. Their length of stay in the United States at the beginning of the study varied from 10 days to 2 years. Almost all of the subjects had studied English in their home countries for a period of at least 5 years. Their ages ranged from 18 to 44 years.

The teacher who taught all three lessons that comprised the treatments in this study was the assistant director of the IELP program. She was a very experienced teacher and familiar with the kinds of students in the classes. However, she had not taught any of the classes previously.

Design

A multi-factorial design with intact groups was used in this study. Existing classes in the IELP were designated as the Premodified Group (N = 18), the Interactionally Modified Group (N = 16) and the Output Group (N = 16)). There was no control group.[3] To establish whether there were any differences in general language proficiency in the subjects in the three groups the Secondary Level English Proficiency Test (SLEP) was administered a few weeks before the commencement of the study. This showed that there were small overall differences between the groups with the means for the Premodified, Interactionally Modified and Output Groups at 46.78, 48.44 and 44.63 respectively. However, a one-way Analysis of Variance (ANOVA) showed that these differences were not statistically significant (F = 2.26; $p > .05$).

The three groups each completed the following:

1. A pre-test, administered one week before the treatment.
2. The treatment, which varied for the three groups.
3. Post-test 1, administered one week after the treatment.
4. Post-test 2, administered two weeks after the treatment.
5. Post-test 3, administered three weeks after the treatment.
6. Post-test 4, administered four weeks after the treatment.
7. Post-test 5, administered at the same time as Post-test 4.

These tests and the different treatments given to the three groups are described in detail below.

Instruments

The pre-test

The purpose of the pre-test was to identify a set of target lexical items related to the domain of furniture that were not known by the subjects. The subjects were asked to read a list of 50 English words and check each word that they recognized. In addition to items labelling furniture, the list included other items to distract the learners (e.g. 'pizza' and 'lemon'). The 10 items that were least known by the subjects were selected for the study. The overall level of non-recognition of these items was 87.8%. The target items all referred to furniture. They were: *recliner, lampshade, comforter, stool, chest of drawers, china cabinet, wardrobe, rocker, dresser, cushion*.

Post-test 1

This was a picture matching test. It was designed to measure the subjects' ability to recognize the meanings of the target words. The subjects were given individual pictures of pieces of furniture and a list of the 10 target words. They were asked to match the pictures and the words. They were awarded one mark for each picture they labelled correctly (total = 10).

Post-test 2

This test was designed to measure the ability of the subjects to produce the target words orally. The subjects were placed in pairs. Each subject was given a matrix picture of an apartment and 10 pictures showing individual pieces of furniture. The researcher quickly read out the words labelling the pictures. Each subject was required to make up a direction instructing where they wanted each piece of furniture to be placed in the matrix picture of the apartment. They then gave each direction orally to their partners who tried to carry it out by writing in the number of the picture in the correct position in the matrix picture. Subjects were allowed to negotiate meaning if they did not understand their partners' directions. After completing this task the students were given pictures of the individual pieces of furniture and asked to label them from memory. They were awarded one mark for each picture they labelled correctly (total = 10).

In effect, this test replicated the treatment for the Output Group (see below). It was administered to approximately half the subjects from each group (i.e. 10 in the Premodified Group, 8 in the Interactionally Modified Group and

9 in the Output Group). In this way, it was still possible to measure the effects of the original treatment on scores obtained in Post-tests 3 and 4 by examining those subjects who did not complete Post-test 2.

Post-test 3

This test was the same as Post-test 1. The orders of the pictures and the words were changed, however.

Post-test 4

This test required subjects to label pictures of the individual pieces of furniture, as in Post-test 2.

Post-test 5

This was the same as Post-test 1 (i.e. subjects completed the picture-matching test for the third time).

Treatment

The treatments provided to all three groups involved the use of a similar kind of task to that described in Chapter Three. The subjects were given a matrix picture of an apartment and a series of small pictures showing individual pieces of furniture. They were asked to listen to or to orally produce directions which gave instructions about where to place the pieces of furniture in the matrix picture of the apartment. As we noted in Chapter Three, one advantage of this kind of task is that it contains an inbuilt measure of the subjects' comprehension of the directions (i.e. by inspecting whether they have written the numbers of the correct pictures in the correct position in the matrix picture). The conditions under which this task was performed in the three experimental groups are described below.

1. The premodified input treatment

Premodified directions were constructed following the same procedures described in Study One in Chapter Three. The following is an example of the kind of premodified directions that were prepared:

Find the cushion. And I'd like you to put the cushion on the sofa. A cushion is like a pad and you put it on the sofa to support your back.

As this example shows, the premodified directions supplied the learners with definitions of the target items. 10 such directions were prepared, one containing each target item. The task was entirely non-reciprocal in kind.

The teacher gave out the matrix picture of the apartment, on which the subjects wrote their names, and the small pictures of the different pieces of furniture, which she very quickly orally labelled. She then read out each direction at a slow rate (approximately 90 words per minute). The students listened to each direction, chose from the pictures of the pieces of furniture, and wrote the number of the picture they had chosen in the matrix picture of the apartment. The students were not allowed to interact with the teacher. To ensure that this treatment took 45 minutes the teacher went through each direction a second time. At the end of the lesson, the teacher collected in each subject's completed matrix picture.

2.   The interactionally modified input treatment

Baseline directions were used in this treatment. As in Study One in Chapter Three, the teacher wrote a number of formulae for requesting clarification on the board (e.g. 'What is a ____?' and 'Could you say it again?'). She then read out each baseline direction at a normal speed (about 180 words per minute). The students were allowed to interact with the teacher using the requesting formulae and she attempted to help them understand by modifying the baseline direction. This involved adding definitional information, as in this example:

T: Here is a cushion. Would you please put the cushion on the sofa?
S: What is a cushion?
T: A cushion is a small bag filled with soft stuff. Got it?
S: One more time please.
T: A cushion is a small bag filled with soft stuff.
S: Where do I put it?
T: On the sofa.

The teacher gave out the matrix picture of the apartment and the small pictures depicting pieces of furniture. After the students had negotiated each baseline direction they made a choice of one of the small pictures and wrote its number in the matrix picture. The teacher went through the baseline directions a second time to ensure the lesson lasted 45 minutes. The completed matrix pictures were collected in at the end of the treatment. The task was primarily non-reciprocal in kind.

3.   The negotiated output treatment

In this treatment, the students were asked to write their own directions containing the target words and then to say their directions to a partner, negotiating for meaning when the need arose. Thus the task became reciprocal in nature as the learners were responsible for performing the directions themselves.

The teacher gave out the matrix picture of the apartment, the small pictures of pieces of furniture and a blank piece of paper. She then read out the words labelling the small pictures and the subjects wrote down each word next to the corresponding picture. The teacher then gave an example of how to write a direction. The students then wrote 10 directions, one for each small picture. When they were ready, the teacher put the students into pairs and asked them to exchange the directions orally. The students were permitted to negotiate meaning if they did not understand a direction. This afforded opportunities for the students to modify their own output. At the end the teacher collected in the matrix pictures. This treatment took 45 minutes.

Results

In this study the independent variable was the kind of treatment which each group received (premodified input, interactionally modified input and modified output). There were three dependent variables:

1.   Comprehension
     This was determined by inspecting the subjects' completed matrix pictures to see how many of the directions they had understood. The maximum score was 10.
2.   Vocabulary acquisition (recognition)
     Vocabulary recognition scores were obtained on three separate occasions from the picture-matching test (i.e. Post-test 1, Post-test 3 and Post-test 5). The maximum score was 10.
3.   Vocabulary acquisition (production)
     Vocabulary production scores were obtained on two separate occasions from the picture-labelling test (i.e. Post-test 2 and Post-test 4). The maximum score was 10.

To determine whether there were any overall differences among the treatment groups across these three dependent variables a multiple analysis of variance (MANOVA) and univariate F-tests were performed using the comprehension scores and the scores for Post-tests 1, 3, 4 and 5. The scores for Post-test 2 were not included in these analyses as this test was administered to only half the sample. The MANOVA realized an overall statistically significant difference (Wilks' Lambda $F = 2.46$; $p > .02$). The univariate F tests showed significant group differences for all three dependent variables.

Descriptive statistics and the results of separate analyses of variance (ANOVAs) will now be reported for comprehension, vocabulary acquisition (recognition) and vocabulary acquisition (production).

Comprehension

Table 1 gives the descriptive statistics for the comprehension scores. These show that the premodified input group scored a mean of 6.67 out of 10, the interactionally modified group 7.13 and the modified output group 8.13. An ANOVA demonstrated an overall statistically significant difference among the groups ($F = 6.31$; $p < .01$). A post-hoc Scheffé test revealed that the modified output group scored significantly higher than both the other groups. However, the difference between the premodified and interactionally modified groups did not reach statistical significance.

Table 1. *Descriptive statistics for the comprehension scores*

	Premodified input group	Interactionally modified group	Modified output group
N	18	16	16
Mean	6.78	7.13	8.12
Std Dev	1.52	.81	.89
Min.	3.0	6.0	6.0
Max.	9.0	8.0	9.0

Table 2. *Scheffé test of differences in comprehension scores among the three groups*

	(1) Premodified input group	(2) Interactionally modified group	(3) Modified output group
(1)		0.35	1.35**
(2)			1.00*

* $p < .05$
** $p < .01$

Vocabulary acquistion (recognition)

In Post-test 1, the modified output group scored a mean of 8.19, the premodified group 6.17 and the interactionally modified output group 7.0 (see Table 3). An ANOVA showed these differences to be statistically significant (F = 7.63; $p < .05$). A post-hoc Scheffé test indicated that the modified output group significantly outscored both the the premodified input and the interactionally modified groups (see Table 4). Again, the difference between the two input groups was not statistically significant.

The results for Post-test 3 differed slightly (see Table 3). Again, there was a significant overall difference in the groups, as revealed by the ANOVA (F = 9.84; $p < .05$). Also, again the post-hoc Scheffé test showed that the modified output group significantly outscored the other two groups (see Table 5). However, in this test the interactionally modified group also scored significantly higher than the premodified group. In other words, both the modified output group and the interactionally modified input groups did better than the premodified input group.

In the final vocabulary recognition test (Post-test 5), administered four weeks after the initial treatment, the results resembled those for Post-test 1. That is, the ANOVA showed a significant overall difference among the groups (F = 6.84; $p < .05$) but the post-hoc Scheffé test indicated that whereas the modified output group again outperformed the other two groups the difference in scores obtained by the two input groups was not statistically different (see Table 6).

Table 3. *Descriptive statistics for the three vocabulary recognition post-tests*

	Premodified input group (N = 18)			Interactionally modified group (N = 16)			Modified output group (N = 16)		
	PT1	PT3	PT5	PT1	PT3	PT5	PT1	PT3	PT5
Mean	6.17	6.33	6.72	7.0	7.56	7.31	8.19	9.0	8.63
Std D.	1.98	2.11	1.84	1.32	1.71	1.35	0.98	1.26	1.26
Min.	2.0	3.0	2.0	5.0	4.0	4.0	6.0	7.0	6.0
Max.	8.0	9.0	9.0	9.0	10.0	9.0	10.0	10.0	10.0

PT1 = Post-test 1
PT3 = Post-test 3
PT5 = Post-test 5

Table 4. *Scheffé test of differences in vocabulary recognition scores (Post-test 1) among the three groups*

	(1) Premodified input group	(2) Interactionally modified group	(3) Modified output group
(1)		0.83	2.02**
(2)			1.19*

*p < .05
**p < .01

Table 5. *Scheffé test of differences in vocabulary recognition scores (Post-test 3) among the three groups*

	(1) Premodified input group	(2) Interactionally modified group	(3) Modified output group
(1)		1.23*	2.67**
(2)			1.44*

* p < .05
** p < .01

Table 6. *Scheffé test of differences in vocabulary recognition scores (Post-test 5) among the three groups*

	(1) Premodified input group	(2) Interactionally modified group	(3) Modified output group
(1)		0.59	1.90**
(2)			1.31*

* p < .05
** p < .01

Vocabulary acquisition (production)

The ability of the subjects to produce the target lexical items was measured by Post-test 2 and Post-test 4. Only a sub-set of the total sample completed Post-test 2 (i.e. those subjects for whom the modified output treatment was repeated). The descriptive statistics are shown in Table 7. An ANOVA demonstrated that there were significant differences among the three groups (F = 8.03; p < .01). A post-hoc

Table 7. *Descriptive statistics for the two vocabulary production post-tests*

	Premodified input group		Interactionally modified group		Modified output group	
	PT2 (N = 10)	PT4 (N = 18)	PT2 (N = 8)	PT4 (N = 16)	PT2 (N = 9)	PT5 (N = 16)
Mean	5.6	6.22	5.75	6.44	7.55	8.19
Std D	1.08	2.34	1.39	1.93	1.01	1.11
Min.	4.0	1.0	3.0	2.00	6.0	6.0
Max.	7.0	9.0	7.0	9.0	9.0	9.0

Table 8. *Scheffé test of differences in vocabulary recognition scores (Post-test 2) among the three groups*

	(1) Premodified input group	(2) Interactionally modified group	(3) Modified output group
(1)		0.35	1.35**
(2)			1.00*

*p < .05
**p < .01

Table 9. *Scheffé test of differences in vocabulary recognition scores (Post-test 4) among the three groups*

	(1) Premodified input group	(2) Interactionally modified group	(3) Modified output group
(1)		0.22	1.97**
(2)			1.75*

*   p < .05
**   p < .01

Scheffé test indicated that the modified output group were able to produce significantly more of the target items than either the premodified or the interactionally modified input groups (Table 8). However, the difference in scores for the two input groups was not statistically significant.

In the case of Post-test 4 results for the total sample will be reported. The descriptive statistics can be seen in Table 7. Again, the ANOVA revealed significant differences among the three groups (F = 6.45; p < .01) and again a post-hoc Scheffé test showed that the modified output group outperformed both the input groups but that the input groups produced the target words at a similar level (see Table 8).

Summary

Overall these results are very consistent. The group that had had the opportunity to produce and modify their own directions outperformed the two groups that had experienced only modified input in their ability to comprehend the directions, to recognize the new lexical items in picture-matching tests and to produce the items in picture-labelling tests. This pattern of results was observed immediately after the treatment and at various times up to four weeks later.[4] In contrast, although the group that had received interactionally modified input consistently outscored the group that had heard only premodified input in comprehension and on the vocabulary recognition and production tests the differences were small and reached significance only in the case of one of the post-tests (Post-test 3; vocabulary recognition).

Discussion

The first research question asked about the relative effects of premodified input, interactionally modified input and modified input on L2 learners' comprehension. The results of this study indicate that reasonable levels of comprehension can be achieved in all three conditions. Learners in the premodified input group had a mean comprehension score of 68%, those in the interactionally modified input group 71% and those in the modified output group 81%. If, as Krashen (1981) has claimed, comprehension is crucial for acquisition, these results are encouraging for pedagogy. They suggest that the kind of listen-and-do tasks used in this study can lead to high levels of comprehension even when they involve listening to or using unfamiliar words. The results also clearly show that the modified output condition worked better than the modified input conditions. However, in contrast to previous studies (Pica, Young and Doughty 1987; Loschky 1994; Study One in Chapter Three) this study failed to demonstrate any advantage for interactionally modified input over premodified input (i.e. the difference in comprehension scores in these two conditions was not statistically significant). One explanation for this finding is that whereas other studies did not control for the time taken to complete a task this study did. When learners were given the same amount of time to process premodified input as to negotiate interactionally modified input their comprehension levels were essentially the same. Below we will argue that, in fact, the activity resulting from these two tasks was very similar while that derived from the modified output task was notably different.

The second research question addressed the effects of the various task conditions on learners' ability to subsequently recognize the target items (i.e. to acquire passive lexical knowledge). Here again the results are encouraging. The learners in all three conditions manifested high levels of acquisition (between 62% and 90%) and, furthermore, there was clear evidence that they were able to remember the words over time.[5] The modified output condition proved superior in promoting retention to either of the input conditions. There is also some evidence that interactionally modified input was more beneficial than premodified input. However, the difference in scores between the two groups was slight and only achieved significance in one of the post-tests. This result again contradicts Study One in Chapter Three, which found a clear advantage for interactionally modified input in a recognition post-test. Again, though this can be explained by the fact that in this study both groups received the same amount of time to complete their tasks and that the tasks involved similar activity.

The third research question addressed the effects of the various task conditions on learners' ability to subsequently produce the target items (i.e. to acquire active lexical knowledge). As was to be expected, the scores on the production tests were lower than those on the recognition tests but were still very respectable (between 52% and 82%). The comparative effects of the different task conditions were very similar to those for comprehension and vocabulary recognition. The modified output group outperformed the other two groups. The difference in scores between the premodified input group and the interactionally modified input were small and did not reach statistical significance.

Why did the modified output group consistently outperform the two input groups in comprehension and vocabulary acquisition? The obvious explanation is that producing new words helps learners to process them more deeply, whether for comprehension or for acquisition, than simply hearing them. However, we feel that there is more to it than this. We believe that the modified input condition afforded the learners a qualitively different discourse experience. To illustrate this let us consider the three protocols below.

(1)   T: Here is a rocker. Please put the rocker next to the sofa. A
              rocker is a chair which can be rocked back and forth.

(2)   T: Here is a rocker. Please put the rocker next to the sofa in the living room.

        S: What is the rocker?

        T: A rocker is a chair that can be rocked back and forth.

        S: One more time.

        T: A rocker is a chair which can be rocked back and forth.

        S: Please repeat.

        T: A rocker is a chaie that can rocked back and forth.

(3)   S1: Please put the rocker on the living room.

        S2: What is rocker?

        S1: Rocker is like chair. You can sit and move. Look at the picture. You know now?

        S2: Yes. Put rocker where?

        S1: In the living room. There are three rooms in your big picture. Put rocker in the room in the middle of the picture.

        S2: OK.

The three groups' comprehension scores for this item were 77%, 75% and 93%. Similar differences were evident in the various vocabulary tests. It is not difficult to see why the modified output group outscored the other two groups. (3) is qualitatively different from (1) and (2) in a number of respects. First, the definitional information provided by S1 is couched in vocabulary ('chair', 'sit' and move') that is high frequency and therefore likely to be familiar to S2. In contrast, the definition supplied by the teacher in (1) and (2) uses a low-frequency item ('rock') that the students may not have known. Second, the subjects in (3) tackle the task facing them systematically by breaking the task into two parts; they begin by locating the correct picture of the rocking chair, dealing with the meaning of the unknown lexical item in the process and then they work out where this piece of furniture is to be placed in the matrix picture of the apartment. S1 scaffolds the task for S2 by encouraging her to relate the definitional information he supplies to the picture and he then checks whether she has successfully accomplished this ('You know now?'). This kind of scaffolding does not occur in (1) or (2). In short, (3) demonstrates how the two learners collaborate effectively to achieve their goal and, in so doing, create what we believe are ideal conditions for language acquisition.

What exactly are these conditions? They can best be described with reference to socio-cultural theory. This emphasizes that participants respond to a task by constructing an activity that matches their own goals (Coughlan and Duff 1994). Thus, although the task was intended to be identical in all three conditions (a requirement of the kind of experimental research we were practising), the activity it generated turned out to differ in ways we had not predicted. In the premodified and interactionally modified input conditions, the teacher treated the task as a kind of test, the goal of which was to measure how well the students could understand the directions and learn the new words.[6] Thus, the teacher engaged in relatively little interactive work to help build what Artigal (1992) has referred to as a 'shared indexical territory'. Even in the input condition that allowed for interaction, the resulting discourse was highly constrained and even mechanical. For example in (2) above, the teacher defined 'rocking chair' using the same item ('rock') and when asked to clarify simply repeated the same definition. In fact, the teacher offered exactly the same definitional information as that provided by the premodified direction. It is not so surprising, then, that the results obtained for the two input conditions were very similar. In contrast, the students treated the task as a collaborative problem-solving activity the goal of which was to help each other to arrive at a successful outcome for the task. To this end, they engaged in the kind of scaffolding that Vygotsky has claimed assists the construction of zones of proximal development. They arrived at a joint, negotiated solution to the task and in so doing ensured that the reference of the new lexical item was fully understood thus enabling the less-expert learner to acquire it.

In short, we believe that the results of this study support Lantolf and Pavlenko's (1995) contention that 'learning hinges not so much on richness of input, but crucially on the choices made by individuals as responsible agents with dispositions to think and act in certain ways rooted in their discursive histories' (p. 116). In this case, the choices made by the learners working in the modified output condition created more opportunities for learning the new vocabulary than the choices made by the teacher in the interactionally modified condition. These choices reflect the different orientations of the learners and the teacher to the task, which, of course, were themselves a reflection of the participants' different 'discourse histories'.

Conclusion

This study was designed to investigate the relative contributions of premodified, interactionally modified and modified output on comprehension and acquisition. It was conducted within the theoretical framework of the Input, Interaction and Output Hypotheses. However, such a framework proved problematic and led us retrospectively to adopt a sociocultural perspective to account for the results we obtained. In such a perspective it is not appropriate to talk of the respective roles of 'input' and 'output'. It is necessary to consider interaction as a totality, a matrix in which learning is socially constructed. Taking this perspective enables us to deal with what we perceived as an inherent problem in the design of our study. This was that whereas it was possible to contrive conditions that distinguished premodified and interactionally modified input quite specifically it was much more difficult to contrive conditions that narrowly distinguished modified input and modified output. Modified output does not occur in a vacuum — it occurs as a response to input and to the opportunity to interact. Thus, the modified output condition in our study did not involve the learners in just production;[7] it also involved providing them with opportunities to talk in pairs in ways that they were familiar and comfortable with. Thus we cannot say that our study has demonstrated that modified output works better than modified input. We can only say that interactions that provide opportunities for learners to use and negotiate new vocabulary items in dialogically symmetrical discourse seem to create better conditions for incidental vocabulary acquisition than interactions in teacher-controlled exchanges that restrict the kind of interpersonal activity claimed to foster learning. We should also note, however, that even the teacher-controlled exchanges in this study were quite successful in promoting vocabulary learning.

Notes

1. Coughlan and Duff (1994) have pointed out that learners may often redefine the activity of a task in accordance with their own goals. A limitation of our study is that no attempt was made to determine to what extent individual learners redefined the focussed task as an intentional vocabulary learning task. From the researchers' observation of the subjects performing the task, however, there were no outward signs of learners' deliberatly attempting to learn the new words.

2. Originally there were 64 students in the study. However, 14 students failed to complete one or more of the pre-test, the treatment, and the post-tests, and so were excluded.

3. No class at the same level was available for use as a control group. However, given that earlier studies (e.g. Pica, Young and Doughty 1987) have found that learners receiving unmodified, baseline input perform consistently worse than learners receiving modified input on measures of comprehension and vocabulary acquisition, the lack of a control group (i.e. a group which received only unmodified input) was not considered a serious threat to the validity of this study.

4. One explanation for the three groups' ability to remember the words over time may have been the opportunity of half of the learners in each group to experience the modified output condition as part of Post-test 2. However, even those subjects who did not have this experience showed relatively high levels of retention in Post-tests 4 and 5. For example, the retention levels for the subjects who did not experience modified output in Post-test 2 in were 48%, 68% and 84% respectively for the premodified input group, the interactionally modified group and the modified output group in Post-test 5.

5. This general finding was also supported by an analysis of those subjects in the premodified and
    interactionally modified groups who experienced the modified output treatment prior to taking
    Post-test 2. These subjects outperformed those subjects who did not experience the modified
    output treatement in subsequent tests.

6. Subsequent discussion with the teacher bore out that she did perceive the task as part of an
    experiment where she should behave more like a researcher than a teacher.

7. It would have been possible to design a condition that involved just production of the target
    items (e.g. the subjects could have been asked to simply write directions containing the items).
    However, such a treatment would not have tapped *modified* output. Indeed, the subjects could
    have responded quite mechanically by simply substituting items in the same sentence frame
    (e.g. 'Find the _____ and put it in the _____.') In fact, many of the directions the students
    actually wrote prior to interacting in pairs were of this kind.

CHAPTER 5

Modified Input, Language Aptitude and the Acquisition of Word Meanings

Hirota Nagata, David Aline and Rod Ellis

Introduction

The studies reported in Chapters Three and Four examined how learners acquire the meanings of new words from modified input and output. The approach adopted in these chapters was a *learning-centred* one; that is, it addressed how the linguistic environment influences vocabulary acquisition by drawing on the universal models of L2 acquisition described in Chapter One. It would seem self-evident, however, that individual learners will vary in the extent to which they are able to benefit from modified input and output. Indeed, there is clear evidence in the studies reported in Chapters Three and Four that this is the case. For example, in Chapter Three it was observed that both the adolescent class-room learners in Study One and the children in Study Two varied in their preparedness and/or ability to signal non-understanding and to negotiate for meaning, with some doing so extensively, some only occasionally and still others not at all. How learners cope with input and with the opportunities to shape input through interaction is likely to differ considerably in accordance with a variety of factors, such as language aptitude, learning style, motivation and personality. However, although there is a substantial body of research that has addressed the impact of such individual differences on language proficiency there is almost a complete absence of research that has examined how such factors impact on specific aspects of the acquisition process, such as the processing of input. Clearly, there is a need to complement the learning-centred approach to the study of the linguistic environment with a *learner-centred* one, where the goal is to discover the extent to which individual learner factors mediate input and output processing. This Chapter reports a study that represents a start in this direction. It addresses the impact of one factor — language aptitude — on learners' comprehension of modified input and their acquisition of word meanings.

Language aptitude

The study of individual differences in second language (L2) learning has
achieved considerable impetus over the last ten years (see Skehan 1989 and
1991; Oxford 1992; Ellis 1994 for surveys of the research). However, the bulk
of the empirical work that has been completed during this period has focussed on
four major areas of individual difference; learning style (Stansfield and Hansen
1983; Willing 1987; Reid 1987), motivation (Gardner 1985; Crookes and
Schmidt 1990), anxiety (MacIntyre and Gardner 1991a and 1991b) and learning
strategies (Oxford 1990; O'Malley and Chamot 1990; Cohen 1998). In contrast,
the role of language aptitude in language learning has received less attention.
This is somewhat surprising, given the importance attached to this factor in
earlier research and to the positive results obtained for this factor in research
carried out in the fifties and sixties.

Gardner and McIntyre (1992) divide the factors responsible for individual
differences in L2 acquisition into two broad classes; affective and cognitive.
Language aptitude is viewed as a cognitive factor. In his review of early aptitude
research, Carroll (1981) defines general aptitude as 'capability of learning a task'
which depends on 'some combination of more or less enduring characteristics of
the learner'. Language aptitude constitutes, therefore, a kind of special gift for
learning languages and is analogous with other special abilities such as a talent
for music or chess. Gardner and McIntyre (1992) view it as a kind of 'cognitive
sponge' in the sense that new skills/knowledge are naturally attracted to existing
skills/knowledge with which they can be readily associated.

Language aptitude is traditionally viewed as the set of variable abilities that
enable some learners to learn new language material more quickly than others.
The identification of these abilities and the development of tests to measure them
owes much to the work of Carroll and Pimsleur. Carroll administered a large
battery of tests to military personnel enrolled in language learning programs and,
through factor analysis, was able to identify a relatively small number of factors
which he interpreted as the abilities underlying successful L2 acquisition.
Subsequent studies confirmed these abilities. Carroll's research led to the
development of the Modern Language Aptitude Test (MLAT) (Carroll and Sapon
1959), designed in the first instance to screen candidates for foreign language
instruction at the Foreign Service Institute in the United States. Pimsleur (1966),
who was considerably influenced by Carrol's work, developed an alternative but
not dissimilar test of language aptitude (the Pimsleur Language Aptitude Battery
— PLAB) for use with foreign language students in the junior high school.

According to Carroll's model of language aptitude there are four major abilities involved:

1. Phonemic Coding Ability (i.e., the ability to code foreign sounds in a way that they can be remembered later). This ability was seen as related to the ability to spell and handle sound-symbol relationships.
2. Grammatical Sensitivity (i.e., the ability to recognize the grammatical functions of words in sentences).
3. Inductive Language Learning Ability (i.e., the ability to identify patterns of correspondence and relationships involving form and meaning).
4. Rote learning ability (i.e., the ability to form and remember associations between stimuli). This ability was hypothesized to be involved in vocabulary learning.

These four abilities constitute what Skehan (1989: 26) calls the 'standard four component view of language aptitude'. Skehan notes, however, that Grammatical Sensitivity and Inductive Language Learning Ability do not appear to be sharply distinguished and argues for a three-component model consisting of auditory ability (corresponding to (1) above), linguistic ability (corresponding to (2) and (3)) and memory ability (corresponding to (4)).

The MLAT consists of five sub-tests; (1) Number Learning, where learners are asked to learn words for numbers in an artificial language, (2) Phonetic Script, where learners are asked to listen to sounds and learn the phonetic symbols for them, (3) Spelling Clues, where learners are required to decipher phonetically spelt English words, which they must then identify with words with the same meaning, (4) Words in Sentences, where learners have to recognize the syntactic functions of words and phrases in sentences and (5) Paired Associates, which is a test of learners' ability to learn and recall paired associates. The PLAB includes a sound discrimination test, a test of sound-symbol association, a test of learners ability to list as many words as possible that rhyme with words provided, a language analysis test that tests inductive language learning capacity, and a vocabulary test that requires learners to identify the meaning of different words. In contrast to MLAT, PLAB emphasizes auditory abilities, which Pimsleur's research showed could be lacking in learners who otherwise demonstrated normal levels of aptitude.

These various tests correspond broadly to particular components of language aptitude. Thus, for example, Phonetic Script and Spelling Clues measure Phonemic Coding Ability, Words in Sentences measures grammatical sensitivity and Paired Associates measures memory. However, as Carroll has been careful to point out, the various tests do not constitute 'pure' measures of the different abilities. Rather each test taps one ability strongly and one or more other abilities more weakly.

Measures of language aptitude obtained from the MLAT or PLAB were found to be consistently related to measures of L2 achievement in the early research. Carroll (1981), summarising years of his own research, reports correlations of between .40 and .60 with a variety of criterion measures (final course grades, objective foreign language attainment tests, and instructors' estimates of learners' language learning abilities). Gardner (1980), in a review of several studies of the relationship between both aptitude and motivation and the learning of French in Canadian schools reports a median correlation of .41 for language aptitude. Gardner also notes that the relationship between language aptitude and achievement is independent of that between motivation and achievement. That is, language aptitude and motivation account for different domains of variance in learners' achievement scores. Language aptitude, however, is 'probably the single best predictor of achievement in a second language' (Gardner and McIntyre 1992: 215).

Whereas much of the research has examined the relationship between global language aptitude and language achievement, one interesting study explored the possibility that learners might vary in the kinds of aptitude they possess and that achievement depends on the extent to which instructional experiences match the learners' aptitude type. Wesche (1981) reports a pair of studies based on a distinction between a Type A learner, who gained a high overall score on MLAT or PLAB, and Type B, who manifested a high level of analytical ability but demonstrated problems with phonetic coding and listening. When these two types of learners were given matching instruction (i.e., Type A learners were taught with an audiovisual, inductive approach and Type B were taught with a more deductive, analytical approach) they did equally well and also outperformed students given complementary instruction. This study is of considerable interest to us because it suggests that different kinds of abilities may be required to perform different types of learning tasks successfully.

There followed a period when there was little interest in language aptitude. The focus of L2 research switched to the universal properties of interlanguage development, as these were manifest in communicative language use. The goals and methods of Carroll's language aptitude research appeared remote from the goals and methods of interlanguage researchers. Whereas Carroll's work lay within the psychometric tradition evident in general psychology, interlanguage research has turned to the descriptive methods of first language researchers (e.g. Brown 1973). However, as is argued below and as illustrated by the study reported in this paper, this separation is not a necessary one; the study of language aptitude can be usefully incorporated into interlanguage research.

More recently, researchers have again begun to show an interest in language aptitude. Horwitz (1986) reports that aptitude scores on MLAT correlated significantly with both scores on a discrete-point written grammar test (0.41) and with scores on a series of oral tasks requiring relatively spontaneous language use (0.40). Ehrman and Oxford (1995) investigated the relationship between a number of factors and speaking and reading proficiency in 282 highly educated learners studying some 32 languages at the Foreign Language Institute in the United States. They found that language aptitude (measured by means of the MLAT) was more strongly related to both proficiency measures than learning styles, learning strategies or personality. They report correlations of up to .51. Sparks, Ganschow and Patton (1995) found that language aptitude (again measured by the MLAT) was one of the two best predictors of the grades achieved by high school foreign language learners, the other being native language (English) grades.

These later studies are important because they address one of the potentially damaging criticisms of Carroll's model of language aptitude; namely, that it addressed only the kind of abilities involved in the acquisition of what Cummins (1981) has termed 'cognitive academic language proficiency' (CALP) and ignored those abilities involved in 'basic interpersonal communication skills' (BICS). As Ehrman and Oxford point out, their results suggest that language aptitude plays a role even with learners who have experienced more communicative methods of language teaching.

Another important study also provides support for the view that language aptitude is a factor in both CALP and BICS. Skehan (1986) used data from Wells' (1985) longitudinal study of the L1 acquisition of English by some sixty plus children in the Bristol area of England. He was interested in (1) the relationship between measures of L1 development and standard measures of aptitude, (2) the relationship between measures of foreign language achievement by the same children at 13 years of age and aptitude, and (3) the relationship between L1 development and foreign language achievement. He reports a number of significant correlations between measures of language aptitude and measures of L1 development. He also found that language aptitude was strongly related to foreign language achievement. However, L1 development was not strongly related to foreign language achievement.[1] Skehan explains these results by suggesting that there are two aspects of language aptitude; an underlying language learning capacity, which is similar in L1 and L2 learning, and an ability to handle decontextualized material, such as that found in discrete item language tests, which is drawn on in formal L2 learning. Such a conclusion is compatible with the results of Sasaki's (1993) study which found language aptitude to be related to both a general cognitive factor (general intelligence) and a general second language proficiency factor. In Sasaki's study both were necessary to account for the language proficiency of Japanese learners of English.

It would seem, then, that language aptitude is involved in both CALP and BICS. In part, language aptitude is related to general intelligence. It is not surprising, therefore, that it is related to CALP, as a number of studies (e.g. Genesee 1976) have found measures of general intelligence to be also related to CALP. Interestingly, intelligence is not strongly related to BICS whereas language aptitude is. Language aptitude, then, is best viewed as a complex construct, involving both a general cognitive dimension and a more specific linguistic dimension.

We might expect that test measures of language aptitude will be related to measures of language development of the kind used in L1 acquisition research and in interlanguage studies. Skehan (1990) provides evidence of this. He reports significant correlations between various measures of language aptitude and such measures of child language development as range of adjectives and determiners, range of modal verbs, aspect and time markers and range of nominal complexity. Skehan's observation that 'most of the higher correlations with the auditory aptitude tests are produced by comprehension/vocabulary indices of first language development' (p. 95) is of particular relevance to the study reported below.

To sum up, the more recent research suggests that there may be no need to reconceptualize the construct of language aptitude to account for functional/communicative aspects of L2 acquisition or for its role in input and output processing. The current model appears to account for these quite well. This conclusion accords with Carrol's (1990) own reassessment of language aptitude. Carrol states that he is 'somewhat sceptical about the possibilities for greatly improving foreign language aptitude predictions' (p. 27). He specifically rejects the need to make any adjustments to the four-component model in order to take account of 'verbal fluency' (a skill likely to figure in BICS), pointing out that in his early research he found that 'tests of various verbal fluency factors failed to make significant contributions to prediction' (p. 23).

However, as Skehan (1989) points out, one conspicuous lacuna in both the early and the more recent research has been any attempt to relate language aptitude to the development of specific proficiency skills such as listening. One way in which this might be undertaken is by investigating to what extent measures of language aptitude are able to predict performance in specific language learning tasks. This approach accords closely with the recommendation that Carroll himself makes in the concluding comments to his 1990 article. He suggests that subsequent research in foreign language aptitude will need to be based on 'a more refined analysis of foreign language learning tasks in terms of the cognitive abilities they call upon' (p. 26).

The Study

The study reported below was designed to investigate the following research questions:

1. Which components of language aptitude are related to and predict the comprehension of oral directions in a non-reciprocal listening task?
2. Which components of language aptitude are related to and predict the incidental acquisition of new lexical items incorporated into oral directions?

Method

The study used a similar task to that employed in the studies reported in Chapters Three and Four. The subjects completed a battery of aptitude tests and a non-reciprocal listening task containing lexical items that were new to them. Subsequently they completed a series of tests designed to measure whether they had learned the new words.

Subjects

The 177 subjects (30 female and 147 male) were English as a foreign language students, aged between 18 and 22. They were enrolled in six intact classes at a major Japanese university in Tokyo, Japan. Two of the six classes consisted of sophomore English major students, while the other four classes were made up of freshman Economic major students. All of these students were registered for the Language Laboratory English Listening Class, which provided them with a one and half hour lesson each week. All the students had received 6 years of formal English instruction at secondary school.

Design

The study was correlational in design. There were five independent variables corresponding to five aptitude tests and four dependent variables represented by comprehension scores derived from the listening task and word-acquisition scores from a test administered on three different occasions after completion of the task.

The subjects completed the following in this order:

1. The pre-test: This was administered to all the participants three months prior to the listening task. This lengthy gap between pre-test and the listening task was intended to ensure that the subjects did not pay focussed attention to the lexical items when they performed the task. It should be noted that the subjects did not receive any opportunity to study the targeted items between the pre-test and the task and that, given the low frequency of the items in the kind of input the subjects experienced, they were extremely unlikely to have been exposed to them in the intervening period.
2. Five aptitude tests: The participants completed these two to three weeks before they were given the listening task.
3. The listening task: The participants completed this in the language laboratory. The task took approximately 30 minutes with each class.
4. Post-tests: The participants completed three post-tests, one forty minutes after the listening task, the second two weeks later and the third eight weeks after the task.

Instruments

The pre-test comprised 75 English words. The words consisted of the names of various cooking utensils, distractor words (e.g., *carpet* and *door knob*) and other high-frequency items likely to be known by all the participants. The subjects were asked to identify whether they knew the meaning of each item on the list. On the basis of the results, 13 words which no subject claimed to know together with a further 5 words which all the subjects indicated they knew were selected.

As in some of the previous studies, the post-tests required the subjects to match the target words with the pictures. They scored one point for each correctly labelled picture.

The five aptitude tests were:

1. Finnish Memory Test (Skehan 1982)
   This test requires subjects to memorize a list of 12 Finnish words in five

minutes. The subjects are then given two minutes to write down the words they can remember. A score of two points was given for a correctly spelt word and one point for an identifiable but wrongly spelt word. Skehan used this test as a measure of learners' ability to rote memorize the graphological form of unknown words.

2. MLAT Part 5: Paired Associates (Carroll and Sapon 1959)
    This consists of a list of 24 Kurdish words together with their English equivalents. The participants were given four minutes to memorize these pairs and then answered 24 multiple choice questions testing their ability to recall the meaning of the Kurdish items. This is a test of associative memory.

3. MLAT Part 4: Words in Sentences (Carroll and Sapon 1959)
    This is a 45 item test of grammatical-semantic sensitivity and inductive language learning ability. Subjects are required to find a word in one sentence which has the same grammatical function as a highlighted word in another sentence. Each correct answer was awarded one point.

4. PLAB Part 5: Sound Discrimination (Pimsleur 1966)
    This tests learners' ability to learn phonetic distinctions and recognize them in different contexts. The learners are required to differentiate Chinese tone patterns and associate them with meanings.

5. PLAB Part 6: Sound-Symbol Association (Pimsleur 1966)
    This is a test of the learners' ability to associate phonological and graphological forms. It requires subjects to identify proper spellings of tape recorded nonsense words such as *tarpdel*.

For each of these aptitude tests a test booklet with Japanese instructions was prepared, although the tests themselves were in English. The subjects completed all the tests in a language laboratory.

The tests were chosen so that they provided measures of the three major components of aptitude discussed by Skehan (1989) — see the previous section. Thus, PLAB Part 5 (Sound Discrimination) and Part 6 (Sound Symbol Association) provided a measure of phonemic coding ability, MLAT 4 (Words in Sentences) provided a measure of grammatical sensitivity and the Finnish Memory Test and MLAT 5 (Paired Associates) provided measures of memory ability.

The language aptitude tests used in this study were designed for native speakers of English. Ideally, tests designed for native speakers of Japanese should have been used. Unfortunately, these were not available to us. However, the content of three of the tests — the Finnish Memory Test, the Paired Associates Test and the Sound Discrimination Test — is language neutral, especially as Japanese instructions for these tests were provided. In the case of MLAT 4

(Words in Sentences), Sawyer (1993) reports a study involving a very similar Japanese population to that drawn on in this study which shows good reliability (Cronbach Alpha = .86). In fact, Sawyer found that the Japanese subjects achieved a higher mean score on this test than an English native speaker group.[2] We conclude that the tests we used provide a valid and potentially reliable measure of the Japanese subjects' language aptitude.

The task

The task used in this study was similar to those used in the studies reported in Chapters Three and Four. It took the form of a set of directions about where to place various kitchen objects (e.g., a ladle, tongs, a toaster) in a matrix picture of a kitchen. The pre-test established that the students did not have prior knowledge of the English names of these objects.

In this study, only premodified directions were given (i.e. there were no baseline directions and no opportunity for the subjects to modify the directions interactionally). The procedure followed for preparing the directions was the same as that described in Chapter Three. There were 18 directions in all, each one containing a single lexical item not known to the subjects. Each direction was spoken once by a native speaker at a speed of about 2 to 3 words per second (i.e., a relatively slow speed). As in previous studies, the subjects demonstrated their understanding of each direction by writing the number of a picture of the relevant object in the correct position in a matrix picture of a kitchen.

A comprehension score was calculated for each student by determining how many of the 13 objects whose names were unknown to the students had been correctly positioned in the matrix picture.

Results

Descriptive statistics are provided in Table 1. The mean Comprehension score exceeded the means of the word acquisition scores by a ratio of more than 2 to 1. It should also be noted that the mean word acquisition score fell from Post-test 1 to Post-test 2 but, surprisingly, rose from Post-test 2 to Post-test 3.

The reliabilities of the instruments used in this study were computed using Kuder Richardson-21 (see Table 2). An acceptable level of reliability was obtained for most of the aptitude tests and for the measure of comprehension obtained from the listening task. However, low reliabilities were obtained for

Table 1. *Descriptive statistics for nine variables*

Variable	Mean	SD	Minimum	Maximum
Finnish Memory Test	9.31	3.76	9.0	20.0
MLAT — 5	15.85	4.89	3.0	24.0
MLAT — 4	23.01	7.12	6.0	39.0
PLAB — 5	22.37	4.22	9.0	30.0
PLAB — 6	14.14	2.90	7.0	22.0
Comprehension	6.72	4.21	0	13.0
Post-test 1	3.23	1.97	0	10.0
Post-test 2	2.82	1.91	0	10.0
Post-test 3	3.16	2.15	0	11.0

Table 2. *Reliability of Nine Variables (Kuder Richardson 21)*

Finnish Memory Test	.93
MLAT — 5	.81
MLAT — 4	.80
PLAB — 5	.70
PLAB — 6	.32
Comprehension	.89
Post-test 1	.41
Post-test 2	.43
Post-test 3	.52

PLAB 6 (Sound-Symbol Association) (.32) and for the three administrations of the vocabulary test (.41, .43 and .52).

Table 3 provides the Pearson Product Moment Correlations. Significant correlations at the .001 or .01 level were obtained between MLAT 5 (Paired Associates) and all four dependent variables (Comprehension, Post-test 1, Post-test 2 and Post-test 3) with that between MLAT 5 and Comprehension the strongest of these ($r = .40$; $p > .001$). MLAT 4 (Words in Sentences) was significantly related to Comprehension ($r = .42$; $p > .001$) and weakly to Post-test 3 ($r = .19$; $p > .01$). However, the coefficients for MLAT 4 and Post-test 1 and Post-test 2 were smaller and did not reach statistical significance. PLAB 5 (Sound Discrimination) was significantly related to Post-test 1 ($r = .20$; $p > .01$) while PLAB 6 (Sound-Symbol Association) was significantly associated with Comprehension ($r = .27$; $p > .001$). All the coefficients involving the Finnish Memory Test were low and non-significant. As a result, this measure was dropped from all subsequent analyses.[3]

Table 3. *Pearson product moment correlations*

Variables	Comprehension	PT1	PT2	PT3
1. Finnish Memory Test	−.0653	.0609	−.0195	.0982
2. MLAT — 5	.4023**	.2286*	.2143*	.2009*
3. MLAT — 4	.4185**	.1451	.1688	.1913*
4. PLAB — 5	.0948	.1992*	.1036	.1547
5. PLAB — 6	.2744**	.0650	.1308	.0285

$*p < .01$; $**p < .001$ (one-tailed)
PT = Post test

Table 4. *Statistically Significant Pearson Product Moment Correlations Corrected for Attenuation ($p < .01$)*

Variables	Comprehension	PT1	PT2	PT3
1. Finnish Memory Test				
2. MLAT — 5	.476	.398	.238	.310
3. MLAT — 4				.297
4. PLAB — 5	.499	.372		
5. PLAB — 6	.414			

PT = Post test

In order to give some indication of the true correlation, all the statistically significant correlations reported above were corrected for attenuation using the results of the Kuder-Richardson-21 analysis. The results are shown in Table 4.

To test the power of different types of aptitude to predict comprehension and word meaning acquisition, multiple regression analyses were run after checking for multicolinearity and ensuring that a minimum number of 40 observations per independent variable was secured (Cohen and Cohen 1975). The results are shown in Table 5. With Comprehension as the dependent variable, three independent variables emerged with predictive value. In stepwise order, they were MLAT 4 (Words in Sentences), MLAT 5 (Paired Associates) and PLAB 6 (Sound-Symbol Association). With Post-test 1 as the dependent variables two variables had predictive value (MLAT 5 and PLAB 5). However, only one variable (MLAT 5) predicted scores on Post-test 2 and Post-test 3.

Table 5. *Stepwise regression analyses for the four dependent variables*

Dependent variables	Predictor variables	Multiple R	R Square	F	p
Comprehension	MLAT 4	.418	.175	37.2	.0000
	MLAT 5	.495	.245	28.3	.0000
	PLAB 6	.522	.274	21.7	.0000
Post-test 1	MLAT 5	.229	.052	9.6	.0022
	PLAB 5	.285	.081	7.7	.0006
Post-test 2	MLAT 5	.214	.046	8.4	.0042
Post-test 3	MLAT 5	.201	.040	7.4	.0073

Discussion

Most of the instruments used in this study were found to be reliable. The failure of the word acquisition test to achieve an acceptable level of reliability in any of its administrations may be due to a variety of factors; the shortness of the test (only 13 items), its difficulty (low scores were the norm) and, possibly, the variable learning difficulty of the target words (see Study Three in Chapter Three).

As in previous studies, comprehension scores exceeded word acquisition scores. In general, though, learners who were successful in comprehending the directions were also successful in acquiring word meanings, as shown by the statistically significant correlations (corrected for attenuation) between Comprehension and all three Post-test scores ($r = .37; .47; .36$).

The word acquisition scores were low on all three post-tests. However, they were of a similar order to those reported for the studies involving high school students (see Chapter Three) and higher than those reported in some other studies of incidental vocabulary learning (e.g. Dupuy and Krashen 1993)

The word acquisition scores rose from Post-test 2 to Post-test 3, despite a gap of some six weeks. The most likely explanation for this is that the learners engaged in deliberate attempts to learn the target words. Informal interviews conducted after the administration of Post-test 3 with 72 of the original sample revealed that nine learners admitted to looking the words up in their dictionary. In effect, this constitutes a new learning task, involving intentional rather than incidental acquisition and, potentially, drawing differently on the various components of language aptitude. It is, of course, not surprising, that the scores obtained by those learners who engaged in intentional learning jumped considerably.

The results of the correlational analyses will now be discussed in terms of the two research question. Research question 1 asked:

Which components of language aptitude are related to and predict the comprehension of oral directions in a non-reciprocal task?

Statistically significant correlations were found between MLAT 4 (Words in Sentences), MLAT 5 (Paired Associates) and PLAB 6 (Sound-Symbol Association) on the one hand and Comprehension on the other. It would seem, therefore, that all three types of aptitude are involved in listening comprehension. In the case of MLAT 4 and MLAT 5 the correlations reached a similar strength to those reported by Carroll (i.e., between .40 and .60). The relationship between PLAB and Comprehension was weaker, the coefficient falling below .40. The multiple regression analysis showed that, of these three variables, MLAT 4 accounted for most of the variance in Comprehension, followed by MLAT 5 and PLAB 6.[4] Together, however, these three aptitudes accounted for only 27% of the total variance in Comprehension. It would seem, therefore, that other factors are needed to account more fully for the variance in the levels of comprehension achieved by the learners. These factors may include factors related to the nature of the premodified input to which the learners were exposed, as indicated in Chapter Three, and factors related to other areas of individual difference (e.g., English language proficiency and motivation).

The second question investigated in this study was:

Which components of language aptitude are related to and predict the incidental acquisition of new lexical items incorporated into a non-reciprocal task?

MLAT 5 (Paired Associates) and PLAB 5 (Sound Discrimination) were significantly but rather weakly correlated with Post-test 1 scores. Also, as shown by the multiple regression analysis, both these variables predicted performance on Post-test 1. Carroll (1990) argues that PLAB 5 tests learners' ability to relate sound patterns with meanings. This ability and memory, therefore, seem to be the important abilities in the incidental acquisition of word meanings from the kind of premodified input supplied in this task. Interestingly, MLAT 4 (Words in Sentences), which was the main predictor variable in the case of Comprehension, was not strongly associated with word meaning acquisition as demonstrated in Post-test 1 and did not enter into the multiple regression analysis. This suggests that different components of aptitude are involved in comprehension and vocabulary acquisition, a point taken up in the Conclusion section.

In the case of Post-test 2 only MLAT 5 (Paired Associates) was found to be significantly related to word order acquisition, again rather weakly (i.e., $r < .40$). MLAT 5 was also related to Post-test 3, but in this case was joined by MLAT 4. However, only MLAT 5 proved to be a significant predictor in the regression analysis for Post-test 3. It is understandable that memory, as measured by MLAT 5, should assume greater importance in relation to other aspects of aptitude where the long term retention of vocabulary is concerned.

Conclusion

This chapter has programmatically explored the role of language aptitude in comprehending premodified input and acquiring the meanings of new words embedded within it. It was motivated by the conviction that second language acquisition researchers need to take greater account of how individual variables such as language aptitude interact with the way learners process input for comprehension and acquisition. The results reported above are sufficiently encouraging to warrant further research in this direction. They show that one learner variable — language aptitude — influences the extent to which learners comprehend oral directions and learn words from them.

The task in this study was designed to provide opportunities for incidental vocabulary acquisition. It is interesting to note that language aptitude was found to be a factor in this kind of acquisition. Krashen (1981) has hypothesized that aptitude only shows a strong relationship to L2 proficiency 'in "monitored" test situations and when conscious learning has been stressed in the classroom' (p. 24). This study demonstrates otherwise. In fact, in discussing his claim, Krashen considers only one component of language aptitude — linguistic ability — and ignores both phonetic coding ability and memory. The results of our study, however, suggest that all three of the major components of language aptitude, including linguistic ability, are involved in listening to and comprehending the task directions. We would argue that the task required learners to engage in very similar input processing to that involved in natural acquisition and that the results of this study suggest that language aptitude is a factor in natural language acquisition. In this respect, the study supports claims that language aptitude is a factor in BICS as well as CALP (see the section on Language Aptitude in this chapter).

Skehan (1998), suggests that there is a close relationship between the components of aptitude and the stages of information processing involved in interlanguage development. Arguing that there are three major components of aptitude (see earlier discussion), Skehan postulates a close connection between each component and a stage in the flow of information processing involved in language acquisition. Thus, phonemic coding ability is related to the processing of input as it defines the auditory ability needed to attend to spoken forms; grammatical sensitivity and inductive language learning ability (viewed as a single component by Skehan) constitute the 'linguistic ability' that is needed to transform input into intake and thereby 'to infer rules of language and to make linguistic generalizations or extrapolations' (p. 5); and, finally, memory is primarily concerned with the storage of linguistic elements in such a way that they can be efficiently retrieved in output.

This study provides some support for such an analysis. Thus, comprehending oral directions appears to have drawn upon all three components of language aptitude, as might be expected. Phonemic coding ability can be hypothesized to have contributed to the learners' ability to segment words in the stream of speech, linguistic ability to the linguistic knowledge the learners needed to decode key grammatical meanings in the directions and memory to the storage and retrieval of previously learned vocabulary items needed to understand the directions. It would seem, then, that listening comprehension — or, at least, the kind of listening comprehension demanded by the task used in this study — requires learners to utilize a broad spectrum of aptitude abilities. In contrast acquisition of the meanings of new words appears to have tapped primarily memory ability. Again, this is to be expected, as it is memory that is involved in the storage and retrieval of new linguistic material. The study, therefore suggests that it may be possible to incorporate language aptitude research, which has been typically psychometric in orientation, into mainstream SLA research directed at understanding how input processing contributes to interlanguage development.

Notes

1. Skehan's finding that measures of L1 learning were not related to measures of L2 learning would appear to contradict the 'linguistic coding deficit hypothesis' of Sparks, Ganschow and Patton (1995), according to which strengths and weaknesses in learners' first language code have an effect on foreign language learning. However, it need not do so. Skehan's study reports no relationship between BICS-like measures of L1 acquisition and foreign language proficiency, whereas Sparks, Ganschow and Patton report a strong relationship between CALP-like measures of native language ability (i.e. English language grades) and foreign language learning. Arguably, it is the CALP like abilities that develop through schooling that correlate with measures of classroom foreign language learning.

2. Sawyer notes that the fact that the Japanese subjects scored higher on the MLAT Words in Sentences score than the native speakers suggests that training or experience may contribute to performance on this test. Japanese students are subjected to intensive explicit instruction in

English grammar throughout high school. The Words in Sentences Test, then, may be measuring something different in Japanese subjects — how good they are in carrying out grammatical analysis in English.

3. In retrospect, it is easy to see that the absence of any relationship between the Finnish Memory Test and Comprehension or Word Acquisition is not surprising as neither the teaching nor the testing tasks involved the ability to memorize L2 graphological forms.

4. It may be thought surprising that PLAB 6 (Sound-Symbol Association) and not PLAB 5 (Sound Discrimination) predicted variance in Comprehension scores. The fact that the ability to relate sounds with symbols played a part in comprehension might suggest that the learners in this study attempted to make connections between the phonological representations of the new words which they obtained from the input and graphological representations which they derived from their existing knowledge of sound-symbol associations in English. It is also possible, however, that PLAB 6 functions as a test of phonetic coding, as Carroll (1990) suggests. He suggests that 'the association may derive from the fact that persons high in phonetic coding ability usually have more accurate perceptions of orthographic conventions in English.

CHAPTER 6

Learning Vocabulary Through Interacting With a Written Text

Hoda Zaki and Rod Ellis

Introduction

The preceding chapters have explored how classroom second language (L2) learners acquire vocabulary from premodified or interactionally modified input when they perform an oral communicative task. This chapter also examines vocabulary acquisition but from input contained in a written text. In accordance with current theories of reading, this input can still be viewed as interactionally derived, although reading involves intrapersonal rather than interpersonal interaction. Readers negotiate meaning from a text by a process of self-interrogation. That is, they comprehend a text by posing and answering questions about it. As we saw in Chapter Two, they can acquire new words by attending to them in context and inferring their meanings through the use of a variety of textual clues.

Reading is not a simple process of decoding a text letter-by-letter, word-by-word, clause-by-clause and sentence-by-sentence. Rather it involves sampling the text, forming hypotheses about what it says, and then confirming and rejecting them. Goodman (1967) has referred to this process as a 'psycholinguistic guessing game'. Smith (1978) emphasizes the role of 'meaningful context' in enabling people to read, pointing out that it makes the identification of individual words unnecessary. When readers make errors (or 'miscues', as Goodman describes them) they generally do so without destroying the meaning of the context. Reading according to this view, then, is a top-down process, involving the activation of the reader's existing knowledge (schemata). Readers guess the meaning of words they do not know or cannot decode using the meaningful context they have created so that even if they 'see' the wrong word the overall meaning of the text is not disturbed.

However, as other reading specialists (e.g. Eskey 1989) have pointed out, reading cannot precede entirely by means of top-down processing. Readers have to decode at least some words in order to create a 'meaningful context' for top-down processing to proceed. Moreover, readers are sometimes confronted with texts on topics for which they lack well-developed schemata, forcing them to rely less on guessing and more on actually decoding the words in the text. L2 readers often lack automatic perception and decoding skills and so have to invest more effort in identifying the words on the page. Reading, then, also involves bottom-up processing. It is best seen as an interactive process, involving both top-down and bottom-up processing. That is, one type of processing facilitates and feeds off the other. Fluent readers need to be able to both decode printed words automatically and to utilize background knowledge efficiently (Grabe 1991). The extent to which they rely on one type of processing or the other will depend on the particular text they are reading. Readers compensate for their inability to employ one type of strategy by utilizing the other (Stanovich 1980).

This interactive/compensatory view of the reading process is relevant to the present study, as we will shortly see, but even more relevant is Widdowson's (1979a, 1984) account of how we read. Widdowson argues that reading involves the same general interpretative processes that occur in spoken communication. Both involve the 'co-operative principle' (Grice 1975). Speakers draw on this principle to help them achieve a degree of commonality of understanding despite the fact that what they say is often vague, imprecise and insignificant. Similarly, reader and writer interact through a text which provides clues that they use to achieve understanding. However, written discourse is non-reciprocal in nature. It requires the reader to function as both addresser and addressee in a 'covert cognitive process' (Widdowson 1979a: 177). The reader engages in an inner dialogue involving question and answer and in so doing creates a meaningful context in which to interpret the text. Reading, then, is an 'ideational matching of frames of reference' (Widdowson 1984) that is achieved through the 'discourse' that a reader creates by interacting with the 'text'. Readers can choose to be 'submissive' or 'assertive' according to whether they give precedence to the writer's frame of reference or to their own in this interactive process.

Compatible with Widdowson's account of the reading process as covert interaction, is Wittrock's (1974) generative model of learning. However, where Widdowson is primarily concerned with how readers create discourse, Wittrock is interested in how reading results in learning. Like Goodman and Smith, Wittrock argues that reading comprehension is facilitated when readers activate schemata to construct meanings from a text and like Widdowson he sees these meanings as individual and idiosyncratic. His generative model predicts that learning from reading (operationalized in a series of experimental studies as the ability to recall the content of a text) is enhanced when readers process a text 'deeply' in the sense that they form hierarchical associations between propositions in the text and construct meaningful elaborations of the text. In a series of studies, (e.g. Wittrock 1974; Wittrock, Marks and, Doctorow 1975; Wittrock and Carter 1975; Doctorow, Wittrock and Marks 1978), he set out to investigate the effects of such processing on both reading comprehension and content learning (ability to recall). These studies used a variety of devices to stimulate deep processing — e.g. inserting one or two word organizers at the top each paragraph, asking subjects to generate a sentence of their own to summarize each paragraph or to form a picture to represent the meaning of particular words). The results demonstrated that such devices lead to both better comprehension and learning.

One particular device for stimulating deep processing is of concern to this study; the use of self-questioning as a generative learning strategy. The device requires readers to construct a series of questions about a text and then answer them themselves. Asking such questions, it is hypothesized, induces readers to focus their attention, to organize the new material, to integrate new information with their existing knowledge and to motivate personal elaborations of the meaning of the text. Self-questioning also serves as a metacognitive strategy as it constitutes a way in which learners can check their understanding of what they are reading. A number of studies involving American high school and adult subjects (see Wong 1985 for a review) have shown that training students to self-question results in better comprehension of a text, with lower ability students benefitting more than higher ability students. In particular, students benefit from training in forming inferential type questions (Davey and McBride 1986). King (1992) used Bloom's (1956) taxonomy of question types as a basis for designing a series of generic question stems which she used to train students to self-question (e.g. the stem 'How does ... effect ...?' was used to help college students form questions relating to cause-and-effect relationships). King's own research was directed at investigating the effects of such training on students' ability to listen to, understand and recall lectures, but her approach is equally relevant to reading and served as a basis for the training used in the study reported in this chapter.

To sum up, the theoretical perspectives on reading outlined above suggest that (1) readers utilize both top-down and bottom-up processes interactively and that they compensate for their inability to use one type of processing by relying more heavily on the other, (2) readers engage in covert interaction with a text by means of an internal discourse which they conduct with themselves, and (3) readers can achieve better understanding and recall of the content of a text if they process it 'deeply' as, for example, when they make use of self-questioning as a reading strategy. These perspectives are best seen as complementary and mutually informing. Thus, self-questioning constitutes one of the primary means by which readers engage in the kind of internal dialogue Widdowson claims is the essential element of the reading process and which necessitates the interactive use of top-down and bottom up strategies.

These perspectives relate to how readers achieve comprehension and store information when they read a text. Our concern here, however, is primarily with how L2 learners acquire vocabulary when they read. We will now turn to this issue, drawing on relevant theories of language acquisition and relating these to the theories of reading outlined above.

As we saw in Chapter One, information-processing theories of L2 acquisition (e.g. VanPatten 1990; Schmidt 1990; Ellis 1993; Robinson 1995) emphasize two principal characteristics of L2 learners. The first is that they are limited capacity processors. That is, they experience difficulty in attending to meaning and form simultaneously, particularly if they have limited L2 knowledge and/or lack control over the knowledge they do possess. As a result, they need to decide whether to attend to meaning, at a cost to their ability to attend to form, or to attend to form, with consequent damage to their ability to decode or encode meaning. The second characteristic of L2 learners is that they can function as 'noticers', consciously attending to the linguistic properties of the input (Schmidt 1990, 1994) and, as a result, possibly storing them in long-term memory (i.e. acquiring them).

The issue that now arises concerns the relationship between the processes of reading and acquisition. This issue is particularly pertinent to vocabulary, as reading serves as a ready means by which L2 learners can extend their L2 lexicons. We will briefly examine three questions. Does reading enable L2 learners to acquire new vocabulary? If it does, how is it achieved? What can be done to facilitate the process of vocabulary acquisition through reading?

As we saw in Chapter Two, there is plenty of evidence to suggest that reading does result in vocabulary acquisition. Thus, while there is wide agreement that direct teaching can promote vocabulary development, there is also recognition that it is not possible for teachers to teach all the vocabulary that children actually acquire.

How, then, is vocabulary learned through reading? One possibility, the one favoured by Krashen (1994), is that the acquisition of new words takes place incidentally and subconsciously as a result of understanding their meanings in context. Such a view, however, contradicts the claim above that acquisition only takes place when learners consciously attend to new words in the input. The theoretical position that informs the study reported in this Chapter is that outlined in Chapter One; it is possible, for learners to acquire vocabulary incidentally (for example, as a result of reading a text) but they do so only if they consciously notice words in the text.

This position also provides a basis for discussing the conditions that are likely to promote incidental vocabulary acquisition through reading. Learners need to notice new words when they read; they need to become conscious of them. In other words, vocabulary acquisition can only take place when learners engage in bottom-up processing as a result of a gap in their mental lexicon (see Faerch and Kasper 1986). Top-down processing, where learners make use of their prior knowledge to construct a meaningful context, does not require noticing and, indeed, may work against it. As we noted in Chapter Two, inferencing through context may impede vocabulary acquisition if a reader can understand a sentence without actually heeding novel items. Only when the inferencing is accompanied with noticing is it likely to lead to acquisition. The kind of reading that is likely to promote vocabulary learning therefore is reading that (1) utilizes bottom-up processing, (2) induces conscious attention to word forms and (3) requires conscious use of inferencing to derive word meanings for the forms attended to. It should be noted that these conditions are different from those needed in order to foster fluent reading and rapid comprehension. In Widdowson's terms, reading is more likely to work for acquisition when the reader is 'submissive' rather than 'assertive'.

How then can these conditions be fostered pedagogically? Two possibilities arise; by manipulating the texts learners are asked to read and by directing the way in which readers read. Two obvious ways of manipulating the text are by increasing the frequency of novel items in the text and by ensuring that there are sufficient contextual clues to make inferencing successful. There is plenty of evidence to suggest that the frequency with which novel words appear in a text affects acquisition (see Chapter Two). However, there is a problem with trying to manipulate the text to ensure the availability of 'rich' contextual clues. Such enrichment may obviate the need for learners to attend to novel items. Learners may find it so easy to recognize the meaning of a word in context that little bottom-up processing of the item takes place. Thus, they understand the word in the context of the reading passage but fail to learn it.

More promising, then, than trying to manipulate the text may be procedures for directing how readers read. Clearly, what is needed is some procedure that will foster careful attention to word forms and their meanings during reading. It is possible that engaging intensively in the covert dialogic activity that Widdowson describes can assist this. One way of achieving such an engagement might be through training in self-questioning strategies, along the lines suggested by King (1992). The process of formulating questions may force learners' attention onto specific words and the process of answering them may involve them in conscious inferencing. Self-questioning is designed to promote the depth of processing which has been claimed to be important for both comprehension and acquisition (see Chapter One). Self-questioning also slows down the reading process and in so doing may provide learners with the time they need to focus on form as well as meaning. Self-questioning, however, does not constitute an intentional vocabulary learning strategy, as long as the primary aim of the questions remains that of understanding the text rather than learning new words.

Research questions

The research questions were:

1. Does training learners to produce 'think-type' questions actually promote the use of such questions when they self-question during reading?
2. Does the production of guided generative output promote comprehension of the content of a text?
3. Does the production of guided generative output promote retention of the content of a reading passage?
4. Does the production of guided generative output promote the acquisition of unknown lexical items embedded in the text?

Here 'guided generative output' refers to the questions readers form when they self-question during reading together with their own answers to these questions.

Method

The study was designed to investigate the effect of guided generative output on L2 learners' comprehension of a reading text and their acquisition of unknown lexical items embedded in the text. It employed a quasi experimental design, involving an experimental group and a control group. The experimental group attended a session where the use of the self-questioning strategy was demonstrated. They then took part in four practice sessions where they had the opportunity to try out this strategy. The control group followed the normal curriculum, experiencing neither the demonstration of the self-questioning strategy nor practice sessions. Both groups subsequently read a test passage, containing words unknown to the subjects, and then wrote down questions based on the text and their answers to them. They also completed a comprehension test consisting of open WH questions and a vocabulary acquisition test. Finally, one week later, they completed a free-recall test and two further vocabulary acquisition tests. The treatment and various tests are described below.

Subjects

The subjects were 28 L2 learners from different ethnic backgrounds, all enrolled in Level 4 (intermediate) of an ESL program in a two-year community college in New Jersey, the United States. All the students had entered the program at Level 1 and proceeded through Levels 2 and 3. The students were divided equally into two sections of a reading course, these comprising the control and experimental groups. Assignment to a section was purely a matter of scheduling (i.e. reflected when the students wished to take the course). The treatment was randomly assigned to the groups by a flip of a coin.

Instruments

All the subjects in both the control and experimental groups completed the following in this order:

1. A vocabulary pre-test
2. A test of background knowledge of the content of the reading passage used in (3) below.
3. A test of the subjects' ability to produce guided generative output based on a reading passage.
4. A reading comprehension test, based on the passage in (3).
5. A vocabulary post test
6. A free-recall test
7. A cloze test

These instruments are described below.

1. The vocabulary pre-test
   The purpose of this test was to identify a set of words that were not known by any of the subjects. The test consisted of 40 words (nouns, verbs, adjectives, and cohesive markers), all extracted from a text, which the subjects did not see. The subjects were required to read each word and

indicate whether they knew it by marking 'No' or 'Not Sure' or by providing a synonym or giving a definition. 12 words that all the subjects had responded 'No' to were chosen as the target words for the study. This test was administered five weeks before the treatment began.

2. The background knowledge test
    This test was designed to establish what the subjects already knew about the content of the reading passage used in (3) below. This was important because one of the aims of the study was to investigate to what extent the use of a self-questioning strategy contributed to content learning and retention. Clearly, this required finding out what the subjects knew about the topic ('smoking') prior to reading. In this test, the subjects answered 7 open WH questions, relating to the main ideas dealt with in the passage (e.g. 'What laws on smoking have you heard or read about?'). This test was also administered five weeks before the treatment began.

3. The guided generative output test
    This test consisted of a reading passage on the topic of smoking (see Appendix A). The choice of reading passage for this test employed the same selection criteria as those used for the reading passages in the treatment (see below). The passage included the 12 target words. However, the subjects were not made aware that these words were the target or alerted to the need to pay attention to difficult words. They were asked to read the passage and to write down 'think-type' questions that would help them to understand the text and relate its content to their own experience. They were also asked to write answers to their questions. While completing this test the subjects were not allowed to interact with the teacher or other students. The students' questions and answers were used to assess their ability to produce guided generative output, as described under 'Scoring' below. This test was administered immediately after the fourth practice session of the treatment.

4. The reading comprehension test
    This test included the 7 open WH questions used in the background knowledge test (see 2 above). In addition, there were a further 7 open WH questions that covered minor ideas, which the students could not have been expected to know prior to reading the passage (e.g. 'What are the examples given by the social psychologists to prove their point?'). This took place immediately after the guided generative output test.

5. The vocabulary post-test
    This test was designed to provide a measure of the subjects' passive knowledge of the target words embedded in the passage used in (3). It took

the same form as the vocabulary pre-test. However, the order of the items in the test was changed. The method of scoring this test is described below. This test was administered immediately following the reading comprehension test. It was also administered a second time one week later.

6. The free-recall test

The purpose of this test was to measure long-term memory of the content of the reading passage used in (3). The subjects were given 50 minutes to recall and write down as much as they could remember of the content of the reading passage. This test was administered one week after the reading comprehension test.

7. The cloze-test

This test was designed to provide a measure of the subjects' active knowledge of the target words. The subjects were given the reading passage used in (3) with the target words deleted. They were asked to fill in the words using the same words as in the original passage as far as they could remember them. This test was also administered one week after the reading comprehension test.

Treatment

The treatment took the form of a demonstration of the self-questioning strategy and four practice sessions where the subjects in the experimental group had the opportunity to engage in producing guided generative output.

The demonstration session occupied a whole class, lasting 1 hour and 45 minutes. The teacher (in this case, one of the researchers) began by describing the self-questioning strategy and by providing a rationale for it. The teacher then modelled the strategy using a 'think aloud' procedure, pointing out how questions could be constructed to link information in one part of the passage to information in another part and to link information in the text to the reader's prior knowledge and, also, what constituted an appropriate response to the questions. She then presented a set of 13 generic question stems (e.g. 'How does … affect …?' and 'Do you agree and disagree with the statement …?' Why or why not?). The subjects then attempted to produce their own questions based on the demonstration passage, using the generic question stems. Finally, the teacher discussed a number of general metacognitive strategies such as monitoring understanding while reading and self-evaluating progress in understanding.

Each practice session occupied 50 minutes. On each occasion the subjects were given a practice text and asked to read it, generating and writing down their own questions as they did so. They were then asked to write answers to their own questions. Finally, they were asked to share their questions and answers with the whole class, which discussed them.

Of critical importance for this study was the choice of reading passages. The six passages used in the treatment and in the guided generative output and cloze tests needed to be of equivalent difficulty and also to pose a reasonable challenge to the subjects. For this reason, a set of explicit criteria were identified to guide selection. These were as follows:

1. The topics of the passage should all be general in nature, so that the subjects could make use of their background knowledge.
2. The level of the reading passages should be judged as 'moderately difficult' or 'difficult but manageable' by two experienced ESL teachers.
3. The texts should be of the same readability level (i.e. fall within the range of 45–60 using the Flesch Formula).
4. The texts should be a similar length and difficulty to those in the reading text books used by the control group.

Scoring

The instruments described above provided the following measures, which constituted the dependent variables of the study:

1. A guided generative output measure
   This was derived from the guided generative output test. The subjects' written questions and answers were collected and evaluated as follows. First, two independent raters scored the questions dichotomously as 'think-type' or 'non think-type' according to whether the response required inferencing from the text, connecting ideas in the text, or using prior knowledge to elaborate on the ideas in the text. Second, the raters classified the 'think' type questions as 'literal', 'inferential' or 'elaborative'. The linguistic accuracy of the questions was excluded from consideration. Overall, the inter-rater reliability was .91 (Pearson Product Moment Correlation). Any differences were resolved through discussion.

2. A reading comprehension score
   The reading comprehension score was computed by adding the score for questions relating to main ideas in the passage to that relating to minor ideas. The distinction between main and minor ideas was made by applying Mayer's (1984) hierarchical model of text content structure. This was used

to present the propositional structure of the text in the form of a tree diagram. 'Main ideas' were those that appeared on the first level of the diagram and were all superordinate in nature. 'Minor ideas' were those that appeared on the various lower levels of the diagram.

One point was awarded for each main idea identified by a subject. A gain score was then computed by subtracting the pre-test background knowledge test score (scored in the same way) from the post-test reading comprehension score. The maximum score for minor ideas was 20. Again, each subject was awarded one point for each minor idea mentioned in his/her written answer to a question. Two scorers worked independently to score major and minor ideas, achieving an interrater reliability of .94 (Pearson Product Moment Correlation). Discrepancies were resolved through discussion.

3. A post-test vocabulary acquisition score (immediate)
    A 'No' or 'Not sure' response to a word in the test was awarded 'zero' points. A satisfactory synonym or definition was awarded one point. The maximum score possible was 12.

4. A post-test vocabulary acquisition score (delayed)
    This was calculated in the same way as (3) above.

5. A free-recall score
    The score was based on the number of different main ideas recalled, the number of different minor ideas recalled, and the number of different elaborations (defined as expansions of ideas in the text and logical inferences from the text). One point was awarded for each idea and elaboration. Linguistic errors were ignored.

6. Cloze score
    The completed cloze tests were scored using the exact word method. One point was awarded for each target word that a subject supplied. No marks were given for synonyms. Spelling errors were discounted providing a word could be clearly identified.

Results

Table 1 gives the total number of questions ('think' and 'non-think') generated by both the control and experimental groups. The experimental group produced more questions overall than the control group. Also, the percentage of 'think' questions was higher (92% versus 69%). The 'think type questions were subsequently broken down into literal, inferential and elaborative types (see Table 2).

Table 1. *Total number of questions generated by both groups*

Group	Think	Non-think questions	Total questions
Control	81	36	117
Experimental	177	16	193

Table 2. *Comparison of groups on types of 'think' questions*

Group	Literal questions		Inferential questions		Elaborative questions		Total questions	
	Mean	SD	Mean	SD	Mean	SD	Mean	SD
Control	3.14	2.85	1.35	1.73	1.64	1.94	6.14	2.68
Experimental	5.64	2.79	5.28	3.53	2.28	3.24	13.21	5.65
t	2.34		3.73		0.64		4.22	
p	.05		.001		.53		.001	

Two-tailed t-tests were calculated to establish whether the differences between the control and experimental groups with regard to these three types were statistically significant. These showed that the experimental group produced significantly more questions overall and also more literal and inferential questions. However, the groups did not differ in the number of elaborative questions produced.

A comparison of the two groups' background knowledge scores and reading comprehension scores for main ideas (see Table 3) was carried out by means of a repeated measures ANOVA. This revealed a significant main effect for time ($F = 41.00$; $p > .001$) and for group ($F = 26.56$; $p > .001$). The experimental group scored significantly higher for comprehension of main ideas than the control group (mean = 4.42 versus mean = 2.62). There was also a significant group by time interaction ($F = 26.56$; $p > .001$). A post-hoc Test of Simple Effects indicated that there were no significant differences between the two groups on the pre-test of background knowledge. Both groups showed significant gains in their scores for main ideas with the experimental group gaining significantly more than the control group.

A two-tailed t-test compared the two groups' scores for comprehension of minor ideas (see Table 3). There were no pre-test scores on this variable. The experimental group comprehended significantly more of the minor ideas than the control group ($t = 4.56$; $p > .001$).

Table 3. *Comprehension of main and minor ideas by both groups*

Group	Main ideas Mean %	Minor ideas Mean %
Control	28.6	9.97
Experimental	50.0	16.92

Table 4. *Free recall of ideas by both groups*

Group	Mean ideas	SD
Control	6.79	2.40
Experimental	14.00	4.99
t	4.88	
p	0.001	

Table 5. *Post-test vocabulary acquisition and cloze scores for both groups*

	Post-test 1		Post-test 2		Cloze test	
	Mean	SD	Mean	SD	Mean	SD
Control	0.9	0.9	0.5	0.8	0.8	1.4
Experimental	1.9	1.3	2.1	1.9	2.6	1.7
t	2.5		2.8		3.1	
p	0.05		0.01		0.01	

The two groups' free recall scores (see Table 4) were also compared using a t-test. The experimental group was found to have recalled significantly more of the ideas (main and minor) in the text than the control group ($t = 4.88$; $p > .001$).

Table 5 gives the control and experimental groups' mean scores for both post-tests of vocabulary acquisition, one administered immediately after the treatment and the other one week later. The mean scores (total possible = 12) were low for both groups but the experimental group achieved significantly higher scores on both tests than the control group.

Also shown in Table 5 are the mean scores for the cloze test, which measure productive knowledge of the target items. Again the scores were low and again the experimental group significantly outscored the control group.

Discussion

The study investigated the effects of training in the use of a self-questioning strategy for reading on intermediate L2 learners' understanding of a reading passage, their ability to recall the content of the passage and their incidental acquisition of unknown words embedded in the passage. The results are very clear cut. The training resulted in the learners producing more 'think' type questions than learners who did not receive the training. It also enabled them to achieve higher comprehension, recall and vocabulary acquisition scores than learners who did not receive the training. Furthermore, these effects were evident immediately after the learners had read the test passage and one week later. Thus, the answers to all the research questions listed on p. 158 are affirmative. The study shows that even a relatively brief period of intervention can make a substantial difference in L2 learners' ability to read with understanding and to learn from their reading.

Prior research has shown that training in the use of the self-questioning strategy is highly effective in helping readers produce generative output that promotes reading comprehension and content learning. Drawing on this research, Mayer (1984) and Wittrock (1990) have concluded that guided generative output helps comprehension and content learning by enabling readers to make explicit connections between the ideas of a text, which in turn enables them to organize the material in meaningful ways and also to integrate new information into existing knowledge structures. However, the research to date has investigated only native speaker readers. This study demonstrates that guided generative output is equally beneficial for L2 learners. L2 readers can also improve their comprehension and ability to learn new content through reading by interrogating a text.

According to Widdowson (1979a), reading is an interactive process, similar to that which occurs in face-to-face communication (see the Introduction to this chapter). This study supports such a view of reading. However, it also suggests that L2 readers can vary considerably in their ability to interact with a text and that specific training in text interrogation can significantly improve individual L2 readers' ability to construct meaningful discourse out of a text. Such training provides a concrete pedagogic tool for enhancing L2 readers' reading comprehension and content learning.

Discussion with the teacher who conducted the training and with the treatment group after the completion of the study indicated a very positive response to the training. The teacher noted that, as the students applied the strategy, they showed conscious awareness of 'comprehension traps' such as over-reliance on their first language in guessing the meaning of words. The learners commented that the strategy had made them more aware of their problems in comprehending English texts. They also noted that they consciously applied the self-questioning strategy when reading texts in their content courses. Thus, it would appear that the strategy transfers successfully from the experimental to the everyday classroom.

The results of this study are also of significance for SLA theory. They indicate that engaging interactively with a text promotes the incidental acquisition of vocabulary. It is important to emphasize that this study addresses *incidental* and not *intentional* vocabulary learning. At no time during the treatment or during the reading of the test passage were the learners aware that the goal was vocabulary learning. In discussions after the study, the learners indicated that they did not make conscious efforts to learn new words in the text. Thus, the vocabulary learning that took place occurred as an offshoot of the learners attempts to grapple with understanding the content of the text and with relating it to their existing knowledge. The study shows that when learners are trained in how to interrogate a text they are more likely to learn and to remember new words.

However, the level of incidental vocabulary acquisition that resulted from the use of the self-questioning strategy was quite low — only an average of 1.9 and 2.1 words per student respectively on the immediate and delayed vocabulary tests and 2.6 on the cloze test. The learners took about 40 minutes to read the test passage and write and answer their questions on it. Thus, the rate of acquisition in the experimental group was only .048 (vocabulary test 1), .053 (vocabulary test 2) and .065 (cloze test). These rates are all lower than the .075 that Dupuy and Krashen (1983) reported in their study (see Chapter Two). However, a direct comparison is not really possible. Dupuy and Krashen used a multiple choice test and also did not pre-test their subjects to establish they had no previous knowledge of the words they tested. This study measured vocabulary by means of tests that required learners to supply their own synonyms or definitions and to produce the items. Arguably, such tests require a greater 'depth' of lexical knowledge than Dupuy and Krashen's test. Also, the learners in this study were pre-tested to ensure that none of the target items were already known by the subjects. Nevertheless, these rates are lower than those reported for Japanese high school students learning vocabulary through oral input (see Chapter Three) and lower than the .25 wpm reported by Nagy, Herman and Anderson (1985) for native speaker readers. The results of this study, therefore, bear out Hulstijn's (1992: 122) general conclusion:

> The retention of word meanings in a true incidental learning task is very low indeed. The chance that L2 learners/readers remember the meaning of a word occurring only once in a text, which is being read for its content, is very small.

We anticipated that the skillful application of a self-questioning strategy while reading would facilitate not just comprehension and content learning but also vocabulary acquisition. This turned out to be correct in so far as the experimental group acquired more words than the control group. Nevertheless, the rate of acquisition in the experimental group was lower than might have been expected. Why might this have been? One possibility is that the self-questioning strategy led the learners to focus primarily on meaning, its primary goal, rather than linguistic form. Thus, in accordance with the view of the L2 learner as a limited language processor, attention to meaning may have occurred at the expense of attention to form, which is considered essential for vocabulary learning to take place.

There is, in fact, some evidence to support this explanation. If learners had paid attention to the target items as they read, made an effort to infer their meaning and found them important for understanding the text, it is reasonable to assume they would have attempted to use the items in their written questions and answers. Table 6 below gives the number of times each target word occurred in both the experimental and control groups' output as they applied the self-questioning strategy. The number of occurrences is higher in the experimental group (total = 33) than in the control group (total = 7), indicating that training in the use of the self-questioning strategy, did indeed promote greater noticing of unknown words, but it is still low. Two of the words ('inclination' and 'weigh-in') did not figure in any of the experimental learners' output, while four others occurred only once. Interestingly, the frequency with which the experimental

Table 6. *Number of occurrences of the target items in both groups' output*

Item	Control	Experimental
enact	2	10
inclination	0	0
weigh-in	0	0
document	0	1
strap	0	1
noxious	0	1
impulsive	4	8
extrovert	1	4
farfetched	0	1
physique	0	3
stance	0	2
abstinent	0	2
Totals	7	33

learners incorporated the target words in their generative output (i.e. their questions and answers) correlated significantly with their cloze scores ($r = .61$; $p > .05$). Thus, the learners' general failure to use the words appears to explain why they acquired relatively few of them.

To sum up, training L2 readers to interrogate a text by posing and answering 'think' type questions promotes both better reading comprehension and content learning from a written text. Also, L2 learners who are trained in the self-questioning strategy achieve higher levels of incidental vocabulary acquisition than learners who attempt to use the strategy without training. However, the strategy itself does not appear to ensure high levels of vocabulary acquisition, even when carried out skillfully. One explanation for this is that it encourages attention to the meaning of a text rather than attention to individual lexical items which may not be essential for comprehension.

Conclusion

The study reported in this chapter bears out earlier observations regarding the complex nature of the relationship between comprehending input and learning an L2 from input. Comprehending input is no guarantee that acquisition will take place. Thus, the application of a reading strategy that focuses on comprehension, such as the self-questioning strategy, may work well in helping learners understand a text and retain information from the text, but may be less effective as a device for promoting acquisition of vocabulary.

It should be noted, however, that in this study no attempt was made to enhance the input so that the target items became more salient to the learners. The text was authentic. The target words occurred once only. Most of the words occurred in contexts that provided few clues as to the meanings. It is possible, therefore, that the self-questioning strategy would be more effective in promoting incidental vocabulary acquisition if the text was 'structured' to promote attention to target items and to assist inferencing their meanings.[1] In other words, the efficacy of the strategy where acquisition is concerned may depend on the availability of suitably modified input.

This suggests an important difference with regard to the kind of negotiation that occurs in face-to-face interaction and that found in reading. As we saw in Chapters Three and Four, the interactionally modified input that arises in oral communication has the potential to supply the learner with additional information relating to the meaning of an unknown item which can assist acquisition. In contrast, the negotiation that occurs during reading is dependent on the learner's own knowledge and strategic ability and, as such, may be less effective in facilitating vocabulary acquisition. With regard to acquisition, then, the interactive processes involved in talking may differ significantly from those involved in reading. It is, therefore, not surprising that the rate of incidental vocabulary acquisition observed in this study is considerably lower than that in the studies of oral interaction reported in previous chapters. As we noted in Chapter Two, modified oral input has several advantages over written input as data for vocabulary acquisition.

Notes

1. The study provides some evidence for the claim that when a word and its meaning are made salient, the self questioning strategy facilitates acquisition. The word 'impulsive' occurred in a context that made its meaning clear. It figured prominently in the experimental learners' guided generative output and was acquired for productive use by six of them.

Appendix A: Treatment Text

(Note: The target words are underlined).

Across the United States, municipal authorities are enacting anti-smoking laws. One third of all American corporations have instituted non-smoking regulations that prohibit smokers from smoking inside the building. The number of these corporations is rapidly growing. Most of the shopping malls across the country do not allow smoking indoor. It is becoming common to have a non-smoking section in every restaurant.

As someone who detests cigarettes, I should be pleased at these developments. Cigarette smoke disgusts me, and in a restaurant, office or airplane full of the stuff, the fumes invariably find their way to my "non-smoking" seat. Never once — not even as an adolescent — can I remember having the slightest inclination to smoke or to even experience the feeling it gives.

So why do I find myself concerned rather than relieved that Hunter College, where I spend a good bit of time, has just instituted tough new regulations against smoking? Frankly, I worry that one day the college authorities may well go after me, too for any of the bad habits I have. While I won't smoke, I also don't do some of the things that many who oppose smoking think I should do — for example, I do not get very much exercise nor do I maintain a low cholesterol diet.

Already some insurance companies offer lower rates to people who exercise and reduce their cholesterol levels. How would I feel if my employees removed egg products and fried foods, both of which I eat regularly, from the menu at the staff lunchroom. Or if I were forced to weigh in or work out each morning before I went to the office? Such scenarios are not so farfetched. Recent studies of so-called wellness programs at work sites have documented the existence of corporate environments in which pressures to shape up and eat right have become extreme. For example, employees who do not join gyms and do not attend scheduled nutrition workshops sometimes find themselves shunned by colleagues and passed over for promotions. If they become ill, colleagues blame them for having brought the illness on themselves.

One might support a ban on smoking while opposing certain other restrictive measures, of course, on the grounds that smoking, unlike eating an egg salad sandwich or flaunting a rotten physique, hurts others as well as oneself. But sustaining such an argument is not easy. Health economists have shown convincingly that everyone pays, through higher insurance premiums and an overtaxed health system, for everyone else's healthy behavior.

I accept the fact that I may be harming myself and others by my actions. Like those who smoke, what I do not accept is that this potential harm is greater than the hardship required to change my ways and develop good habits. It might not be a terrible burden to give up fatty foods and to strap oneself into a rowing machine. No doubt some people accomplish such things easily. As for myself, every low cholesterol diet I have ever tried has left me hungry all the time and frustrated, and I have not yet found an exercise machine that makes me look forward to exercise and lose weight.

In surveys, the major reasons smokers give for their habit is that they enjoy it and find it relaxing. Those are exactly the reasons I eat what I do and spend my spare time with a book or in front of a television screen. These choices fit my personality and life style. To oppose a ban on smoking is to object to the demand upon a group of people to give up their particular stance toward life-one that, for all its noxious qualities, has contributed much to the American character.

Social psychologists have found that, as a group, smokers differ from non-smokers. Smokers are more likely to be impulsive — they take chances in a variety of areas of their personal lives that abstinent types like me shy away from. They have also found out that smokers tend to be extroverted risk takers Smokers tend to drive faster, for instance, and to make more venturesome business decisions that might have negative effects or lead to company losses.

The important point is that we all take unnecessary risks at times and behave in ways that upset others. Smokers may be doing the same thing in more areas of life, or in different ways, than nonsmokers. But we nonsmokers who believe that we have a right to our own idiosyncrasies, have an obligation to defend smokers' rights as well.

SECTION 3

Interaction and Grammar Learning

In the previous section we considered how input and interaction create conditions for the learning of vocabulary. This section reports two studies which have examined the relationship between interaction and grammar learning.

In fact, there have been few studies that have investigated whether and how interaction contributes to the development of L2 grammar. There is an obvious reason for this. Whereas some acquisition of word meanings can take place rapidly, in some cases instantaneously, the acquisition of grammatical forms and rules is typically a slow process involving access to multiple exposures and opportunities for use over a long period of time. Ideally, then, the study of grammar learning requires longitudinal studies that can plot the gradual process of acquisition in relation to the particular interactional opportunities that learners experience. Such studies are time consuming and difficult to conduct, not least because it is difficult to control the variables that can impact on acquisition and thus to determine the particular effects of the learners' interactional opportunities.

It is, therefore, not surprising to find that, to date, researchers interested in the relationship between interaction and grammar learning have plumped for experimental studies, which are less demanding on time and make it easier to determine the particular role that interaction can play. The studies that have been completed to date are reviewed in Chapter 1 and so will be mentioned just briefly here. Loschky (1994) investigated the effects of baseline, premodified and interactionally modified input on the acquisition of locative structures by English speaking learners of L2 Japanese, but contrary to expectations, failed to find any advantage for modified input, either premodified or interactionally. This study tested the early version of the Interaction Hypothesis (IH), namely that interaction assists learning by supplying learners with comprehensible input. More recent studies have focussed on the effects of the negative evidence that learners receive through interaction (i.e. relate to the claims of the later version of the IH). These have produced more encouraging results. Experimental studies of the effects of recasts on grammar learning (Mito 1993, Long, Inagaki and Ortega 1998 and Mackey and Philps 1998) provide some support for Long's claims that negative feedback in the context of message-focussed interaction can assist learning. Other studies have examined another claim of the revised IH, namely that pushed output helps learners acquire L2 grammar. Nobuyoshi and Ellis (1993) found that two out of the three learners they studied appeared to benefit from being pushed to reformulate utterances containing past tense errors. Mackey (1995) found that active participation in meaning negotiation by L2 learners led to greater progress through the stages of acquisition of English question forms. In general, though, it is probably fair to say that these studies provide only limited support for the claim that interaction contributes to grammar learning. This is an area of SLA where theory has tended to run ahead of empirical inquiry.

The first study reported in this section (Chapter 7) builds on Nobuyoshi and Ellis' research. That is, it investigates the effects of pushing learners to reformulate utterances containing past tense errors on the acquisition of this grammatical structure. The second study (Chapter 8) is based in part on the early version of the IH and in part on my own claims (see Ellis 1991 and 1993) relating to the value of tasks designed to develop learners' explicit knowledge of grammar. This seeks to show that such tasks can serve a double purpose; they can successfully help learners to discover grammatical rules for themselves and they can also stimulate the kind of meaning negotiation that Long claims facilitates acquisition. Both studies were designed to demonstrate how theoretical ideas drawn from SLA can be operationalized for language pedagogy.

These two studies have drawn on the dominant experimental tradition of research in SLA. It should be noted, however, that some SLA researchers are turning to more qualitative methods to examine how interaction contributes to grammar learning. Research based on socio-cultural theory draws on Vygotsky's microgenetic method, attempting to demonstrate how learners' participation in specific exchanges enables them to perform grammatical structures that initially they were incapable of. In such studies, in accordance with the precepts of the theory, acquisition is equated with learners' manifest ability to use structures, the assumption being that what is used is subsequently internalized. Examples of such studies were discussed in Chapter 1 (see the references to Donato 1994, Ohta forthcoming and Swain forthcoming). Such studies are likely to become increasingly important in helping to develop our understanding of the role that interaction plays in grammar learning.

CHAPTER 7

Output Enhancement and the Acquisition of the Past Tense

Hide Takashima and Rod Ellis

Introduction

This chapter has two major purposes. It aims to contribute to theory by testing the claims of the Interaction Hypothesis as these relate to the role of modified output. It also aims to illustrate how a theoretical construct can be applied in the second language classroom.

The current version of the Interaction Hypothesis (see Long 1996) draws on Swain's Output Hypothesis (Swain 1985, 1995) in proposing that 'pushing' learners to produce output that is precise, coherent and appropriate can induce learners to engage in the kind of bottom-up processing necessary for extending interlanguage grammar. There are potentially many ways of 'pushing' learners to produce such output but here we will be concerned with just one — the use of clarification requests.

When a learner produces an utterance that is not comprehended the listener may respond with a clarification request, which causes the learner to subsequently reformulate the problematic utterance, as in this example:

(1)   Student: Cinderella change into the beautiful girl.
        Teacher: Sorry?
        Student: Cinderella changed into a beautiful girl.

Here, the learner, who is attempting to tell the story of Cinderella, says something that the teacher does not understand. The teacher requests clarification, causing the learner to reformulate his utterance, substituting the target language verb form ('changed') for the non-target-form in the initial utterance ('change').

The result of this negotiation is what Takashima (1995) calls 'enhanced output' (i.e. output that has been 'grammaticalized' as a result of 'pushing').

Pushing learners through clarification requests can have three possible outcomes. First, learners may simply repeat rather than reformulate their utterances, as in this example:

(2)   Student: Cinderella have to go home.
       Teacher: Cinderella? I beg your pardon?
       Student: Cinderella have to go home.

In this case, the output is not enhanced. That is, the learner simply repeats the initial utterance without making any grammatical modification. Second, it can lead to reformulation where the learner fails to use the correct target language form but does substitute a more advanced interlanguage form, as in this example:

(3)   Student: The prince fall in love at first glance.
       Teacher: Sorry?
       Student: The prince falled in love at first glance.

Here the learner modifies the initial utterance by substituting 'falled' for 'fall'. This is ungrammatical, but it represents a form that typically occurs later in the acquisition of irregular past tense (see Doughty and Varela 1998). The third possibility is that the clarification request causes the learner to substitute the correct target language form for an initial incorrect interlanguage form, as in (1) above. Enhanced output arises when learners grammaticalize their output either through the use of more advanced interlanguage forms or of target language forms.

As we saw in Chapter 1, a question of considerable importance is whether learners do indeed produce enhanced input when they are pushed through meaning negotiation. We considered the study by Pica, Holliday, Lewis and Morganthaler (1989), which showed that 10 adult Japanese learners of L2 English modified their output by making it more grammatical when one particular type of negotiation took place — that involving requests for clarification, as in the above examples. This study showed that, in contrast to requests for clarification, confirmation requests, were less likely to lead to enhanced output, as this type of feedback supplied learners with a reformulation of their initial utterances, thus obviating the need for them to reformulate. This finding is supported by Lyster and Ranta's (1997) study of learner 'uptake' in response to corrective feedback in French immersion classrooms. This study found that learners were much less likely to incorporate corrections provided via teachers' 'recasts' (which, like confirmation checks, reformulate a learner's utterance) than they were if the teachers' corrections took the form of clarification requests.[1]

We also noted in Chapter 1 that it is not sufficient to show that learners reformulate by grammaticalizing their output; it is also necessary to demonstrate that enhanced output contributes to acquisition (i.e. has some long term effect on learners' use of grammatical forms). This was the goal of Nobuyoshi and Ellis' (1993) study. Although no conclusions are possible from such a small-scale study (see Krashen 1998 for a critique), this research does suggest that, for some learners at least, the opportunity to produce enhanced output aids acquisition. Nobuyoshi and Ellis' study raises two interesting possibilities that are worthy of further investigation; not all learners produce enhanced output when given an opportunity to do so and only those learners who do modify their output benefit acquisitionally.

But how does enhanced output contribute to acquisition? In the case of recasts, learners are exposed to grammatical forms that may not yet be part of their L2 competence. Thus recasts can potentially help learners to acquire completely new forms. However, it is self-evident that learners cannot themselves reformulate using grammatical forms that they have not yet acquired. Thus, if a learner modifies output by substituting a correct target language form for an incorrect form, as in (1) above, this must be because (s)he already knows the target language form. What then is acquired from enhanced output? Possibly, reformulating helps the learner to produce grammatical forms that have already entered their interlanguages but which they have difficulty in accessing, particularly in the context of on-line communication. According to this argument, then, enhanced output does not result in the acquisition of *new* forms but in greater control of those forms that have already been acquired. This is the most likely way in which pushed output contributes to acquisition. However, pushing learners to reformulate may also motivate the kind of overgeneralization error observed in (3) above. That is, faced with the need to make their output more comprehensible, learners may apply a grammatical rule they have acquired inappropriately, resulting in transitional constructions such as 'falled'. If such interim stages of acquisition are seen as an essential feature of interlanguage development, as suggested by research on developmental sequences (see Ellis 1994, Chapter 3), it might be claimed that pushing learners to modify their output induces learners to engage in the kind of restructuring that McLaughlin (1990) has claimed to be a key aspect of language acquisition. Finally, it can be hypothesized that clarification requests alert learners to potential gaps in their interlanguage which they seek to fill by paying closer attention to input (see Swain 1995).

The study[2] which we now report was designed to examine the effects of 'pushing' learners through clarification requests on both their immediately reformulated output and on their acquisition of past tense verb forms over time. It sought answers to the following questions:

1. When pushed to modify their own output by means of clarification requests, do L2 learners reformulate by 'grammaticalizing' their speech (i.e. by using target language or more advanced interlanguage forms)?

This question is motivated by Nobuyoshi and Ellis' (1993) suggestion that learners may vary in the extent to which they reformulate when pushed.

2. Does pushing learners to modify their output by means of clarification requests result in subsequent increase in the grammatical accuracy?

Assuming that at least some learners reformulate grammatically when pushed, this question addresses whether there is any effect on acquisition (i.e. do grammatical reformulations lead to subsequent gains in grammatical accuracy).

3. Do learners who are pushed to modify their output by means of clarification requests show greater gains in grammatical accuracy than learners who just overhear the modified output?

Pushed output may be important for acquisition not because it involves learners in production but because it provides a particularly rich kind of input. In the case of the speaker who produced the output, this would constitute 'auto-input' (Schmidt and Frota 1986). In the case of learners who overhear the modified output produced by other learners it would constitute modified input. Krashen (1985) has argued that speaking in itself does not cause acquisition. To test whether modified output contributes to acquisition by providing opportunities for production it is necessary to demonstrate that learners who produce modified output outperform learners who do not produce it but overhear it.

Method

The specific grammatical features investigated were English irregular and regular past tense forms. These are typically acquired in a series of stages, with the first stage characterized by the use of a simple form of the verb (e.g. 'fall' and 'show') in contexts calling for past tense followed by acquisition of the past tense form (e.g. 'fell' and 'showed'). In the case of irregular verbs, learners frequently pass through a stage where they overgeneralize the past tense form -ed (e.g. 'falled') before finally returning to the target form ('fell'). As Bardovi-Harlig and Reynolds (1995) have shown, learners find it easier to mark certain classes of verbs for past tense than others. For example, they mark verbs referring to events (e.g. 'arrive') first, then activity verbs (e.g. 'sleep') and finally state verbs (e.g. 'want'). It is clear from the available research that the acquisition of past tense forms is a slow and complex process. It should also be noted that in many contexts the marking of the verb for past tense is redundant, as either the situation or the linguistic context makes it clear that the time referred to is past. As a result, there may be little communicative pressure on learners to supply past tense forms.

Subjects

The subjects were 61 second-year students[3] in a Japanese national university enrolled in required English courses. They had studied English for seven years prior to the study but had only limited communicative proficiency, as their previous instruction involved grammar translation and had been largely conducted in Japanese. There were 19 males and 42 females. In general, the students were not strongly motivated to learn English.

The subjects were taught in intact classes, making random distribution for purposes of the experiment impossible. However, the two classes used in the study did not differ in the scores they obtained on the English language section of the national university entrance examination ($F = .8361$; $p = .36$).

Design

The study was designed to investigate the effects of two kinds of clarification requests. An experimental group received clarification requests only when a learner produced an utterance that contained an error in the use of the past tense (e.g. used the simple form of the verb or overgeneralized the regular form with an irregular verb). This occurred irrespective of whether the hearer (the teacher) had actually understood the utterance. However, the learners in the experimental group were not aware that the teacher's clarification requests were focussed on use of the past tense. They were led to believe that they occurred in response to the teacher's failure to understand something they had said. In contrast to this 'focussed negotiation', the control group received clarification requests only when there was a genuine breakdown in communication. That is, the negotiation they took part in was 'unfocussed'.

Both the experimental and control groups experienced the following:

1.   A pre-test (week 1)
2.   The treatment (weeks, 2, 3 and 4)
3.   Post-test 1 (week 5)
4.   Post-test 2 (week 6)
5.   Post-test 3 (week 11).

Instruments

The pre-test and the three post-tests took the form of oral narratives based on two series of four pictures. One series of pictures ('The Monkey and the Crab') was used for the pre-test and post-test 1. While a second series ('The Three Little Pigs') was used for post-test 3 and post-test 4. In this way, the subjects did not become over-practised by telling the same story four times but it was possible to make a direct comparison between the pre-test and immediate post-test scores on the same materials. Accompanying each picture series was a list of 12 to 15 words (nouns and verbs in the infinitive form) which the subjects could use to help tell the story. Such support was considered necessary given the limitations in the students' English proficiency. To provide a trigger for the use of the past tense, students were instructed to begin their stories with 'Once upon a time ...' or 'One day ...'.[4]

The treatment utilized a further three sets of pictures. In the first week of the treatement, the subjects in both the experimental and control groups narrated 'Beauty and the Beast', in the second week they narrated 'Cinderella' and in the final week 'The Grateful Stone Statues'. Thus, all the subejcts had the opportunity to work with three different stories.

Procedures

The students told the oral narrative for the pre-test in a language laboratory. They were first given a picture series ('The Butcher and a Dog') to practise telling a story orally and then given the materials for the pre-test. They were placed in groups, each student receiving one picture. They were allowed five minutes to talk to each other about their pictures, in either Japanese or English. After the five minutes was up, they individually recorded their stories in English on cassette. After recording, the tapes were collected for transcription.

The same procedures were followed for the three post-tests. Each test involved a group planning phase followed by the production of an oral narrative individually by each student.

The treatment for the experimental (output enhancement group) involved the following:

1. The subjects were organized into groups of four or five.[5] Each subject was then given one picture from a series of four pictures. In groups with five subjects, two of the students shared one picture. The subjects were told to elect a representative for their group who would later have to tell the complete story to the whole class. Each subject then described the picture (s)he was holding without showing it to the others in the group. In this way, the subjects prepared for step 2. Step 1 took 15 minutes.

2. The representatives of the groups took it in turn to tell the story with the rest of the class listening. Whenever a student representative produced a sentence containing an error in the use of the past tense (e.g. by substituting an incorrect simple verb form or using an overgeneralized verb form) the teacher immediately requested clarification by means of a standard formula (e.g. 'Sorry?', 'I beg your pardon.'). In this way, the subjects telling the stories were pushed to reformulate. However, if they failed to produce a correct past tense form in their reformulations no further attempt to push them was made. The other subjects were motivated to listen carefully because they had been told that their grades would be based on their representatives' narratives and, therefore, were presumed to be interested in how well (s)he performed. This step took 30 minutes. The representatives' oral narratives with the teacher's feedback were audio recorded.

This treatment was repeated three times using different series of pictures. It took place over a three week period, with one treatment occurring each week. The student representatives were not changed; thus, the same representatives told all three stories. However, the order in which the representatives were asked to tell the stories varied on each occasion in an attempt to ensure that the order of telling did not unduly effect their performance. The narratives were audio-recorded.

In the case of the control group, the first step of the treatment was the same as for the experimental group. However, the second step differed. While the groups' representatives were telling the stories the teacher intervened with a request for clarification only when he was not clear of the meaning of what was said. This did not involve utterances with a past tense error as such errors did not affect the comprehensibility of the narratives. Again, this procedure was repeated three times with different sets of pictures but with the same representatives. The narratives were audio recorded.

Scoring

The audio-recordings of the subjects' oral narratives produced during the pre-test, the three treatments and the three post-tests were transcribed in normal orthography by four researchers. Each researcher was allocated a quarter of the narratives. To ensure reliability, each transcription was then checked by another researcher. Working in pairs, the researchers discussed any occasion where they differed (e.g. 'walked' vs. 'walks') by replaying the recording.[6]

The obligatory occasions for the use of the past tense in the transcriptions of the oral narratives were then identified and both the number and percentage of correctly supplied past tense forms calculated. All the students made some attempt to tell the stories using the past tense (i.e. no student tried to use the historical present tense).

Based on the transcripts of the subjects' oral narratives produced during the treatments, charts were prepared for each narrator showing which past tense verbs were incorrectly produced, whether the teacher requested clarification (occasionally the teacher failed to notice an error), and the nature of the subject's response (i.e. whether (s)he reformulated using the target language form or an interlanguage form or whether the error went uncorrected).

Results

Table 1 shows the number of obligatory occasions for past tense that the individual subjects who acted as group representatives created during the three oral narratives produced as part of the experimental treatment (column a). It also shows the number of past tense forms incorrectly supplied in their initial utterances (column b) and correctly supplied in their reformulated utterances (column c). The final column shows the percentage of past tense forms that the subjects corrected in their reformulated utterances (column d).

It is clear that the subjects varied considerably in the extent to which they attempted to reformulate their utterances by correcting past tense forms. Subject 1, for example, corrected rarely, only once out of 16 opportunities (6.2%). In contrast, subject 7 corrected 6 of 9 utterances (66.7%). The average rate of correction for all seven subjects was 29%.

Table 2 provides the scores of these seven subjects (i.e. those who performed the narratives publicly in class) on the pre-test and subsequent post-tests. Here again we see considerable variation in the pattern of scores. Subject 1, for example, shows no improvement, whereas subject 7 shows steady improvement,

Table 1. *Individual narrators' reformulations during the treatment (experimental group)*

Subject	Task 1				Task 2				Task 3			
	a	b	c	d	a	b	c	d	a	b	c	d
1	7	3	1	33	16	11	0	0	9	2	0	0
2	23	13	3	23	21	7	3	43	–	–	–	–
3	11	4	1	25	13	3	2	67	11	4	0	0
4	21	8	1	13	17	5	1	20	20	4	1	25
5	12	5	1	20	13	3	2	67	15	3	1	33
6	17	5	2	40	14	8	1	13	22	2	2	100
7	12	3	1	33	17	4	4	0	17	2	1	50

a = total obligatory occasions for past tense
b = number of errors in initial utterances
c = number of errors corrected in reformulated utterances
d = percentage of errors corrected in reformulated utterances

Table 2. *Individual narrators' percentage scores on the pre- and post-tests (experimental group)*

Subject	Pre-test	Post-test 1	Post-test 2	Post-test 3
1	86	90	74	64
2	72	66	68	62
3	22	11	55	78
4	75	71	62	82
5	82	63	73	70
6	68	80	73	94
7	46	79	86	95

advancing from 46% accuracy in the use of past tense forms in the pre-test to 95% accuracy in the final post-test. Comparing the scores for the pre-test and post-test 1 (which were based on the same picture series) we find that only three out of the seven subjects showed improvement.

To examine the relationship between the subjects' preparedness to reformulate using correct past tense forms and their subsequent performance on the post tests Spearman Rank Correlation coefficients were calculated using percentage reformulation scores and percentage gain scores between the pre-test scores and each of the post-test scores. The results are shown in Table 3. None of the coefficients reached statistical significance, although the correlation between reformulations and Post-test 2 came close ($p = .06$).[7]

Table 3. *Spearman Rank Correlation coefficients between percentage reformulations and post-test percentage gain scores (n = 7)*

	Gain scores		
	Post-test 1	Post-test 2	Post-test 3
Reformulations			
r	.14	.64	.32
p	.38	.06	.24

Table 4. *Comparison of pre- and post-test past tense accuracy scores for 'narrators' and 'listeners' in the control and experimental groups*

	Pre-test	Post-test 1	Post-test 2	Post-test 3
Control group:				
Narrators (N=4)	28.9	63.0	54.5	47.9
Listeners (N=30)	42.2	41.7	40.2	45.9
Experimental group:				
Narrators (N=7)	64.4	65.6	70.7	78.1
Listeners (N=20)	47.8	59.6	58.2	67.7

Table 4 shows the mean pre-test and post-test past tense accuracy scores for subjects in the control and experimental groups according to whether they were 'narrators' (i.e., were given the opportunity to produce reformulated utterances as they narrated) or 'listeners' (i.e., just listened to the reformulated utterances produced by the narrators). In the case of the control group, the treatment had a clear effect on the narrators, as reflected in the gain in past tense accuracy from the pre-test to post-test 1, although there were no subsequent gains in post-tests 2 and 3. In contrast, the listeners in the control group showed little improvement. In the case of the experimental group, both narrators and listeners showed improvement, with the listeners improving more. It should be noted that the experimental group narrators' score was quite high in the pre-test (64.4%), notably higher than that of the control group narrators.[8] Two repeated measures ANOVAs were computed for the control and experimental groups to test whether these differences between narrators' and listeners' test scores were significant. In both cases the difference in scores was found to be statistically non-significant (Control group — $F = .67$ and $p = .42$; Experimental group — $F = 1.4$ and $p = .24$). However, there was a clear effect for time, with the subjects in both the control and experimental groups showing a significant improvement in past tense accuracy in the post-tests.

Table 5. *Test of Simple Main Effects*

Test	F	p
Pre-test	4.01	.05
Post-test 1	7.64	.008
Post-test 2	7.77	.007
Post-test 3	13.21	.001

Finally, an ANOVA was computed, with test as the repeated measure and group as the between subjects factor, to investigate whether the overall performance of the experimental and control groups was different. This found a statistically significant overall difference between the groups (F = 12.50; p = .001). Table 5 gives the results of the follow-up Test of Simple Main Effects, showing that there were significant differences between the two groups on the pre-test and each of the three post-tests. It can be seen, then, that the experimental group outperformed the control group on all the tests, with the difference least evident in post-test 1 and most evident in post-test 3.

Discussion

As Tables 4 and 5 show the experimental and control groups were not equivalent at the beginning of the study. This was because some of the subjects in the experimental group had been used six months previously in a pilot test to ascertain the viability of the enhanced output treatment and thus had already benefited from being pushed to reformulate utterances containing past tense forms. The lack of equivalence of the two groups at the beginning of the study makes it difficult to carry out a reliable comparison of the effects of the two treatments. Overall, the experimental group outperformed the control group in accurate use of the past tense on all the post-tests, but, because of the experimental group's high score on the pre-test the gains it manifest were smaller than those evident in the control group. It should be noted, however, that the experimental group's access to focussed feedback are reflected in a general increase in accuracy in the use of past tense forms over the three post-tests whereas the overall scores of the control group improved from pre-test to post-test but then evened out.

Overall, then, the results indicate that focussed feedback is effective in promoting learning (operationalized as improved accuracy in the use of a grammatical feature), particularly if credit is given for the effects of the focussed negotiation the subjects in the experimental group experienced during the pilot-test. They also suggest that unfocussed feedback can lead to gains in grammatical accuracy. We will now turn to what was the main purpose of the study — what it was in the treatment received by the experimental group that helped acquisition. It was this issue that the research questions were designed to address.

The first research question asked whether the subjects who were asked to narrate the stories in front of the whole class actually reformulated by correcting their past tense errors when pushed. Overall, the narrators self-corrected 29% of their past tense errors. This seems quite a low rate of repair. It indicates that the subjects did not become aware that the requests were focussed on past tense and also that they may have experienced difficulty in correcting errors because the pressure to tell the story in real time led to a focus on message content rather than form. It is interesting to note that the rate of repair in this study is almost identical to the 28% of repaired utterances following requests for clarification that Lyster and Ranta (1997) report in their study of teacher feedback in Canadian immersion classrooms.

Lyster and Ranta do not provide any information on individual learners but Nobuyoshi and Ellis (1993) found that their subjects varied considerably in the extent of their self-corrections. We also found considerable variation in this study. While some of the narrators self-corrected their use of past tense frequently others did so rarely. We can only speculate why this might be so. One possibility, as suggested by Nobuyoshi and Ellis, is that learners vary in their orientation to learning, with some motivated to attend to the norms of the target language and others more concerned with functional language use. Another possibility is that the subjects varied in their existing knowledge of past tense forms. As we noted in the introduction to this chapter, learners can only self-correct if they already know the correct form. Another possibility is that there is a trade-off effect between fluency and accuracy, with less fluent speakers less able to devote time to accuracy (see Skehan and Foster 1987).

It is of course one thing to show that focussed feedback results in enhanced output and quite another to claim that the enhanced output leads to long-term gains in accuracy (i.e. acquisition). The second research question, therefore, asked whether pushing learners to modify their output resulted in a subsequent increase in grammatical accuracy. In fact, only three out of the seven narrators in the experimental group showed gains in past tense accuracy from the pre-test to any of the post-tests; four actually declined in accuracy. Furthermore, there was no relationship between the subjects' rate of repair and their post-test scores. In other words, contrary to expectations, this study failed to show that enhanced output had any effect on learners' subsequent ability to use past tense forms accurately. In this respect, then, self-correcting a grammatical feature in the context of a message-focussed task does not appear to promote the acquisition of specific grammatical forms, although, it should be noted, that individual learners (e.g., learner 7) did appear to benefit from such an opportunity.

If there is no relationship between self-correction and acquisition, the question arises as to why the experimental group as a whole improved in past tense accuracy. The answer to this lies in the answer to the third research question addressed in this study; do learners who are pushed to modify their output show greater gains in grammatical accuracy than learners who just overhear the modified output? The results reported in Table 4 indicate that the narrators did no better than the listeners in the experimental group. It would seem then that learners who have the opportunity to produce enhanced output are not advantaged in comparison to students who simply listen to such output. Indeed, in the experimental group it was the listeners who showed the greater gain from pre-test to post-test 1 (47.8% to 59.6% compared with 64.5% to 65.6%). The results of this study, therefore, reflect those of Pica (1991) for comprehension; Pica found that learners who functioned as observers achieved a similar level of comprehension to learners who were active negotiators in a communicative task (see Chapter 3). Thus, pushing learners to self-correct while publicly performing a message-focussed task may not necessarily lead to the performers achieving higher levels of grammatical accuracy than the listeners. However, such pushing is not without value as it does lead to the listeners being exposed to valuable input which they can use to advance their interlanguages.

It would be mistaken to conclude, therefore, that pushing learners to enhance their output through focussed feedback is of no pedagogic value. Indeed, this study suggests that it is. First, some of the narrators who experienced focussed feedback and enhanced their output appeared to benefit acquisitionally. Second, the enhanced output produced by the narrators served as input to the listeners that benefitted them acquisitionally. Perhaps enhanced output of the kind elicited through focussed feedback provides a particularly rich source of input that enables listeners to notice the targeted form, to compare it with an inter-language form, and thereby to acquire it. Exchanges such as the one below seem to afford listeners just this kind of opportunity:

(4)   Student: And she (i.e. Beauty) said 'I love you'. And she, she fall down on her cheek.
        Teacher: Sorry?
        Student: Fell down tears? Oh Beauty's tears fell down, fell down on her cheek.

Here the narrator responds to the clarification request by both changing the subject of the verb (from 'she' to 'tears') and correcting 'fall'; in so doing, she repeats the past tense form, 'fell', three times, thus affording the listeners ample opportunity to notice it.

To sum up, although it would obviously be premature to dismiss enhanced output as of no acquisitional value to the learners who actually produce it, this study shows that enhanced output appears to work because of the rich input it supplies rather than because of the opportunities it provides learners to practise the production of problematic forms.

Conclusion

The study reported above investigated the effects of 'focussed feedback' on learners' use and acquisition of past tense forms. Focussed feedback was operationalized as requests for clarification that pushed learners to reformulate their output in the context of a message-focussed task. The study indicated that (1) focussed feedback resulted in learners self-correcting past tense forms 29% of the time, (2) the learners' modified output was not related to the accuracy with which they used past tense forms in subsequent tasks, (3) learners who overheard the modified output did improve in past tense accuracy, and (4) that in each post-test the group that received focussed feedback was more accurate in its use of past tense than the group that received unfocussed feedback (i.e. requests for clarification that occurred when a learner utterance was not understood).

The study addresses an issue of considerable theoretical importance to SLA. What is the role of feedback in the acquisition of specific grammatical forms? Two broad explanations of the role of feedback are possible, as shown in Figure 1 below. The first (A) is that feedback results in modified output, the production of which has a direct impact on L2 acquisition. The second (B) is that feedback results in modified output which affects acquisition via the 'enriched input' that it supplies. (A) represents the position adopted by the Output Hypothesis advanced by Swain (1985) and also with skill-building theories that emphasize the importance of obtaining feedback on performance under real-operating conditions (Johnson 1996). In contrast, (B) can be seen as an extension of the Input Hypothesis in that it views modified learner output as contributing to acquisition through the input it supplies. The results of the study are clearly more supportive of B. However, given the small scale of the study and the fact that only one type of feedback was examined, this conclusion is necessarily tentative.

A. learner output → feedback → modified learner output → acquisition

B. learner output → feedback → modified learner → enriched → acquisition
output input

Figure 1. *Two models of the role of feedback in L2 acquisition*

This study also addresses a number of issues of pedagogical significance. First, it demonstrates that 'focussed feedback' in the form of requests for clarification directed at utterances containing specific errors is pedagogically feasible. This was questioned by Hopkins and Nettle (1994) who, responding to the feedback treatment used by Nobuyoshi and Ellis (1993) commented

> constant requests for clarification are likely to interfere with a communicative activity, if not disrupt it; and learners are likely to be demotivated by such interruptions (p. 159).

In fact, the focussed feedback treatment we used differed from that of Nobuyoshi and Ellis, which occurred in one-on-one interactions between teacher and student. In this study we introduced focussed feedback into the public performance stage of a communicative task, finding that the requests for clarification did not interfere unduly with the activity and that the learners were not demotivated by the 'interruptions'.[9] Furthermore, the results of the study indicate that such feedback is beneficial to the other students in the class who function as listeners. We would claim, therefore, that this study shows that focussed feedback is a viable pedagogic option, even in large classes. It constitutes one way of achieving what Long (1991) has called a 'focus on form' — an attempt to draw students' attention to linguistic features in lessons where there is an overriding focus on meaning or communication. Furthermore, focussed feedback via clarification requests provides a way of achieving such a focus on form relatively unobtrusively.

There are several questions raised by this study. Why are some learners more inclined to self-correct than others when pushed? Why does self-correction of errors in a communicative task appear to assist some learners' acquisition of grammatical forms but not other learners? To what extent does enhanced output function as 'auto-input' (i.e. do speakers attend to their own output)? These questions are of obvious theoretical and pedagogical importance and await further study.

Notes

1. It does not follow, of course, that clarification requests are more effective in promoting language acquisition than recasts. Recasts supply learners with modified input and as such may help acquisition. Studies by McKay (1995) and Doughty and Varela (1998) demonstrate that recasts are effective in helping learners develop grammatically.

2. For a report of the complete study see Takashima (1995). Takashima also examined the effects of reformulation on the use and acquisition of plural -s.

3. Initially there were 91 subjects but 30 of these missed one of the tests or the treatment and so were excluded from the study.

4. Four native speakers were also asked to perform the tasks. Their narratives, which were audio recorded, demonstrated that the tasks did elicit natural use of the past tense.

5. As far as possible, groups of four students were formed. Sometimes, however, a group of five was needed to ensure all the students in the class participated.

6. In one of the control group's treatments, a failure in the recording apparatus led to the oral narratives not being recorded. Also, some students' voices were so faint that a complete transcription was not possible. As a result, data were available for only four narrators in this group.

7. Nor was the coefficient that was computed between the percentage of reformulations and the average gain score for the three post-tests statistically significant ($r = .28$; $p = .27$).

8. The experimental group had had prior experience of telling oral narratives, albeit six months previously, as they had been used in a pilot test. As is pointed out in the discussion section, this may explain why the pre-test scores of narrators in this group was notably higher than that in the control group, which had not been used in the pilot test. If this explanation of the difference is correct it points to a strong positive effect for the focussed negotiation treatment and one that is surprisingly durable!

9. In fact, the requests for clarification received by each student were not excessive, varying from a maximum of 11 to a minimum of 1. The teacher who carried out the treatments reports that the requests for clarification did not interfere unduly with the students' performance of the task.

CHAPTER 8

Communicating About Grammar

Sandra Fotos and Rod Ellis

Introduction

A continuing controversy in second language pedagogy is whether grammar should be taught. On the one hand, there are those who adopt a "zero position". They maintain that the teaching of grammar has only a minimal effect on the acquisition of linguistic competence in a second language. Krashen (1985), for instance, argues that "acquisition" only takes place when learners are exposed to roughly tuned input which they are able to comprehend and that "learning" is limited to a few simple portable rules. On the other hand, there are those who argue for grammar teaching. White (1987) claims that some grammatical forms cannot be acquired solely on the basis of comprehensible input and that formal instruction may be necessary to ensure that learners obtain the data they need to acquire these forms.

In contrast to the disagreement over the role of grammar teaching, there is now broad agreement that learners need opportunities to engage in communication based on an exchange of information. As we have seen in the preceding chapters, having learners participate in a variety of tasks which encourage them to negotiate meaning when communication problems arise is considered essential, both to ensure that they obtain sufficient comprehensible input and opportunities for pushed output that facilitate acquisition of linguistic competence, and to provide the real operating conditions needed to develop the kind of strategic competence which is necessary for the development of fluency (Brumfit 1984).

The purpose of this chapter is to demonstrate that it is possible to integrate the teaching of grammar with the provision of opportunities for communication involving an exchange of information. This can be achieved by giving learners grammar tasks which they solve interactively (see Dickens and Wood 1988).

Following a discussion of the roles of formal instruction and communicative language teaching in L2 acquisition, this chapter reports on an exploratory study designed to investigate whether this kind of task is successful in developing L2 linguistic knowledge and in promoting the kinds of interaction which the Interaction Hypothesis (IH) claims will facilitate L2 acquisition.

The role of formal instruction in L2 acquisition

Bialystok (1981) hypothesizes that learners formulate two distinct kinds of knowledge, "explicit" and "implicit" (p. 34). The former refers to knowledge that is analyzed and abstract. It is available to learners as a conscious representation, so that, if called upon, learners are able to say what it is that they know. Explicit knowledge is not the same as metalinguistic knowledge (i.e., knowledge of grammatical terms), although this may help in its articulation. Implicit knowledge refers to knowledge that is intuitive and procedural. It is not consciously available to learners. Native speakers, for example, are generally unable to describe the rules they use to construct actual sentences. Both explicit and implicit knowledge can be used in communication, but there are limits on learners' ability to access the former. Effective participation in face-to-face conversation, for instance, requires implicit knowledge.

A key issue is the relationship between explicit and implicit knowledge, in particular, whether the two types of knowledge are completely distinct (Krashen 1981) or whether one type changes into the other (Sharwood Smith 1981). The position we wish to adopt lies somewhere in between these. Our position is based on studies which have investigated the effects of formal instruction on the acquisition of grammatical knowledge. (For detailed reviews, see Ellis 1994, Larsen-Freeman and Long 1991 and Spada 1998). These studies suggest the following tentative conclusions:

1.   Formal instruction helps to promote more rapid L2 acquisition and also contributes to higher levels of ultimate achievement (Long 1988).

2.   There are psycholinguistic constraints which govern whether attempts to teach learners specific grammatical rules result in, implicit knowledge. Formal instruction may succeed if the learners have reached a stage in the developmental sequence that enables them to process the target structure (Pienemann 1984). Conversely, it will not succeed if learners have not reached the requisite developmental stage.

3. Production practice is not sufficient to overcome these constraints. There is no clear evidence to suggest that having learners produce sentences that model the target structure results in its acquisition as implicit knowledge. Studies by Schumann (1978), Ellis (1984a), Kadia (1988) and VanPatten and Sanz (1995), among others, suggest that formal instruction directed at developmental or difficult grammatical structures has little effect on performance in spontaneous language use. (The term developmental refers here to structures that are acquired in stages and involve the learner passing through a series of transitional phases before mastering the target structure. Examples of developmental structures are negatives and interrogatives.)

4. It is possible, however, that formal instruction directed at relatively simple grammatical rules (such as plural and third-person -*s* or copula be) will be successful in developing implicit knowledge, as such forms do not require the mastery of complex processing operations (Pica 1983; Pienemann 1984).

5. Formal instruction is effective in developing explicit knowledge of grammatical features. There is substantial evidence to suggest that formal instruction is successful if the learning outcomes are measured by means of an instrument that allows for controlled, planned language use (e.g., an imitation test, a sentence-joining task, or a grammaticality judgment task). It is in this kind of language use that learners are able to draw on their explicit knowledge. Studies by Kadia (1988); Lightbown, Spada, and Wallace (1980); Schumann (1978); and Zobl (1985) all support such a conclusion.

6. Formal instruction may work best in promoting acquisition when it is linked with opportunities for natural communication (Spada 1987; Doughty and Williams 1998).

Ellis (1990, 1993) suggests that the main mechanism by which formal instruction works is by developing explicit knowledge of grammatical features which, subsequently, helps learners to acquire implicit knowledge. Explicit knowledge contributes to L2 acquisition in two major ways. First, knowing about a grammatical feature makes the learner more likely to notice that feature in input and, therefore, to acquire it as implicit knowledge. But implicit knowledge will not be achieved until learners are ready to integrate the L2 feature into their interlanguage systems and, in many cases, this will be subject to developmental constraints. Second, explicit knowledge can be used to construct planned utterances, which then serve as input for the language processing mechanisms. The role of explicit knowledge, however, is a limited one because there are restrictions on how much explicit knowledge the typical learner can learn. As indicated above, formal instruction can accelerate knowledge while failing to contribute directly to implicit knowledge of specific linguistic features. Also, explicit knowledge plays only a "monitoring" role in communicative language use. This is a positive role, however, because it accelerates the process of acquiring implicit knowledge and may even be necessary for the acquisition of certain kinds of grammatical rules that evidence suggests (Hammerly 1987) cannot be acquired solely by means of input derived from communicative language use.

This model, shown schematically in Figure 1, has a number of implications for formal instruction. First, it suggests that the goal of formal instruction should be directed at explicit rather than implicit knowledge. Although formal instruction may succeed in developing implicit knowledge of simple rules (see Conclusion 4 above) and also of developmental rules if the learner is ready for these (see Conclusion 2 above), it is not possible to predict easily and with sufficient precision when these conditions have been met. At the present time, it is more useful, therefore, to limit the formal instruction to explicit knowledge.

Second, Ellis' model suggests that formal instruction should be directed at ensuring that learners know about a target structure and can monitor with it (i.e., consciously correct their own erroneous output) but not at enabling them to use the structure in free communication. This in turn suggests that the kind of grammar teaching that is required is one that aims at consciousness-raising rather than practice. Most traditional approaches to grammar teaching are based on providing the learners with opportunities to use the target structure, first in controlled production, and subsequently in free or communicative practice (see Ur 1988). These opportunities constitute "practice". The approach we have in mind is one that downplays the role of production and, instead, emphasizes the role of cognitive understanding. One way in which this can be achieved is by constructing various problem-solving tasks that require learners to consciously

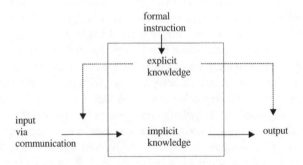

Figure 1. *A model of instructed second language acquisition*

analyze data in order to arrive at an explicit representation of the target feature. Third, this proposed model suggests that formal instruction needs to be accompanied by instruction that provides learners with opportunities for authentic communication (see Conclusion 6 above).

Communicative language teaching and second language acquisition

One of the main aims of communicative language teaching is to provide opportunities for learners to participate in interaction where the primary goal is to exchange meaning rather than to learn the L2. How does this help acquisition?

According to the IH, the comprehensible input which results from attempts to negotiate communication difficulties helps to make salient grammatical features which are problematic to learners and thus facilitates acquisition. The hypothesis emphasizes the importance of interactional adjustments (e.g. requests for clarification and confirmation checks) which arise in two-way communication when a communication problem arises. As we saw in Chapter 1, the later version of the IH (Long 1996) also incorporates a role for 'pushed output' in L2 acquisition, as initially proposed by Swain (1985). Although the IH hypothesis, in its original and revised forms, does not specifically make the distinction between explicit and implicit knowledge, it is clear that, in fact, "acquisition" refers to implicit knowledge.

The comprehensible output hypothesis has been proposed by Swain (1985) as a complement to Long's interaction hypothesis. It claims that learners need the opportunity for pushed output (i.e., output that is precise, coherent, and situationally appropriate) in order to develop advanced levels of grammatical competence. Allen, Swain, Harley, and Cummins (1990) show that classrooms with abundant comprehensible input, such as immersion classrooms, may not typically afford many opportunities for such pushed learner output. This may explain why immersion learners often fail to acquire certain marked grammatical features, such as the distinction between French *imparfait* and *passé composé*. Pica, Holliday, Lewin, and Morgenthaler (1989) have observed that learners produce pushed output when they are required to respond to clarification requests.

A task-based approach to language pedagogy can provide opportunities for the kinds of interaction which have been suggested to promote acquisition. Long (1989) proposes four general points regarding the effectiveness of different task types:

1. Two-way, reciprocal tasks produce more negotiation of meaning than one-way, non-reciprocal tasks, since the former make the exchange of meaning obligatory, whereas the latter do not.

2. Planned tasks, where learners prepare their speech or think about what they will say beforehand, encourage more negotiation than unplanned tasks.
3. Closed tasks, where there is a definite solution or ending, produce more negotiation than open tasks, where there is no clear resolution.
4. Convergent tasks, where the participants must agree on a solution, promote more negotiation than divergent tasks, where different views are permitted.

The adoption of a task-based approach in language pedagogy is closely linked to the use of pair/group work (see Nunan 1989). A survey of research on pair/group work conducted by Long and Porter (1985), together with the results of studies by other researchers (Doughty and Pica 1986; Pica and Doughty 1985; Porter 1986; Rulon and McCreary 1986), indicate that learners produce more in pair/group work, use longer sentences, and do not speak any less grammatically than they do in teacher-fronted lessons. Learners also negotiate meaning more, provided that the task requires information exchange. One disadvantage, though, is that the input they receive from other learners may be less grammatical than what they obtain from the teacher.

Grammar tasks for communication

Formal instruction and communicative language teaching can be integrated through the use of grammar tasks designed to promote communication about grammar. These grammar tasks have two primary aims: to develop explicit knowledge of L2 grammatical features and to provide opportunities for interaction focused on an exchange of information. They can be completed in teacher directed lessons or they can be used in pair/group work in order to increase opportunities for negotiating meaning.

Grammar tasks aim at raising the learner's consciousness about the grammatical properties of the L2. Such tasks are designed to provide multiple opportunities for producing sentences containing the target features. Any production that occurs will be incidental and not directed at "acquiring" the target features, only at "learning" them. Also, the grammar tasks can incorporate a multi-way information gap which requires the exchange of information in order to reach an agreed solution to a problem. The tasks can be designed so that they are closed, i.e., there is a single solution.

An example of such a task is shown in the appendices. The task consists of four task cards (Appendix A) and a task sheet (Appendix B). The task cards list a number of grammatical and ungrammatical sentences illustrating the use of dative verbs. They specify which sentences are correct and which are incorrect. The task sheet provides the learners with some basic grammatical information concerning dative verbs and also supplies them with some useful metalinguistic terminology (e.g., *direct* and *indirect object*). In addition, the task sheet contains a chart to fill in for each of the verbs for which data has been supplied. Finally, it instructs the learners to formulate three rules about the different kinds of dative verbs in terms of the sentence patterns they permit. This task was designed for use in pairs or groups of four learners. It required learners to (a) exchange the information on their task cards in order to complete the chart on the task sheet, (b) talk about the information in order to agree on the results, and (c) report to the class the rules they had formulated.

The study which we now report was based on this task. It was set up to investigate to what extent the task was successful in developing an explicit understanding of how dative verbs work and also whether the task produced the kind of interactions which have been suggested to facilitate L2 acquisition.

The study

The two research questions addressed were:

1. Is study of a specific linguistic feature (dative alternation) through performance of a grammar task as effective as study of the same feature through traditional, teacher-fronted grammar instruction, as measured by test scores on a grammaticality judgment test?
2. Is the grammar consciousness-raising task used here interactive in the sense that its performance results in the same kinds and quantity of interactional adjustments which have been reported in other studies based on reciprocal tasks performed in pairs/groups (see Doughty and Pica 1986)?

Subjects and Design

The subjects for this research were two groups of Japanese EFL college students: first-year English language majors at a women's junior college, determined to be intermediate level on the basis of listening subtest scores of the Michigan English Placement Test and the listening and grammar subtest scores of the Comprehensive English Language Test (CELT), and first-year Business Administration majors, predominantly male, at a private 4-year university. Standardized test scores were not available for the latter group but these students were considered to be "basic level", having received scores below 60% on a department listening exam. In each case, students from two Oral English classes were combined and assigned to one of three groups on a random basis. In one group, the grammar task was performed by groups of four students and dyads in one classroom, and all participation patterns were audio-taped. (Students were divided into two participation patterns to investigate the findings of Doughty and Pica (1986), who reported that pairs of students tended to produce more negotiations than did groups.) In another classroom, a traditional, teacher-fronted grammar lesson was presented in English by the native-speaker instructor to the second group; the lesson was audiotaped only at the university. The remaining students served as the control group and worked on a reading assignment in a separate classroom during the treatments.

The design of the pre- and post-tests, data sheets, and data cards required several steps. As mentioned, the problematic grammar feature selected was dative alternation. This refers to the position of the indirect object in the sentence. There are three patterns of indirect object placement in English verbs. The first allows placement of the indirect object either after the verb or as a prepositional phrase at the end of the sentence ('I gave her the book'; 'I gave the book to her'). The second pattern permits placement of' the indirect object only as a prepositional phrase and generally is the case with Latinate verbs ('The teacher pronounced the word for the students'). The third pattern is applicable only to a limited set of verbs, such as the verb 'ask' meaning inquire, and necessitates placement of the indirect object immediately after the verb ('She asked the teacher a question').

Ten verbs were selected on the basis of observed errors in student usage and, a pilot grammaticality judgment test of 20 sentences, 2 per verb, was designed. A grammaticality judgment test was chosen as our measure of language proficiency because, as we have suggested, testing instruments which allow controlled, planned language promote the use of explicit knowledge. In the pilot study, the test was administered to 18 second-year women's junior college English majors. These students were then given a pilot task sheet which listed the verbs used on the test and required the students to generate two rules explaining the possible position of the indirect object and to place the verbs given under the appropriate rule. The students performed the task in groups of four, and two groups were taped for negotiation counts.

Negotiation was obligatory since each student had a task card with five sentences marked correct or incorrect which she had to read to the other group members, who noted the position of the indirect object on their task sheets.

Negotiations were observed to consist of comprehension checks, clarification requests, confirmation requests, and repetitions as students listened to and tried to understand the sentences being read, and checked whether they were correct or incorrect. After students performed the task, which took 30 minutes, the same test was given again as a post-test. A significant difference was obtained for pre- and post-test scores (n = 18, pretest m = 15.94, post-test m = 19.17, paired t = −10.825, $df = 17$, $p < .001$) and negotiation counts were greater than 15 for each group.

The test was then redesigned to exclude items which were not problematic and the task sheet and task cards were rewritten. Figures 2 and 3 display the final form of the task sheet and task cards, and the grammaticality judgment test is included in Appendix C. These were administered to the two groups of subjects described above. Two weeks after each grammar treatment, the same test was administered again as a final test to measure longer term learning.

The content of the traditional grammar lesson was identical to the information given on the task sheet and task cards and took the same amount of time to cover — 20 minutes. The teacher wrote the correct and incorrect sentences on the board and pointed out the placement of the indirect object, asking the students whether they thought the sentences were correct or incorrect. The teacher then provided the answer and, at the end of the lesson, wrote out the three rules governing indirect object placement, and indicated which verbs fit each rule. The board was then erased, and the post-test administered.

Audio recordings were made of all groups and dyads and, for consistency, were transcribed for 10 minutes from the same starting point on all tapes, the reading of the first sentence. Negotiations were considered to consist of the following:

1. Clarification requests, made by listeners when they haven't understood (e.g., 'What is question?' or 'Which one is correct?')
2. Confirmation requests, made by listeners when they believe they have understood but want to make sure (e.g., 'Is it incorrect sentence?' or 'Plan is indirect object?')
3. Comprehension checks, made by the speaker to be certain that the listener has understood (e.g., 'Do you have any questions?' or 'Are you satisfied?')
4. Repetitions, which in the data examined consisted largely of restatements of another subject's utterance as a type of confirmation check (e.g., 'Correct?' or 'Is it incorrect?')
5. Request for repetition, which consisted of the listener's requests for the speaker to repeat a previous utterance (e.g., 'Once more please' or 'Please repeat').

Results

Statistical analyses of differences in pretest and control means were performed using a one-way analysis of variance (ANOVA). Paired t tests were used to examine the significance of differences between pre- and post-test scores and unpaired t tests for determining the significance of differences between post-test scores for the two treatments and between the treatments and the control group. A one-way chi-square test corrected for continuity (Hatch and Farhady 1982) was used to examine the significance of any differences between negotiation counts for the groups and the dyads.

Statistical Analysis of Test Scores

Table 1 gives the pretest, post-test, and final test score means for all treatment groups and controls. Because of absences, the number of students taking the final test at the university differs from the initial number.

For students of the women's junior college, no significant difference existed among the three pretest means as determined by a one-way analysis of variance (ANOVA) (F[2, 53] = .5309, $p > .05$). However, differences were significant at the .05 level between the means of the scores of the pre- and post-test for the task treatment (paired t = −6.497, df = 17) and for the grammar treatment (paired t = −4.535, df = 17), as well as for both treatments' post-test scores compared with the control group's post-test scores (task vs. control: unpaired t = 6.926, df = 36; grammar vs. control: unpaired t = 7.644, df = 35). It is notable that no significant difference was found to exist between the means of the post-test

Table 1. *Mean scores for the pretest, post-test, and final test*

	Pretest	Post-test	Final test	p*
Women's Jr. college (n = 56)				
Task treatment (n = 18)	14.39	18.94	16.33	<.05
Grammar treatment (n = 18)	115.00	18.69	17.83	<.05
Control (n = 20)	14.20	14.25	14.50	*ns*
University (n = 34)				
Task treatment (n = 12)	13.00	16.17	15.20 (n = 10)	<.05
Grammar treatment (n = *I*o)	12.70	19.10	16.83 (tn = 6)	<.05
Control (n = 12)	12.17	12.42	11.63 (n = 8)	ns

* Significance refers to paired t tests between pre- and post-test means

scores of the task treatment and the grammar treatment (unpaired t = −.0574, df = 33, p = .570). Regarding the final test given 2 weeks after the treatments, no significant difference existed between the scores of the post-test and the final test for the grammar treatment, indicating that no significant loss of proficiency occurred (paired t = 1.399, df = 17, p = .180). However, for the task treatment, the difference between the post-test and the final test 2 weeks later was significant (paired t = 3.803, df = 17, p < .05), indicating a loss of proficiency. Nevertheless, comparing the results of the final test to the initial pretest revealed a significant difference (paired t = −2.475, df = 17, p < .05) between the scores before performing the task and the proficiency remaining after 2 weeks. No significant difference was found among the control group scores (Hotelling's T2 = .19231, p = .590).

For the students at the university, the one-way ANOVA indicated no significant difference existed among the three pretest means (F[2, 31] = .3345, p > .05), although there was a significant difference between the pretest scores for the basic non-English majors and the junior college intermediate-level English majors (unpaired t = 5.562, df = 4, p < .05), indicating a significant difference in initial proficiency levels between the two groups of students. Differences were significant at the .05 level between the means of the pre- and post-test scores for both the task treatment (paired t = −3.245, df = 11) and the grammar treatment (paired t = −8.552, df = 9), as well as for both treatments' post-test scores compared with the control group's post-test scores (task vs. control: unpaired t = 2.837, df = −22, p < .05; grammar vs. control: unpaired t = 5.094, (If = : 20, p < .05). However, unlike the results obtained with the intermediate English majors, the intermediate post-test scores for the grammar treatment were significantly higher than the task treatment's post-test scores (unpaired t = −2.449, df == 20, p < .05).

Comparison of the University students' final test scores with the previous scores was complicated by the fact that fewer students took the final test. For the task group, the difference between the pretest scores and the final test scores is not significant (paired t =: −2.141, (df = 9, P = .061) at the designated level of .05, although the value of p was quite close, at .061. Nor was the difference between the post-test and the final test significant (paired t = 1.118, df = 9, p = .293), suggesting that there was no substantial loss of proficiency between the two tests in the reduced sample. However, the differences between both pre- and post-test scores and the final test scores were significant for the grammar group (pretest vs. final test paired t = −2.652, df = 5, p < .05; post-test vs. final test paired t = −2.936, df = 5, p < .05), indicating a significant gain in proficiency over the pretest but a subsequent significant loss 2 weeks later. Again, no significant differences among the control group scores were observed (Hotelling's

T2 = .3343, p = .774).

Combining the task treatments from both schools gives a total of 20 students performing in groups of four, and 10 students in dyads. No significant difference (unpaired t = 362, df = 28, p = .362) was found between the post-test scores of students, regardless of whether they performed the task in groups or in dyads.

Quantitative and qualitative analysis of negotiations

Table 2 gives the total negotiation frequencies in both English (the L2) and Japanese (the L1), and the negotiation frequencies in English only during the 10 minute sample period for the groups and the dyads for the task treatment and the grammar treatment at each school.

No significant difference in the number of negotiations made by the two types of participation pattern was found for the total number of negotiations produced (X2 = .253, df = 1, p > .05) or for negotiations in the L2 only (X2 = 2.542, df = 1, p > .05) produced by the four groups and four dyads which were recorded performing the task. At the junior college three pairs and three dyads participated in the task, but because of mechanical failure the data for one group and one dyad could not be obtained.

Although the grammar treatment at the women's junior college was not taped, the teacher stated that no student made any comment, except to answer yes or no when asked if sentences were correct. The grammar treatment at the university was taped, and there was no audible participation by any student during the 20 minute presentation.

At the women's junior college, where the students were strongly requested to use only English during the task, negotiations were almost entirely in English, with only one negotiation each in Japanese for the groups and dyads respectively. At the university, however, where the teacher did not emphasize the need to use only English, the proportion of the L1 used was much higher, with 13 negotiations in English and 31 in Japanese for the groups, and 50 in English, and 18 in

Table 2. *Total negotiations and L2-only negotiations for the different participation patterns*

School	Grammar	Task group (Total/L2 only)	Task-dyad (Total/L2 only)	Total/L2 only
Junior college (n = 30)	0 (n = 18)	49/48 (n = 8)	33/32 (n = 4)	82/80
University (n = 22)	0 (11 = 10)	44/13 (ti = 8)	68/50 (n = 4)	112/63

Japanese for the pairs.

Finally, the negotiations made by both groups were found to be qualitatively limited in either language and consisted of asking whether a sentence was correct or incorrect, asking for a repetition of a sentence, part of a sentence, or a single lexical item, or making a comprehension check, as in the following portions of protocols from a university group and dyad and a junior college group and dyad:

1. University Group
   A: Ready? (Student reads sentence and indicates correctness.)
   B: Yes. (Other three reply in unison.)
   A: All right? (Student reads next sentence and indicates correctness.)
         Huh'? (One student only.)
   A: (Student repeats sentence.) One more time?

2. University Dyad
   A: (Student reads sentence.)
   B: Correct?
   A: Yes. (Student reads next sentence,.)
   B: Please again.
   A: (Student repeats sentence.)
   B: Incorrect?
   A: Yes. (Student reads next sentence,)
   B: Correct?
   A: Yes.

3. Junior College Group
   A: (Student reads sentence.) Are you satisfied?
   B: Yes. (Other three reply in unison.)
   A: (Student reads next sentence.) Do you have any questions?
   B: No. (Other three reply in unison.)
   A: Ready?
   B: Yes. (Other three reply in unison.)
   A: (Student reads next sentence.)

4. Junior College Dyad
   A: (Student reads sentence and indicates correctness.)
   B: Is it the answer?
   A: Yes. (Student reads next sentence but does not indicate correctness.)
   B: Is it correct?
   A: Yes.
   B: Once more please.
   A: (Student repeats sentence.)

B: *Plan* is indirect object?
A: Yes.

Discussion

The Grammar Task Versus the Grammar Lesson

The first research question was to compare the effectiveness of a task approach and a traditional grammar lesson. It should be recalled that no discussion of the grammar point was included in the task treatment except for what was written on the task sheet and task cards, and the students' mastery of the form was gained solely from performance of the task activity. For the English majors at the junior college, the initial mean percent correct for the task group was 72%, which increased to 95% on the post-test, but then dropped to 82% after 2 weeks — a net gain in proficiency of 10%. In comparison, the grammar-lesson students started at an initial mean of 75% correct, increased to 93% correct after the lesson, then decreased to 89% correct after 2 weeks — a net gain of 14%. Whereas the post-test scores of the task group and the grammar-lesson group were not statistically different, the task group's mean score on the final test 2 weeks later was significantly lower than the mean score for the grammar-lesson group but was nonetheless significantly higher than the pretest score. Thus, the task appeared to have functioned equally well as the grammar lesson in the short term, and was only slightly less effective in maintaining proficiency than the grammar lesson after 2 weeks.

For the basic level non-English-major university students, the initial mean percent correct for the task group was 65%, which increased significantly to 81% after the task, a gain of 16%. In comparison, the grammar group's initial mean percent correct was 64%, which increased to 96% after the grammar lesson, a gain of 32%. Thus, the gain in proficiency for the task group was significantly lower than for the grammar-lesson group. Longer-term proficiency gains for the grammar-lesson group were more difficult to assess due to absences. However, even with fewer students, the grammar-lesson group showed maintenance of significant proficiency gains after 2 weeks although the task-treatment group did not.

Two possible explanations for the less successful results of task performance by this group compared with the English majors are (a) their lack of familiarity with pair/group work, and (b) as indicated by their comments and questions during the audio recordings, their imperfect understanding of the goals and procedures of the task, information which was presented to them in the second language. It is likely, therefore, that proficiency gains would have been higher with a more detailed explanation of the requirements of the task and previous experience in the pair/group participation pattern. In contrast, the English majors were familiar with both group work and performance of information-gap activities, and were better able to comprehend the L2 explanation of the task procedures. Furthermore, to prevent the teacher from giving formal instruction about the grammar point, neither group of students received subsequent teacher feedback on the success of their task work. It is reasonable to assume that the learning of explicit knowledge of a grammatical point gained from performance of a grammar task would have been enhanced by feedback concerning how effectively the groups had performed the task.

As a final consideration, it is necessary to establish that there was no practice effect occurring when students took the same test three times, otherwise the favorable results reported above regarding the effectiveness of the grammar task in promoting proficiency gains are questionable. First, the three test scores for the control groups at both the junior college and the university showed no significant variation and, furthermore, the final control group score was actually lower than the previous two control group scores at the university. Second, a similar observed decline in test scores for both task and grammar treatment groups after 2 weeks is additional evidence against the operation of a practice effect.

The Grammar Task and Negotiation of Meaning

One of the problems with communicative task performance is that there have been few ways other than analysis of the nature and frequency of interactions to determine the success of the task in promoting language acquisition. On the other hand, with task types such as listening or reading comprehension tasks, the students' performance in answering questions serves as a criterion-referenced indication of the success of the task. With the type of grammar task presented here, it is possible to test for proficiency gains as well as to analyze the quality and quantity of interactions. The second research question addressed in this report concerned the amount and qualitative nature of the negotiations produced by the grammar task.

The mean number of negotiations reported in a previous study (Doughty and Pica 1986) for performance of a two-way information gap task during a 10-minute period by three groups and three dyads combined was 64. With the grammar task investigated here, the total negotiation counts in both the LI and L2 for groups and dyads combined were 82 for the junior college and 112 for the university. If the LI negotiations are removed, the L2 negotiation counts come to a combined total of 80 for the junior college groups and dyads (2 of each) and

63 for the university groups and dyads (2 of each). These figures are similar to the average combined count of 64 previously reported for a greater number of groups/dyads. Thus, the grammar task appears to promote similar amounts of interaction in the limited data presented here.

The Doughty and Pica study also hypothesized that in terms of amounts of negotiations, dyads would produce the most, followed by groups, with the least being produced by the teacher-fronted activity. This pattern was found in the data here, with no negotiations produced by the grammar lesson, 61 L2 negotiations produced by the four groups, and 82 L2 negotiations produced by the four dyads. Although the difference between these figures was not significant, the pattern for the junior college indicates that groups produced more negotiations than dyads.

Why did the university dyads produce so many more negotiations? Examination of the transcripts shows that the extra negotiations made by the university dyads consisted of the words *correct or incorrect* asked as confirmation requests, as shown in Example 2. In the junior college transcripts, such usages were rare since the sentence readers usually supplied the information to the students who were listening. As mentioned, task performance took 20 minutes, with the bulk of the negotiations occurring during the first 10 minutes, during the reading of the sentences. During the final portion, the students were relatively quiet as they wrote out the rules and did not discuss the nature of the rules in either language. An explanation for this finding is that the students, who had 6 years of previous English study, already possessed explicit linguistic knowledge of the general grammar rules governing English dative alternation and did not have to consult on this point.

We must now consider the broader question of whether the qualitatively limited negotiations observed during performance of this task can be regarded as requests for modifications of input in the sense that the term has been used (see Doughty and Pica 1986; Long 1983b; Pica and Doughty 1985; Pica et al. 1989). Again, it must be recalled that the students heard their interlocutors read a sentence, and requested one of the following: (a) a repetition of the sentence or of part of the sentence, (b) an explanation of an unfamiliar word in the sentence, or (c) confirmation of their guess that the sentence was either correct or incorrect. Their interlocutors' response options were to read the sentence again, say yes or no regarding correctness, repeat the questionable word, or make their own comprehension checks, as shown in Examples 1 and 3. Since the students reading the sentences were not originating the language, there was no modification of output taking place and the language was "planned" to the extreme. Does such limited discourse represent negotiated interaction?

We suggest that the exchanges observed during performance of this particular grammar task are within the limits of the construct because the focus of the interaction was on meaning, and the negotiations performed were essential to the comprehension of meaning. However, it is clear that a more detailed investigation of the qualitative nature of the negotiated interactions promoted by different types of grammar tasks in different settings is an important future research question. This point is equally true with regard to the quality of interactions analyzed in other published studies. Further research in the area of negotiated interaction must deal with qualitative aspects of the data, particularly in situations where both interlocutors are non-native speakers.

Conclusion

This chapter has presented the case for use of a particular type of language learning task — one which encourages communication about grammar. It has been argued that such grammar tasks may contribute to L2 acquisition in two ways. They may contribute *directly* by providing opportunities for the kind of communication which is believed to promote the acquisition of implicit knowledge, and they may also contribute indirectly by enabling learners to develop explicit knowledge of L2 rules which will later facilitate the acquisition of implicit knowledge.

The results of the exploratory study reported in the previous section lend some support to these claims. This study demonstrated that Japanese EFL learners at the college level were able to increase their knowledge of a difficult L2 rule by completing a grammar task. It also showed that the interaction which resulted from grammar task performance was characterized by a similar quantity of conversational modifications to those reported to occur in other two-way information-gap tasks. The learners performing this task had the opportunity to learn about grammar while taking part in communication centered on an exchange of information.

In addition, a number of considerations have been raised. First, the grammar task used here did not result in the same level of longer-term learning as did the traditional, teacher-fronted grammar lesson. As mentioned, possible reasons for this may have been the learners' lack of experience in working in small groups and the absence of teacher feedback on their solution to the task. Clearly, though, it is important to establish that group work discussion can result in development of explicit knowledge, given the importance attached to this in the theoretical framework illustrated in Figure 1. We still need to discover whether and how, group work can be made as effective as teacher-directed explanations in developing explicit knowledge.

Second, although the grammar task produced a large number of interactional modifications, the nature of the exchanges which took place was rather mechanical, as the examples given in the previous section illustrate. This leads us to ask whether it is the quantity of speech modifications that is important for acquiring implicit knowledge, as suggested by the Interaction Hypothesis, or whether it is some yet undetermined qualitative aspects of communication which are more important (see Bygate 1988). The nature of the relationship between interaction and language acquisition is still poorly understood.

Grammar tasks which emphasize consciousness-raising rather than practice appear to be an effective type of classroom activity, and their use is supported by what is currently known about the way a second language is acquired. Furthermore, such tasks provide serious content, in contrast to the trivial content of many information-gap activities, and they accommodate learners who believe that it is important to learn about grammar. They provide opportunities to communicate in the L2 in groups or pairs, and they encourage an active, discovery-oriented approach on the part of the learners, which accords with current views about good educational practice. It should be possible to develop a wide range of grammar tasks, including those which focus on sociolinguistic learning problems as well as on purely formal problems, such as the grammatical feature which was the focus of this study. Hopefully, through experimentation, it will be possible to devise tasks which result in interaction which is qualitatively richer than what we obtained in this exploratory study.

Grammar tasks also have their limitations, however. Some learners may not wish to talk about grammar. They may find it a boring topic, or they may find it difficult to discuss because they lack the basic metalinguistic knowledge needed to do so. Learners may resort extensively to the use of their first language during a grammar task, as is seen in the case of the university group in this study. However, with training in task performance, it should be possible to overcome this limitation, as the English language majors at the junior college demonstrated. It is also possible that grammar tasks are less suitable for beginners, partly because such learners are not able to talk in the second language, and partly because grammar as a discussion topic is less appropriate at this level. In general, we suggest that grammar tasks seem best suited for intermediate/ advanced learners who are motivated to study grammar as subject matter.

The use of communicative, problem-solving grammar tasks remains an intriguing proposal in need of further study. Future research will need to address a number of issues. These include (a) developing different formats for grammar tasks, (b) examining the effect of these different formats on the quality and quantity of interaction, (c) examining the effect of the different formats on gains in explicit knowledge, (d) investigating the effect of teacher feedback on the learner's solutions to grammar tasks on learning, and (e) investigating the role of metalinguistic knowledge in task performance.

Appendix A. Task Cards

Students in groups of 4–one different card to each member
Students in pairs-two different cards to each member

1.	Correct:	I asked my friend a question.
1.	Incorrect:	She asked a question to her mother.
2.	Correct:	Kimiko reviewed the lesson for John.
2.	Incorrect:	Kimiko reviewed John the lesson.
3.	Correct:	The teacher calculated the answers for the students.
3.	Incorrect:	The teacher calculated students' answers.
4.	Correct:	The secretary reported the problem to her boss.
4.	Incorrect:	The student reported the teacher the matter.
5.	Correct:	I offered her a cup of tea.
5.	Correct:	I offered a cup of tea to the president.
6.	Correct:	The teacher pronounced the difficult word for the class.
6.	Incorrect:	The teacher pronounced the class the difficult word.
7.	Correct:	I bought many presents for my family.
7.	Correct:	I bought my family several presents.
5.	Correct:	She cooked a delicious dinner for us.
8.	Correct:	She cooked us a wonderful meal.
9.	Correct:	She suggested a plan to me.
9.	Incorrect:	She suggested me a good restaurant.
10.	Correct:	The teacher repeated the question for the student.
11.	Incorrect:	The teacher repeated the student the question.

Appendix B. Task Sheets

There are some verbs in English which can have two objects. One of the objects is called the *direct object. The* other is called the *indirect object.* An indirect object names the person for whom the action of the verb is performed:

	indirect object	direct object
She wrote	Susan	a letter.

Different verbs may have the objects in different order, and this is often a problem for students of English. The following exercise will help you understand some confusing verbs.

Directions:

In groups, you are to study correct and incorrect sentences using different verbs. You all have different sentences. You must read your sentences to the rest of the group. *Do not show your sentences to the other members. Only read the sentences as many times as necessary.* Work together as a group and decide on the basis of the correct and incorrect sentences where the indirect objects should be located. Fill out the rest of this page. Choose one student to report your results to the rest of the class. Please speak only in English during this exercise.

Verbs: Possible correct order of direct and indirect object
1.   asked:
2.   reviewed:
3.   calcuated
4.   reported
5.   offered:
6.   pronounced:
7.   bought:
8.   cooked:
9.   suggested:
10. repeated

Conclusion: Write 3 rules concerning the possible order of objects.

Rule 1: _____
verbs which follow this rule: _____
Rule 2: _____
verbs which follow this rule: _____
Rule 3: _____
verbs which follow this rule: _____

Appendix C. Grammaticality judgment test on dative alternation

Directions: Read the sentences. Decide if they are correct or incorrect. Write (0) if correct, or (X) if incorrect.

1.   She asked the class a question.
2.   She asked a question to the class.
3.   She reviewed the sentences for Mary.
4.   She reviewed Mary the sentences.
5.   She calculated John the math problem.
6.   She calculated the math problem for John.
7.   She reported the police the problem.
8.   She reported the problem to the police.
9.   She offered her friend a chocolate.
10. She offered a chocolate to her friend.
11. She pronounced the difficult word for me.
12. She pronounced me the difficult word.
13. She bought her friend a dress.
14. She bought a dress for her friend.
15. They cooked a meal for their friends.
16. They cooked their friends a meal.
17. They suggested the children an idea.
18. They suggested an idea to the children.
19. She repeated the word for me.
20. She repeated me the word.

Section 4

Pedagogical Perspectives

The previous sections have been primarily concerned with theoretical aspects of interaction as it relates to second language (L2) acquisition, although Section Three also dealt with pedagogical issues. The chapter in this section addresses directly how teaching can create the kinds of interactional opportunities likely to promote acquisition.

There are two ways in which we can view teaching; the **external** and **internal** views. When we adopt an external view of teaching we see it in terms of curricular goals (the syllabus), materials for realizing these goals, classroom activities (e.g. 'drills' or 'information gap tasks'), methodological procedures, viewed either in macro terms (e.g. small group work vs. lockstep teaching) or in micro-terms (e.g. using situational props to drill a grammatical structure) and devices for measuring student progress. The external view of language teaching is enshrined in handbooks for language teachers (e.g. Harmer 1985, Ur 1996). It provides the main content for courses on syllabus design, language teaching materials, TESOL methods and language testing. It is what teachers orient to when they are in the process of learning how to teach a second/foreign language. When teachers contemplate and discuss language teaching they are likely to adopt an external view. It constitutes the traditional way of looking at teaching.

An internal view of teaching requires us to see teaching as an interactional event — or, more properly, as a series of interactional events. Teachers talk to students. Students sometimes talk to teachers and, more often perhaps, talk to each other. How is all this talk accomplished? What kinds of speech events do teachers and students enact when they talk to each other? In what way does classroom talk vary from one interactional event to another? What are the factors that cause this variation? To think of teaching in this way calls for a very different vocabulary — we need to talk about 'speech acts', 'turn-taking', 'questioning behaviour', 'negotiation', 'exchange structure', 'topic control' etc. Such terms help us to describe how interactional events are constructed as teachers actually teach. They provide a language for talking about teaching as a *process* of classroom communication and what Barnes (1976) has called the 'hidden curriculum'. However, it is not a language with which teachers are generally familiar. For this reason, teachers rarely conceive of their teaching in terms of this internal view.

There are, however, good reasons for adopting an internal view of teaching. One is that ideas about teaching that seem different when viewed externally may in fact turn out to be very similar when examined internally. Also, ideas that are apparently similar may turn out to be very different in classroom process terms. In other words, the constructs that inform an external view of teaching may lack validity when viewed from an internal perspective.

Teachers, I would argue, need to adopt both an external and an internal perspective. The external perspective is important for *planning* lessons. Teachers need to decide on the aims of their lessons, the particular activities they are going to use, and the methodological procedures they will employ. The internal perspective is important for understanding how what teachers accomplish through their teaching creates conditions in which language learning can take place. For, ultimately, teaching is about managing classroom interaction to provide opportunities for learning (cf. Allwright 1984a).

Theory and research relating to the roles of interaction in L2 acquisition clearly speak to an internal view of teaching and it is such a view that is adopted in the following chapter. Through the notion of 'discourse control' I suggest ways in which teachers can bring about the kinds of interaction that theory and research suggest are important for L2 acquisition.

CHAPTER 9

Making the Classroom Acquisition Rich

Rod Ellis

Introduction

This chapter will explore one particular aspect of classroom interaction that appears to be central to understanding how interaction creates opportunities for language learning. This is **discourse control**. I shall begin by discussing what is meant by this term and then illustrate how discourse control affects a number of qualitative aspects of classroom discourse. Subsequently, I shall draw on different theories of language learning to support my central thesis, namely that giving learners the chance to control the discourse helps to make the classroom acquisition rich.

'Topic' and 'activity' in classroom discourse

The term 'discourse topic' is not easy to define. Brown and Yule (1983) consider it a 'pretheoretical notion'. McCarthy (1991) suggests that 'topic' can be defined in different ways — formally (i.e. as stretches of talk bounded by transactional markers such as 'right', 'now', 'by the way'), semantically (i.e. by using words or phrases to state what is being talked about), interactively (i.e. in terms of whether an utterance produced by one speaker is relevant to an utterance produced by another speaker, in terms of cohesion (i.e. a topic can be said to end when patterns of cohesion peter out) or pragmatically (i.e. whether the participants in a conversation perceive themselves to be talking on a single topic). McCarthy suggests that the semantic definition predominates in language teaching, so, as my perspective here is a pedagogic one, I will adopt this definition. The terms 'discourse topic' will be taken to refer to what the speakers are talking about.

Clearly, whenever people talk to each other they have to talk about something. Sometimes, however, what they are talking about seems to be immaterial — as, for example, in phatic communication. In such cases, saying what the topic is (e.g. 'the weather') does not really tell us what the conversation is about. This is because it is not what we are talking about but what we are doing that is important. This distinction between what is talked about and what is done in a conversation is also relevant to the language classroom. As Van Lier (1988) has pointed out, talk in the classroom is often focussed on how things are said or what is done rather than on what is talked about. He uses the term 'activity' to refer to this aspect of discourse. He suggests that classroom discourse can be classified according to the extent to which the emphasis is on 'topic' or 'activity'. I would like to explore this distinction by examining two extracts from sequences of classroom interaction.

Extract (1) consists of a stretch of talk that took place in the context of a language drill designed to teach students how to use markers of plurality (as in 'These are pencils.'). We might say that the topic of this sequence is 'pencils' and 'rulers' but this does not capture what is going on. This is because the topic is not really what matters here (the participants could just as well be talking about 'books' or 'shoes'). In this sequence it is 'activity' that is dominant — the display of grammatically correct sentences.

Extract 1
(The teacher is drilling the student in the use of plurals).

1. T: Now, Tasleem.
2.   What is this? (T. holds up pen.)
3.   S: This is a pen.
4. T: What are these? (T holds up two pens.)
5.   S: This are a pen.
6. T: These are _____?
7.   S: Are pens.
8. T: What is this? (Teacher holds up a ruler.)
9.   S: This is a ruler.
10. T: What are these? (Teacher holds up two rulers.)
11.   S: This is a.. are..
12.   This are a rulers.
13. T: These are rulers.
14. T: What are these?
15.   S: This are a rulers.
16. T: Not 'a'.

17.   These are _____?
18.   S: Rulers.
19. T: Rulers.
20.   S: Rulers.
(From Ellis 1984b: 103–4)

Extract (2) is taken from an ESL lesson where the students have just finished reading a newspaper article about making a Hollywood movie. Here it is clear what the teacher and the student are talking about — 'favorite movies'. There is a definite topic. In a sense, though, the sequence also involves 'activity', as the teacher's pedagogic goal is to provide an opportunity for the students to practise using English, albeit much more freely than is the case in Extract (1). It is, in fact, rare for discourse in the language classroom to avoid some degree of orientation towards 'activity', given that the mental set of the participants is towards using language to learn rather than to communicate. Nevertheless, the primary orientation in Extract (2) is towards 'topic' rather than 'activity'.

Extract 2
The teacher is asking students about their favourite movies).

1. T: Vin, have you ever been to the movies?
         What is your favourite movie?
2.   V: 'Big'.
3. T: 'Big'. OK, that's a good movie. That
         was about a little boy inside a
         big man, wasn't it?
4.   V: Yeah, boy get surprise all the time.
5. T: Yes, he was surprised, wasn't
         he. Usually little boys don't do
         things that men do, do they?
6.   V: No, little boy no drink.
7. T: That's right, little boys
         don't drink.
(From K. Johnson (1995: 23).

Another way of capturing the difference between the nature of the discourses in these two extracts is in terms of the descriptive framework proposed by Willis (1992). She suggests that a basic distinction can be made between 'outer' and 'inner' language in the classroom. Outer language consists of utterances which provide a framework for the lesson, enabling pedagogic activities to take place. Such utterances are produced by both the teacher and the students. Inner language consists of those utterances produced during the course of a pedagogic activity; it is comprised of the samples of language designated as the goal of the activity. There are no examples of outer language in extracts 1 and 2 but it is not difficult to supply some. For example, in extract 1, the teacher might have prefaced the drill by saying something like 'Right. I'm going to hold up some things and I want you to tell me what they are. Ready.' while in extract 2, the teacher might say 'Okay, now we've read about how to make a film, let's talk a bit about your favourite films'. As presented, though, extracts 1 and 2 consist entirely of inner language. However, they differ in the kind of inner language they illustrate. Willis further distinguishes 'pseudo' and 'free' inner language. Pseudo inner language is strongly oriented towards activity; free inner language is oriented more towards topic.

These distinctions — between topic and activity and between inner pseudo and inner free language — are important for understanding how the classroom can afford qualitatively different discourses that can have a significant effect on language learning.

Discourse control

In natural settings (i.e, outside the classroom) we can distinguish two broad types of discourse — that which is co-constructed by participants who function as social equals and that which arises out of unequal encounters. Conversation is an example of the former; a job interview is a good example of the second. These two basic types of discourse differ in terms of how a topic is chosen and how that topic is subsequently developed. How the discourse is controlled and managed by the participants influences the nature of the talk in various qualitative ways.

A good example of these differences can be found in the samples of mother-child talk discussed by Wells and Montgomery (1981). Mothers can treat their children as equal partners in conversation (as in extract 3) or they can assume a more tutorial role (as in extract 4). The resulting discourses are very different.

Extract 3
(Mark is talking to his mother about a man who was in their garden and has just left).

1.	M:	Where man gone?
		Where man gone?
	M:	I don't know. I expect he's gone inside because it's snowing.
3.	M:	Where man gone?
4.	M:	In the house?
5.	M:	Uh?

6.		M:	Into the house.
7.	M:	No. No. Gone to shop, mummy.	
8.		M:	Gone where?
9.	M:	Gone shop.	
10.		M:	To the shop?
11.	M:	Yeh.	
12.		M:	What's he going to buy?
13.	M:	er — biscuits.	
14.		M:	Biscuits — mm.
15.	M:	Uh?	
16.		M:	Mm. What else?
17.	M:	er– meat.	
18.		M:	Mm.
19.	M:	Meat. er — sweeties.	
		Buy a big — bag — sweets.	
20.		M:	Buy sweets?
21.	M:	Yeah. M — er — buy — man	
		— the man — buy — sweets.	
22.		M:	Will he?
23.	M:	Yeah.	

(From Wells and Montgomery 1981).

Extract (3) is characterized by a focus on topic, rather than activity. That is, we feel that Mark and his mother are taking part in a real conversation where what is said is important. It is the child that nominates the topic with the question 'Where man gone?' and it is the child who stays in control of the topic throughout. The mother helps the conversation along in a number of ways. She requests clarification (e.g. 'Gone where?') and confirmation (e.g. 'To the shop? and 'Buy sweets?') and she encourages Mark to extend the topic (e.g. 'What else?'). This discourse, then, is highly collaborative in nature, with the child in charge of the topic and thereby how the discourse proceeds and the mother playing a supporting role, encouraging and helping the child to say what he wants to say. Mark's utterances during this sequence become progressively more linguistically complex.

Extract 4
(Thomas is talking to his mother about some people who visited them last weekend).

1.	T:	Biscuits.
	M:	Those were got specially — we had visitors at the weekend.
		Who came to see — Tommy? Who came in a car?
3.	T:	See Grannie Irene — e — car

4.	M:	Grannie Irene's coming. But who came last weekend?
5. T:		Auntie Gail *in — a — train*.
6.	M:	*Auntie* Gail's coming. They're coming on the train — yes.
7. T:		Colin in -a train.
8.	M:	Colin — Colin er — and Anne came in a <car>, didn't they?
9. T:		Colin — Anne Colin — Anne
10.	M:	Yes.
11. T:		Colin — Anne Colin — Anne
12.	M:	Colin and Anne came in the train.
13. T:		In train. Auntie train.
14.	M:	No, not auntie train — darling. Auntie Gail — and Grannie Irene — are coming on the train — on Friday.
15. T:		Auntie Gail — in — a -train.

Extract (4), it seems to me, involves more of a focus on activity than topic. We have here 'pseudo inner language' not so different from that found in language classrooms. Although, the sequence begins with Thomas nominating a topic ('Biscuits') which elicits a contingent response from his mother, she then nominates a topic of her own ('Who came to see Tommy?'), which relates to a displaced event rather than to the here-and-now of Thomas' topic. What follows is an attempt by the mother to get Thomas to display the 'right answer' to her question. The mother takes complete charge, insisting on her own topic even though Thomas does not seem able to go along with it ('But who came last weekend?') and correcting Thomas when he is wrong ('No — not auntie train, darling.'). Here, then, it is the mother who establishes the goal of the conversation and who insists on it being achieved, even though the goal is apparently beyond the linguistic (and perhaps cognitive) abilities of her child. Thomas' utterances in this sequence are repetitive and linguistically very simple, similar to the kind of utterances found in a language drill.

In the classroom, it is the teacher who typically takes control of the discourse. When the focus is on activity (as in extract (1)), the teacher is more or less obliged to dictate how the interaction will proceed to ensure that the language produced by the learners conforms to the goal of the activity. This control is achieved by means of a particular exchange structure where the teacher initiates, the learner responds and the teacher then supplies feedback of some kind. This IRF exchange structure is ubiquitous in classrooms where the interactions are activity-centred. It is evident in extract (1). When the focus is on topic in the classroom the teacher is still likely to remain in control of the discourse. The teacher typically nominates the topic that is to be talked about. She is also likely to try to manage the way in which it develops. Thus extract (2) also consists of a series of IRF exchanges. In this respect it differs markedly from the discourse structure found in extract (3), where Mark does the initiating and the mother responds and where there is no separate feedback move.

However, topic-oriented classroom interaction can afford opportunities for the learners to take control of the discourse, if only for a short time. This involves what Van Lier (1988) has called **topicalisation**–the process by which learners take up what a teacher (or another learner) has said and make it into a sub-topic of their own.

Extract (5), which is in fact a continuation of extract (2), illustrates this process. Here a learner, Wang, takes the initiative by naming a film he wants to talk about. Note that he does this by taking rather then by being offered a turn. The teacher responds in a similar way to Mark's mother — by encouraging Wang to elaborate on the topic. In particular, the teacher uses expansions to help Wang say what he wants to say. The resulting discourse structure is also more like that in extract (2) — i.e., it departs from the standard IRF structure. This seems to help Wang as, like Mark, his utterances become progressively more well-formed as the interaction continues. At the end of the sequence, however, the teacher takes over control of the discourse once more, perhaps so as to allow other learners in the class the opportunity to participate. She achieves this skillfully. She might have resorted to outer language (e.g. by saying 'OK, does anyone else have a film he wants to talk about?') but she maintains the free inner language of the topic Wang has established.

Extract 5
(Wang is talking to the teacher about a film he has seen).

8.   Wang: Kung Fu.
9. T: Kung Fu? You like the movie Kung Fu?
10.   Wang: Yeah ... fight.
11. T: That was about a great fighter? ...
          A man who knows how to fight with his hands.
12.   Wang: I fight ... my hand.
13. T: You know how to fight with your hands?
14.   Wang: I fight with my hand.
15. T: Watch out guys, Wang knows karate.

The effects of discourse control on the quality of discourse that arises in the classroom are clearly demonstrated in Ernst's (1994) study of one particular

classroom event which occurred regularly in the elementary ESL classroom she
was studying. The event was the 'talking circle', where the students were asked
to gather round the teacher in a semi-circle in order to share and discuss
experiences and to introduce the weekly theme of the class. Ernst notes that this
repetitive event had a clear five-part structure consisting of (1) getting ready, (2)
entry into the circle, (3) a core phase, when students had the chance to talk about
topics of interest to them, (4) the teacher's exposition of her agenda for the week
and (5) moving on. Ernst provides a detailed analysis of one 16 minute talking
circle in order to demonstrate how the five phases differ with regard to topic
development, the social demands placed on the children and the particular
communicative functions performed by the teacher's and the students' speech. A

Table 1. *Comparison of the discourse in two phases of a classroom event (based on Ernst 1994)*

Phase	Core	Teacher's Agenda
1. Topic control	– teacher nominates student but student nominates topic – students able to freely express and share personal experiences – sustained talk on a single topic. – student talk occupies 71.4% of total time	– focus on classroom management and information giving – topics controlled entirely by teacher – teacher talk occupies 63.1% of total time.
2. Social demands	– students able to bid for floor – one single conversational floor (i.e. whole group attended to one speaker) – long turns by individual students – teacher signals continuance	– opportunities for students to talk highly constrained – students required to call out answers to teacher's questions
3. Speech functions	– teacher's talk has many continuing and supporting moves (e.g. prompts and requests for clarification) – student talk contains considerable explaining, extending and elaborating moves.	– teacher's talk dominated by explaining and holding moves and display questions – students' talk made up of minimal responses and repeating moves.

summary of Ernst's analysis of the two key phases (i.e. (3) and (4)) is shown in Table 1. It demonstrates clearly that when the students are in control of the topic the quality of the discourse is markedly richer than when the teacher is in control. Ernst suggests that when students have control of the topic they are more likely to take risks in using the L2 and to develop their strategic competence by using communication strategies to overcome problems.

Another study referred to in Chapter One also suggests that when learners do not control the discourse communication problems can ensue. Polio and Gass (1998) compared the comprehension scores of two sets of dyads performing an information-gap task in an experimental setting. They found an unusual amount of "leading" on the part of the native speakers in the dyads with the lowest comprehension scores. In contrast, the learners with higher comprehension scores were more in control of the interactions they took part in. Polio and Gass suggest that when native speakers take over the discourse learners may be robbed of the chance to focus on their comprehension and language problems.

To sum up, I have tried to show that when 'novice' language users (young children or L2 learners) are able to control the way in which the discourse unfolds the resulting interactions are likely to be qualitatively richer than when 'expert' language users (mothers or teachers) take control. I have suggested that classroom learners are more likely to achieve control of the discourse when the focus is on topic rather than on activity and when the teacher permits learner topicalisation. In the resulting interactions, learners receive assistance from the teacher in expressing and developing their own ideas. If it can be shown that such interactions contribute to language acquisition, then it can be argued that giving learners control of the discourse is one way of making the classroom acquisition-rich.

Discourse control and language acquisition

We can consider the relationship between discourse control and language acquisition empirically or theoretically. That is, we can carry out studies in classrooms to try to discover how discourse control is achieved and what impact it has on L2 acquisition. Alternatively, we can use theory to advance hypotheses about how discourse control will influence acquisition.

Classroom studies of discourse control and language acquisition

What evidence is there that discourse control is a factor in L2 acquisition? There is, in fact, remarkably little research that has addressed this issue. In general, researchers have chosen to look at particular aspects of discourse in the language classroom, such as teacher-talk (Gaies 1977), teacher questions (Long and Sato 1983), teacher feedback (Lightbown and Spada 1990), learner participation (Day 1984) and interactional modifications (Pica and Long 1986). There has been relatively little research that has examined classroom discourse holistically from the perspective of how the participants structure and manage interaction. Yet it is this, I would argue, that is the central factor which governs other more micro aspects of the discourse. *Tls control over disc*

Important exceptions to this generalization are Van Lier (1988) and Johnson (1995). Van Lier makes a special point of examining the overall organization of second-language lessons. In an ethnographic study of classrooms he shows that although teachers typically control the discourse by telling learners what, when and how to talk about a topic, there are some teachers who are less controlling and permit learner topicalisation. He notes that in some classes there is 'a significant degree of improvisation and variation' (p. 179). Van Lier argues that learners need such opportunities because they cater for experimentation with language that is at the cutting-edge of their linguistic development. Van Lier also illustrates how the question of discourse control impacts on other aspects of discourse. For example, teachers who seek to control the discourse do so by means of closed questions (e.g. 'What is the capital of England?') and reactive feedback. It is these strategies that lead to the familiar IRF pattern. Van Lier argues they 'interrupt the flow of the discourse' and the learner's 'interactive work', and, thereby, interfere with interlanguage development.

Johnson (1995) adopts a similar holistic approach to that of Van Lier. She seeks to show how the patterns of classroom communication are governed by 'academic task structures' (i.e. how the subject matter is sequenced in a lesson and the sequential steps involved) and 'social participation structures' (i.e. how the allocation of interactional rights and obligations shapes the discourse). These two structures are inter-related. Where the academic task structure is rigid (as for example in the kind of drill shown in extract (1)), the social participation structures are also tightly controlled. In such cases, classroom communication becomes ritualized. In contrast, when the academic task structure and social participation structure are more fluid, classroom communication can become highly spontaneous and adaptive. Johnson considers that topic control plays a crucial role in determining how fluid the communication is. Drawing on Ellis

(1990) and Van Lier (1988), Johnson then suggests the 'optimal conditions' for L2 acquisition. These include, creating opportunities for students to have a reason for attending to language, providing ample opportunity for students to use language, helping students to participate in language-related activities that are beyond their current level of proficiency and offering a full range of contexts that cater for a 'full performance' of the language. Johnson argues that these optimal conditions are more likely to occur in discourse where the academic task structure and social participation structure are more relaxed.

Van Lier and Johnson offer a wealth of descriptive information about the general patterns of classroom discourse and offer compelling accounts of how interaction affects acquisition. However, neither of them provides actual evidence to support their claims; they do not show how interaction actually leads to acquisition. There are, of course, enormous methodological problems in establishing a direct link between discourse events in the classroom and language acquisition. The studies that I will now consider constitute attempts to establish such links.

One way of trying to establish links is through the kind of detailed ethno-methodological examination of specific sequences of classroom acquisition proposed by Markee (1994). As Markee puts it 'dissecting a single cadaver is sufficient to demonstrate (explain) that the heart does indeed function as a pump' (p. 98). As Markee's own attempts at such an examination have dealt with interactions between learners in small groups and in this chapter I am primarily concerned with teacher-student interaction, I will attempt to illustrate this approach through a more detailed analysis of the same sequence which I discussed in Chapter 1 (see p. 18). The sequence is reproduced as extract (6) below.

Extract 6
(The teacher is talking to the student, R, about a What's Wrong Card).

1. T: I want you to tell me what you can
         see in the picture or what's wrong
         with the picture?
2.   R: A /paik/ (= bike)
3. T: A cycle, yes. But what's wrong?
4.   R: /ret/ (= red)
5. T: It's red, yes. What's wrong with it?
6.   R: Black
7. T: Black. Good. Black what?
8.   R: Black /taes/
                             (= tyres)

In this sequence, a teacher is talking to R, an 11 year old Pakistani boy, whose English is very limited. R was the subject of a longitudinal study (see Ellis

1984b). The teacher shows R a picture depicting a bicycle with the pedals missing. He begins by stating the pedagogic goal of this 'activity', i.e. 'saying what is wrong with the bicycle'. R, however, is unable to understand the academic task structure, probably because he does not understand the teacher's instruction. He, therefore, establishes his own, alternative goal, which might be glossed as 'naming objects and stating their colours'. Thus, the teacher and R, talk to different topics. The result is what Keenan and Schiffelin (1976) refer to as 'discontinuous discourse' (i.e. the discourse topics of consecutive utterances are not linked in any obvious way). In an attempt to give the interaction some coherence and perhaps also out of desire to be supportive, the teacher does acknowledge R's contributions to the discourse (e.g. 'A cycle, yes.'; 'It's red, yes.') but on both occasions reasserts his own topic. In turn (7), however, he adopts a different strategy. Once again he acknowledges R's contribution ('Black. Good.') but this time instead of repeating 'the question of immediate concern' he accepts R's topic and provides a prompt ('Black what?') to encourage him to develop it further. In other words, topicalisation by the learner occurs. In turn (8) R says 'Black /taes/'. As I pointed out in Chapter 1, this utterance constitutes the first occasion R produced a two-word utterance in my longitudinal data. It is tempting to see the teacher's relinquishing of topic control as the discourse mechanism that enabled this learner to advance his interlanguage.

An alternative method for trying to demonstrate how discourse control affects acquisition can be found in Slimani's work on 'uptake' (see Slimani 1989 and Study Three in Chapter Three). Slimani investigated a series of lessons taught to a group of adult Algerian students. At the end of each lesson she asked the students to record on an 'uptake chart' what they thought they had learned. In the main, they listed vocabulary items. She then examined transcripts of the lessons to try to identify what it was in the classroom interactions that might have caused them to learn the items. In general, the lessons were activity oriented and the teacher controlled the discourse. However, there were occasions when individual students nominated their own topics, i.e., learner topicalization occurred. Slimani found that 'whatever is topicalized by the learners rather than the teacher has a better chance of being claimed to have been learnt'. In other words, as in extract (6) above, it was when the learners took control of the discourse that opportunities for acquisition arose.

To date, there have been few classroom studies of how discourse control affects the course of interlanguage development. What research there has been suggests that when teachers allow learners the chance to topicalize, acquisition is more likely to take place.

Theoretical accounts of how discourse control affects language acquisition

While there is an obvious need for more empirical studies of classrooms to show how interaction creates opportunities for language learning, there are strong theoretical grounds for claiming that discourse control is a key factor. I would like now to consider two theoretical positions that address this.

As we have seen in the preceding chapters, the Interaction Hypothesis claims that acquisition is promoted when the input to which learners are exposed is made comprehensible through the interactional modifications that arise when meaning is negotiated. Chapters 1 and 3 described research showing that negotiation does help to make input comprehensible and also enables learners to acquire new lexical items.

However, most of the research based on the interactional hypothesis has not taken place in actual classrooms but under pseudo-experimental conditions involving dyads consisting of either a native speaker and a non-native speaker or two non-native speakers. For this reason, we do not know much about when and how meaning negotiation takes place in classrooms. Long and Sato's (1983) work on teachers' questions and Pica and Long's (1986) study of experienced and inexperienced teachers suggests that there may not be much negotiation taking place in many language classrooms. It is pertinent to ask why. One possibility is that negotiation is to a large extent dependent on learners' control of the discourse. When teachers control the discourse, learners may be reluctant to signal their lack of comprehension and to negotiate understanding, preferring instead to either wait and see if they can work things out later or, alternatively, to abandon any attempt to comprehend. The socio-cultural norms of some classrooms, such as those in many parts of Asia, may also mitigate against students actively negotiating meaning. To some extent, the reluctance of students to negotiate can be overcome by providing learners with the formulae they need to carry out negotiation (e.g. a list of ways of requesting clarification) and placing them in a situation where they have to negotiate in order to complete a task (as in the non-reciprocal listening tasks described in Chapter 3). However, a better way of promoting negotiation in classroom discourse involving the teacher might be to encourage learner topicalization. In contrast to students, teachers are not hesitant to negotiate when they fail to understand something a student has said.

I would like to suggest, therefore, that acquisition can be promoted when learners have the chance to control the discourse because this enables them to engage in meaning negotiation. In this way the notion of topic control can be incorporated into what is currently the favoured theoretical position in SLA.

Negotiation is, however, only a part, and perhaps only a small part, of the kind of discourse work that can help to make a classroom acquisition-rich. In extract (5) the teacher is not negotiating in the sense intended by the Interaction Hypothesis. She seems to understand what Wang says without any difficulty and yet the discourse work she engages in assists Wang in expressing what he wants to say in a more target-like way. The same might be said of the teacher in extract (5). He understands what R is trying to say and by finally accepting his topicalization helps him to produce an utterance that is more complex than he had previously been capable of. How can we explain this? I would like to suggest that socio-cultural theory can provide a more encompassing framework for understanding how discourse control impacts on acquisition.

As we saw in Chapter 1, socio-cultural theory views speech as one of the principal ways of mediating learning, including language learning; learning takes place when children are helped to perform functions in the zone of proximal development. This is achieved through interaction, with new functions first evident in interpersonal activity and only subsequently available for independent use. According to socio-cultural theory, then, cognitive development arises interpsychologically through interaction in concrete social situations. It is facilitated when learners have the opportunity to interact with a more experienced person who can guide, support and shape their actions (i.e. scaffold their attempts to perform new functions).

This theory provides a way of explaining why learner control of the discourse is so important. First and foremost, it ensures the learner's interest. Learners are more likely to be motivated to talk about topics they themselves have nominated. Next, it provides the teacher with information regarding what learners are capable of saying on their own. This helps the teacher to identify what speech forms may lie within the learner's zone of proximal development and provides a basis for determining the kind of scaffolding needed to assist the learner to use and subsequently internalize more complex language. The teacher's efforts can then be directed at helping the learners note the difference between what they have said and the 'ideal solution' (i.e. the target-language version of their utterances) and to modelling such a solution. In the process, the teacher may need to simplify the task and to deal with frustrations learners experience.

Extracts (2), (5) and (6) provide clear examples of scaffolding. Mark's mother helps her son to maintain the conversation, allowing him to build on and extend his own utterances. Wang's teacher also encourages Wang to pursue his topic and in the process provides him with target-language versions of what he is trying to say. R's teacher deals with R's frustration by accepting R's topical-isation, thereby simplifying the task he initially posed, which clearly lies outside R's zone of proximal development, and encouraging him to pursue his own goal.

Of course, this kind of scaffolding is not restricted to sequences where the learner is in control of the discourse, as extract (2) shows. Here the teacher engages in very similar interactional behaviour to that found in extract (5), although it is notable that, on this occasion, the learner is unable to incorporate the teacher's idealized versions of what he is trying to say into his own speech. It may be that scaffolding is more effective when learners control the topic. When the discourse is controlled by the expert, there is always a danger of operating outside the learner's zone of proximal development, as I think is the case in extracts (1) and (4).

The Interaction Hypothesis and socio-cultural theory provide ways of accounting for how classroom discourse can affect acquisition. I have tried to show how the notion of discourse control is important for both theories. Of the two theories, socio-cultural theory has the greater potential as it emphasizes the collaborative nature in meaning making in discourse in general, not just in exchanges where communication breakdown occurs.

Conclusion

This chapter has sought to demonstrate the importance of an internal perspective on language teaching for understanding how classrooms can be made acquisition rich. In this respect it has focussed on a key aspect of classroom interaction — discourse control. By way of conclusion, I would like to address how external and internal views of language teaching can be inter-related. How can a teacher make external decisions about what and how to teach that will help to create an acquisition-rich classrooms? What kinds of pedagogic tasks and methodological procedures are available that will enhance learners' opportunities to control the discourse and thereby their own language learning?

I have argued that learners' control of the discourse is more likely to occur when instruction involves a focus on 'topic' rather than on 'activity'. One way of creating such a focus is by means of task-based language teaching of the kind advocated by Prabhu (1987) and Skehan (1996). Tasks, in the sense intended here, are meaning-based activities. That is, they are activities that require the learners to attend primarily to **what** is talked about rather than **how** language is used. Thus, they are topic- rather than activity-centered. Examples of tasks are the various kinds of information- and opinion-gap activities now common in communicative language teaching, including the non-reciprocal tasks described in Chapter 3 and the consciousness-raising task illustrated in Chapter 8.

Task-based language teaching (and research, too) is generally based on the assumption that tasks will be performed by learners working in pairs or small groups. Clearly, this is one way of ensuring that learners have control of the discourse. With the teacher out of the way learners are free to manage the discourse for themselves. Also, because learners participate in tasks as social equals the management of the discourse is likely to be shared more equitably, leading to greater negotiation of meaning (Pica 1987) and mutual scaffolding (Donato 1994). In cases, where the learners differ in proficiency, giving the key information to the less rather than more proficient learner is likely to result in longer interactions and more successful task-outcomes (Yule and McDonald 1990). Thus, one reason why group-work is so important for language learning, is that it fosters learner discourse control and thereby ensures opportunities for language learning. However, there are also problems associated with asking learners to perform tasks in small-groups. In monolingual classrooms, the students may rely extensively on their L1. Also, as Foster (1998) found, students may not take the tasks seriously and, as a result, the level of talk and negotiation may be quite low. Foster, in fact, believes that 'the claims made for group work tasks by previous researchers are surely overconfident when applied to the realities of the classroom' (p. 28).

However, task-based language teaching need not involve small group work. It can also be carried out by teachers interacting in lock-step with the whole class, as we saw in Chapter 3. Indeed, Prabhu (1987) has argued that in the teaching context he was concerned with (low-level classes of secondary school students in southern India), task-based teaching is better carried out in lockstep as this ensures the students access to the teacher's better formed samples of the target language. In such a case, however, the role relations are likely to be asymmetrical and the turn-taking rights inequitably distributed. As a result, there is a danger that the teacher will take control of the discourse and the structure of the discourse revert to the familiar IRF pattern. If the arguments relating to discourse control that I have presented in this chapter are correct, this will result in learners being less likely to experience the opportunity to negotiate meaning and to benefit from the scaffolding provided by an expert.

An interesting methodological question, therefore, is how lockstep task-based teaching can be conducted in such a way that it creates the interactional conditions believed to facilitate language acquisition. The answer may lie, in part, in ensuring that the learners rather than the teacher are in control of the information that needs to be communicated. For example, in a non-reciprocal task, such as symbol-drawing, giving the learners the information (i.e. pictures of the symbols to be drawn) and having them communicate the information so that the teacher can complete the task may help learners to take greater control of the discourse. Another way, is to provide learners with time to plan how to perform the task before the task is actually undertaken. Such planning may make learners more prepared to advance their own ideas in an opinion-gap task and thus more eager to take control of the discourse. Tsui (1996) provides evidence to show that Chinese learners are more likely to participate in classroom discourse when they have had the opportunity to plan what they want to say. It is, perhaps, a pity that so much of the task-based research has focussed on group performance of tasks rather than whole-class performance. We need to understand more about the kind of discourse that results from tasks performed in lockstep under different conditions.

A second way of fostering learner control of the discourse is by setting aside regular time for a 'talking circle', as described by Ernst (1994). In the classroom she investigated, the students were asked to physically regroup themselves in a semi-circle around the teacher, thus signalling to them that a different type of discourse from that prevailing in other classroom activities was socially possible. During the core phase of 'talking time' the students competed for the floor and were able to nominate and talk about their own topics, but the teacher maintained orderliness in the discourse by exerting her right to nominate speakers. In large classes, it may be difficult to conduct a 'talking circle' with the whole class, but the teacher may be able to set aside time to engage with groups of students in such an activity.

A third way in which learner control of the discourse can be fostered in the classroom is by ensuring that 'framework' communication in the classroom is conducted in the target language. What Willis (1992) has called 'outer language' is perhaps the only language in a classroom that is truly communicative in so far as it serves as the medium for accomplishing language lessons — the raison d'etre of teacher and students alike. In many instances it will be the teacher who controls the outer-language as it he/she who has the primary responsibility for ensuring that lessons are accomplished in an orderly fashion. However, my own research in beginner-level ESL classrooms in London (see Ellis 1984b and 1992), showed that the need to get on and stay on task motivated the learners to frequently produce their own outer-language. The learners used English (the L2) to request the goods they needed for an activity, to seek clarification when they did not understand what to do, to request assistance when they were stuck and to make public announcements about their progress. In such interactions, the learners controlled the discourse, both nominating the topic and managing its subsequent development. These interactions, then, were built around the learners' own communicative needs and, I believe, contributed greatly to their early interlanguage development. Of course, it is much easier to use the target language for 'framing' lessons in the kind of multilingual classroom I was studying. However, it can also be achieved in monolingual classrooms (see, for example, Mitchell's (1988) account of foreign language classroom in Scotland).

Thus, teachers can do much to foster learner control of the discourse through the decisions they make externally about what kinds of activities to use and how to use them. In this respect, it is possible to *plan* for learner discourse control. However, as Van Lier (1991) has pointed out much of teaching involves *improvisation*: 'in any lesson, planned and improvised actions and interactions may be tightly interwoven' (p. 47). It is because of this that we must talk about lessons being accomplished rather than being enacted. Opportunities for giving learners control of the discourse will arise naturally in the course of a language lesson. The extent to which teachers grasp these opportunities, for example, by permitting learner topicalisations, may well prove more crucial for creating the optimal conditions for acquisition than any planned decisions they make.

Finally, I would like to mention two caveats in the position I have adopted. First, in arguing that opportunities need to be created for learners to control the discourse, I do not want to suggest that there is no place for teacher discourse control. Teachers have a responsibility to ensure that lessons are accomplished in an orderly fashion and this alone will necessitate they take responsibility for managing classroom discourse. Also, there are many legitimate pedagogic procedures that are 'activity' rather than 'topic' oriented and that presuppose teacher control of the discourse. A good example might be the use of structured input tasks to focus learners' attention on specific linguistic features (see VanPatten 1993; Ellis 1995). Another example are the non-reciprocal tasks that figures in the various studies reported in Chapters 3 and 4. Such tasks allow little opportunity for learner discourse control but can contribute to acquisition through the rich input they supply. Nevertheless, a classroom where there is very little opportunity for learner discourse control, particularly for learners who have progressed beyond the beginner stages of acquisition, may impede the development of communicative proficiency. Thus, viewing the classroom in terms of how much opportunity there is for learners to take charge of interactions constitutes a powerful way of evaluating how acquisition-rich a classroom is.

The second caveat concerns the cultural expectations that exist in many language classrooms regarding the roles of the teacher and the students. In situations, where the teacher is viewed as a 'knower' and the students as 'receivers of knowledge', it may prove very difficult to create the conditions necessary for learner discourse control (see, for example, Li's (1998) account of the difficulty Korean teachers experience in implementing communicative language teaching). Stevick (1993) has shown how the choices teachers make from the options available to them convey social messages. Conversely, the social messages teachers wish to convey are likely to influence both the planned and improvised decisions they make in accomplishing lessons. Teachers who wish to assert their authority as teachers, because this is their socio-historically constructed understanding of what a teacher is, may be reluctant to engage in classroom discourse where learners are in charge. They will be happier with what McArthur (1984) has called the 'monastery tradition' (i.e. with containerization of life, clearly-defined norms and strict discipline) rather than the 'marketplace tradition' (i.e. the rough and tumble of life where 'anything that works is welcome', p. 279). Yet, it may be something akin to the market-place tradition that is needed if learners are to have the chance to control the discourse. There is, then, a potential conflict between the psycholinguistic rationale I have evoked to argue the need for learner discourse control and the socio-historical rationale that many teachers may draw on, implicitly or explicitly, to justify a style of teaching where they remain, more or less exclusively, in charge.

If the central premise of this chapter is accepted, namely that classroom learners' language development is, like all language learners' language development, tied to the kinds of interaction they are involved in, the key issue is as follows: how can teachers provide opportunities for students to participate in the broad range of interactive behaviours that learner discourse control affords without relinquishing their culturally constructed identities, and accompanying responsibilities, as teachers? This is a key question, to which there are no easy answers.

A socio-historical theory of language use and development, such as that proposed by Hall (1994) emphasizes the way in which engagement in particular interactions are shaped by the language user's previous experience of such interactions and their social identity. However, according to Hall, L2 learners need to not only learn what constitutes appropriate linguistic practices in different interactional events but also how to challenge these practices by using their linguistic resources creatively to negotiate new meanings. Becoming competent in a language involves being able to utilize language for one's own purposes as well as conventionally. If pedagogic practice serves only to socialize learners into the rigidly institutionalized discourse of teacher dominated classroom interaction, learners will have no opportunity to develop 'the range of voices' that constitute the kind of practical and critical language competence they need to become effective communicators.

SECTION 5

Conclusion

This book has sought to give answers to three key questions concerning the role of interaction in second language (L2) acquisition. These are:

1. In what ways does interaction/input contribute to L2 acquisition?
2. Which types of interaction/input promote L2 acquisition?
3. What kind of language pedagogy is needed to ensure that classroom learners experience acquisition-rich interaction?

In this concluding chapter I would like to try to bring together the various insights provided by the preceding chapters in order to provide possible answers to these three questions. In addition, I would like to suggest some future directions for research.

CHAPTER 10

Retrospect and Prospect

Rod Ellis

The contribution of input/interaction to L2 acquisition

In order to consider how interaction/input contributes to L2 acquisition it is obviously important to have a clear understanding of what is meant by the term 'acquisition'. In fact, 'acquisition' can mean very different things in the SLA literature. Too many researchers take the term for granted, even though the measures that they use to investigate it differ widely, indicating that they are in fact studying very different phenomena. To unpack precisely what is meant by 'acquisition' it is necessary to examine (1) the *kind* of acquisition, (2) the *aspect* of acquisition and (3) the *object* of acquisition under study.

Recent discussion of acquisition by researchers drawing on information processing models (e.g. Schmidt 1994; Robinson 1995; Skehan 1998) makes two important distinctions. The first relates to how the L2 learner orientates to the task of learning the language; if the learner approaches the task with the deliberate attention of learning (e.g. by studying rules of grammar or memorizing vocabulary) then the acquisition is said to be *intentional*. If, on the other hand, the learner treats the L2 as a tool for communicating messages in reception and production so that any learning that occurs is only a by-product of the efforts to make meaning, then the acquisition is *incidental*. The second distinction concerns whether the learning that takes place is *implicit* or *explicit*. In the case of implicit learning the learner is not aware of what has been learned; that is, changes to interlanguage occur without consciousness. In the case of explicit learning the learner is aware of the changes that are taking place; acquisition is a conscious process. While there is wide acceptance among SLA researchers that acquisition can be intentional or incidental there is less unanimity regarding the possibility of both implicit and explicit learning, with some researchers (e.g. Krashen 1981) maintaining that acquisition is necessarily implicit, others (e.g. Schmidt 1994) suggesting that it may be explicit (i.e. involve a degree of consciousness), and yet others (e.g. DeKeyser 1995) arguing that it is necessarily explicit.

A number of further issues are raised when the aspect of acquisition that is to be studied is considered. A number of models of acquisition (e.g. Sharwood-Smith and Bialystok 1985; DeKeyser 1998) assume that acquisition involves both *knowledge* and *control* or *declarative knowledge* and *procedural knowledge*. Thus, acquisition can refer to either the internalisation of some previously unlearned item or rule (i.e. the learner learns something new) or to an increase in control over the use of previously acquired items, as evident, for example, in increases in production accuracy over time. Information processing models identify a number of stages of acquisition. In particular, they distinguish *intake* from *interlanguage restructuring* (Gass 1997). Acquisition is initiated when learners notice forms in the input (i.e. intake occurs); however, only some of these temporarily stored forms will enter interlanguage. Viewed from a process perspective, then, acquisition can refer to intake or to interlanguage change and in the case of the latter the change can involve the addition of some new item or rule or an increase in control over previously acquired material.

Finally, fairly obviously, acquisition can be distinguished in terms of what is being internalized — whether it is a feature of pronunciation, a lexical item, a grammatical rule or some other aspect of language. It is not self-evident that acquisition of these different features involves the same processes. Indeed, there is ample evidence that they do not. For example, learners appear to draw more heavily on their first language resources where pronunciation and pragmatic aspects are involved than they do for grammar. In the case of grammar, there is also evidence to show that different processes may be at work depending on whether learners are acquiring syntax or morphology. It has been suggested for example, that interaction may be important for the acquisition of syntax but not for morphology (Sato 1986). Over and above the question of what level of language involved is also the type of knowledge at stake. The knowledge learners internalize can be *implicit* (i.e. it is represented in a form that does not permit awareness but does permit easy and rapid access) or *explicit* (i.e. it is represented in a form that permits awareness but not easy access).[1] Thus, in the case of implicit knowledge learners are not aware of what they know whereas in the case of explicit knowledge they are.

All these distinctions are premised on a computational model of language acquisition and assume that a general distinction needs to be made between 'competence' and 'performance'; 'acquisition' is viewed as the process by which learners build their competence in the L2. However, sociocultural theories of acquisition, as we saw in Chapter One, dispute this distinction, arguing that 'acquisition' occurs initially interpsychologically in social exchanges. It follows from such a premise not just that acquisition derives from performance but that performance itself constitutes acquisition. Learners are acquiring new structures when they learn how to perform these in interaction. However, as I point out below, this position is quite problematic.

This deconstruction of the term 'acquisition' allows us to examine the role of interaction more precisely and to consider what the foregoing chapters have contributed to our understanding of this role. It also allows us to identify alternative lines of enquiry for addressing important issues that have not been considered.

In accordance with the computational model of language acquisition, the Interaction Hypothesis breaks down 'interaction' into its component parts (i.e. input, feedback and output) and posits that these contribute to acquisition by facilitating learners' attention to new linguistic forms and by providing opportunities for learners to practice using them. The Interaction Hypothesis was designed to address *incidental acquisition*; that is, it does not aim to account for *intentional* language learning. It is less clear, however, whether its compass is restricted to *implicit learning* or also includes *explicit learning*. Potentially, interaction can contribute to both. The original IH, with its emphasis on the role of comprehensible input, would seem to have been primarily concerned with explaining how learners acquire *new* linguistic knowledge but the revised IH, which incorporates a role for output, is more widely directed, incorporating a potential effect of interaction on learners' *control* of existing knowledge. The revised IH, with its emphasis on the role that interaction plays in stimulating learners' attention to form, draws heavily on current models of acquisition that view *intake* as a preliminary stage in the acquisitional process. The IH can be used to address all levels of language — pronunciation, lexis, grammar and discourse. Its primary concern is with how learners develop *implicit knowledge*. It is clear, then, that although there are some aspects of acquisition that the IH does not address (e.g. intentional learning and its role in acquisition) it is a theory with the potential to explain many of the key elements in a computational model of language acquisition.

Much of the research reported in this book was informed by the IH. The studies reported in Chapters Three, Four and Seven were all designed to test claims of the hypothesis. They explicitly concerned themselves with *incidental acquisition*, demonstrating that the interaction and input derived from non-reciprocal tasks that required learners to listen to directives and perform actions to show their understanding can facilitate the acquisition of *new* L2 lexical knowledge (Chapters Three and Four) and an increase in *control* over a grammatical form (past tense) that learners had already partially acquired (Chapter Seven).

Taken together, these studies lend broad support to the claim that interaction, specifically that which arises when there is an attempt to repair some communication problem, can contribute to acquisition. Negotiated interaction serves as a source of data on which learners can draw to extend their interlanguages.

In contrast to the IH, the two other theories discussed in Chapter One (sociocultural theory and the depth-of-processing model) have figured less strongly in this book. Chapter Seven drew on sociocultural theory to explain why learners' performance of the task in the output condition (i.e. one that required them to actually produce the target words) seemed to work so much better for the incidental acquisition of new words than either a premodified or interactionally modified input condition. There it was suggested that it might not be possible to examine the independent effects of input and output on acquisition as both occur together when learners negotiate for meaning. In addition, it was suggested that much depends on how learners construct the 'activity' that arises from a task, with very different kinds of activity arising from the same task depending on how the participants view it. Chapter Five drew on the depth-of-processing model. It provided evidence to suggest that, with guidance, learners are capable of interacting within themselves by posing and answering questions about a written text and that this can have beneficial effects on the incidental acquisition of new words. This study forces us to recognize that interaction does not need to be social to work for acquisition. Chapters Five and Seven suggest that the role of interaction in language acquisition cannot be fully accounted for by the IH, which focuses narrowly on a single type of social interaction. They point for the need for a broad, general theory of interaction or for the acceptance of the kind of multiple theories that I (Ellis 1994) and Lantolf (1996) have argued for.

The research reported in this book is not atypical of the research on interaction to date. Its limitations are a reflection of the general state of interaction-oriented research. The following is a list of some of the more obvious problems and limitations of the research to date. The list points to possible directions that future research might follow.

1. There is an obvious need to pay more attention to the role of interaction in providing learners with *positive evidence* about the L2. The IH has led to researchers focussing overly narrowly on interaction as a source of *negative evidence*. There are theoretical grounds (e.g. in Chomsky's theory of Universal Grammar as this has been applied in SLA; see White 1989) for acknowledging the importance of positive evidence. There are also obvious methodological problems in trying to isolate the effects of positive and negative evidence, as in naturally occurring interaction the provision of

negative evidence frequently depends on the prior provision of positive evidence, the two working together.[2]

2. Similarly, as has already pointed out, there are obvious difficulties in attempting to distinguish the separate effects of interactionally derived input and output on acquisition.

3. Much of the research to date has focussed on vocabulary learning. The reasons for this have already been mentioned. The trigger for a communication problem in negotiation sequences is frequently lexical in nature. Also, lexical learning can occur as a result of relatively small amounts of interaction/input/output whereas other levels of language may require much more extensive opportunities to hear and use the target forms.

4. There have been very few attempts to examine what effect interaction/input/output has on learners' *intake* (i.e. what they notice and take into short term memory).[3] Researchers have instead focussed on what learners take into the interlanguage systems. In this respect, the research may be seriously underestimating the effects of interaction, as it is likely that learners intake more than they actually store in long-term memory. Furthermore, there is an obvious need to investigate the relationship between what is intaken and what is finally stored and whether interaction influences this.

5. The instruments used to measure what is acquired from interaction are insufficiently sensitive. In particular, they do not distinguish between the measurement of implicit and explicit knowledge. The kinds of testing instruments used in the studies reported in Chapters Three and Five, for example, all lend themselves to learners accessing explicit knowledge of the target lexical items (i.e. they do not require learners to access their knowledge rapidly). In contrast, the instrument used in Chapter 7 (the production of an oral narrative) is more likely to tap implicit knowledge. Measurement is also a problem for socio-cultural researchers who assume that 'use' is equivalent to 'acquisition'; it does not follow that because learners are helped to use a new form in interaction that they have stored it in such a way that it is subsequently available for independent use. Ultimately some kind of distinction between 'initial performance' and 'acquisition' will have to be maintained.

6. Related to this point, the existing research has not examined what kind of learning (implicit or explicit) arises as a result of opportunities to interact in the L2. To what extent are learners aware of what they have learned? In this respect, Allwright's (1984b) suggestion that researchers obtain measures of learners' 'uptake' (i.e. what they can report learning after a period of

exposure to the L2) is worth pursuing (see Ellis 1995 for a study examining the use of this measure). In general, researchers have been content to work with rather vague and inexplicit notions of 'acquisition'.

7. Researchers have focussed almost exclusively on social interaction, paying little attention to the interactions that learners engage in inside their heads. In this respect, there is a distinction to be made between the relative roles of oral and written input. Social interaction is typically an oral event whereas the kind of intrapersonal interaction studied in Chapter Six is often stimulated by written input. Also neglected in this book and elsewhere is the relationship between interpersonal and intrapersonal interaction.

8. The research reported in this book has been experimental and quantitative in nature. Again, this reflects its origin in the IH hypothesis, which has been traditionally investigated by research in the nomothetic tradition. However, there is an obvious need for more qualitative studies of interaction that explore how learners gradually master the ability to perform particular language forms and functions over time. In this respect the 'microgenetic method' employed by sociocultural researchers is promising, particularly if this involves the analysis of data collected longitudinally.[4]

9. Researchers have been preoccupied with identifying the universal roles of interaction, in accordance with SLA's overriding concern with developing a general theory of L2 acquisition. There has been very little research that has investigated the ways in which opportunities to interact and their effects on acquisition are mediated by individual learner factors. Chapter Five showed that learner differences in language aptitude can influence what they learn from modified input. Other chapters have indicated that learners vary markedly in their preparedness to engage in interaction. Factors of potential importance in explaining this are age, personality, learning style, communication style and motivation but we currently know very little of how these influence social (let alone intrapersonal) interaction. Future research on interaction needs to complement the current *learning-centred* approach with a *learner-centred* one.

There is now a strong theoretical and empirical base for claiming that interaction plays an important role in L2 acquisition. There are, however, major questions that have not been answered. One general question concerns whether interaction is *necessary* for acquisition. The answer to this question depends on part on how interaction is defined. If it is defined as 'social interaction' the answer is probably no; it is facilitative in a number of ways (see following section) but it is not necessary. There is plenty of evidence, including that from the studies reported in Chapters Three, Four and Five, to show that learners can learn from non-interactional input. However, if interaction is held to include the intra-personal, mental activity that occurs when learners 'talk' to themselves, then the answer is less clear-cut. Sociocultural theorists would maintain that all learning is mediated and that one form of mediation is private speech (see Chapter One). Some form of interaction, then, may be necessary for learning.

In this book I have argued for a broadly based definition of interaction. The various limitations of the research to date listed above are a reflection of the need I see for such a definition. There are, of course, advantages of restricting the focus of research in ways that the IH has encouraged. It has enabled researchers to address fairly precise research questions of the kind posed in this book. But there are obvious dangers of such an approach, not least in the assumptions it makes. For example, it seems to me that there is neither a strong theoretical or empirical base for assuming that interactions that arise as a result of communication problems are privileged with regard to their contribution to language acquisition. Prospective research can benefit by continuing to work from a narrow theoretical base, for example by exploring how opportunities to negotiate for meaning impact on intake (see note 3), but should also widen the scope of enquiry, for example by exploring the role of intrapersonal interaction. There is also an obvious need also for more attention to be paid to the dependent variable (acquisition) in order to demonstrate how interaction affects different aspects of this complex phenomenon.

The contribution of different types of interaction/input

Arguably a more interesting issue than the general nature of the contribution that interaction makes to acquisition is the effect of different types of input/inter-action. Indeed, it is this issue that has motivated much of the research to date, including that reported in the preceding chapters. Here I would like to review a number of features of input/interaction that have been found to impact on L2 acquisition and, at the same time, identify possible avenues of future inquiry.

Comprehensible input and L2 acquisition

The starting point for much of the research was Krashen's claim that input works for acquisition when it is comprehensible. Krashen (1985, 1994, 1998) views his Input Hypothesis as 'fundamental' to a theory of L2 acquisition. According to this hypothesis, learners will advance when they receive input that contains linguistic forms (phonological, lexical and grammatical) that are slightly beyond their current stage of interlanguage development. Krashen argues that this can be achieved when learners comprehend the input to which they are exposed and that, therefore, there is no need to 'fine-tune' the input to ensure that it is at the i + 1 level. 'Rough-tuning' is sufficient. This arises automatically when interlocutors adjust their input to learners to ensure that they comprehend. However, learners may tune-out input even when it is comprehensible if their 'affective filter' is high. In short, then, Krashen claims that acquisition will take place when:

1. the input is modified to ensure that it is comprehensible.
2. it contains linguistic features just beyond the learners' current level
3. the learner is affectively disposed to 'let in' the input.

It would seem to follow from this position that we should expect a strong correlation between measures of comprehension and measures of acquisition. The studies reported in Chapters Three and Four reported a number of such correlations but with very mixed results. In some cases the correlations were significant but by no means strong while in others the correlations were weak and statistically non-significant. Taken together, these studies do not suggest that a high level of comprehension of input is needed in order for acquisition to take place. Input, it would seem, does not have to be that comprehensible. But what exactly does this mean and why might this be so?

A limitation of Krashen's position is his failure to specify what he means by 'comprehension' and what the internal mechanisms are that are responsible for processing comprehensible input. As I pointed out in Chapter One, there are degrees of comprehension — for example, one can understand the general purpose of a message or just some of the individual words that comprise it. What exactly does a learner have to comprehend in order to acquire? Also, it was noted that the processes of comprehension and acquisition are not isomorphic. Learners can comprehend using their schematic knowledge and context, so obviating the need to attend to the linguistic composition of the input. Further, learners can presumably attend to linguistic form without necessarily comprehending the message. Thus, whereas we can expect some kind of general relationship between comprehension and acquisition (for, after all, if learners do not comprehend they are likely to lose interest and switch off their attentional mechanisms), we should not necessarily expect a strong relationship. The results of the research reported in the previous chapters are indicative of this.[5]

The role of comprehension in L2 acquisition remains an uncertain one and is clearly in need of further research. Such research will need to examine exactly what it is that learners comprehend when they are exposed to input and also whether they notice forms that they do not comprehend and what effect such noticing has on acquisition. If acquisition is taken to involve both attention to linguistic forms and to the meanings they convey in communication, then, it would seem reasonable to assume that the acquisition of form can precede without comprehension but that the acquisition of form-meaning mappings will require at least 'local' comprehension. Researchers will need to distinguish between the acquisition of form and form/meaning mappings if progress in investigating the role of comprehension in acquisition is to be made. They will also need to theorize comprehension more explicitly and develop measures that are sensitive to different types and degrees of comprehension in learners.

Input/interactional modifications and acquisition

One of the main purposes of the various studies reported in this book was to examine the relative effects of different kinds of modifications on learners' L2 acquisition. In particular, the studies investigated the effects of input as opposed to interactional modifications on learners' acquisition of new lexis. This comparison was motivated by research which has shown that interactional modifications are in general more effective than input modifications in promoting comprehension and, thus, in accordance with the Input Hypothesis, may also be more effective where L2 acquisition is concerned. The comparison was also theoretically motivated. The IH claims that the modifications that arise when learners negotiate for meaning are especially beneficial for acquisition because they create the conditions needed for noticing form to take place (Long 1996). In addition, the studies explored the contributions made by specific input and interactional modifications on the learners' acquisition of new L2 words.

With regard to the relative effects of input and interactional modifications the studies produced somewhat mixed results. Study 1 and Study 2 reported in Chapter Three both found that learners who were given the chance to interact acquired more new words than learners who received premodified input. However, the study reported in Chapter Four found almost no difference. Furthermore, Study 3 in Chapter Three found that with regard to the number of words acquired per minute of exposure to the L2, premodified input was more efficient than interactionally modified input. What these studies seem to suggest, then, is that interactionally modified input is not necessary for acquisition to take place and not necessarily more facilitative; learners can learn very effectively from premodified input. Second, they indicate that the real benefit of interactionally modified input may lie less in the qualitative differences between this kind of input and premodified input and more in quantitative differences and the extra processing time it affords learners. Giving learners the opportunity to interact results in more input and provides them with more time to process the input. Perhaps it enables learners to divide their time between attending to form and to meaning, avoiding the trade off between these two types of processing which research (e.g. VanPatten 1990) has shown can occur, and thereby facilitating both acquisition and comprehension. However, once time is controlled for this advantage disappears; when there is no difference in the quantity of premodified and interactionally modified input there is no difference in the extent of learners' lexical acquisition.

In fact, Study 3 in Chapter Three shows that there is a real danger in interactionally modified input. It can result in input that is overelaborated with the result that learners fail to comprehend and also fail to learn. In other words, interactionally modified input serves as an effective data source for acquisition when it supplies input that learners are able to process but as ineffective when it overloads learners with information that they are unable to process. This suggests that where interactionally modified input is concerned much depends on the skills of the interactant who is supplying the modified input. A skilful interactant is able to respond to signals of non-comprehension by providing input that is transparent and frugal. In contrast a less skilful interactant may impede acquisition by providing input that is too embroidered and therefore too complex for learners to process.

In general, SLA researchers have been overly concerned with investigating the relative effects of premodified and interactionally modified input on acquisition. This has been motivated in part by the rival claims of the Input and Interaction Hypotheses. There are obvious problems in making this comparison, in particular, the question of time. Also, the comparison may be fundamentally mistaken at a more theoretical level. I have argued above that the kind of interaction that is crucially important for acquisition is the intrapsychological activity that results from learners' attempts to process input for comprehension and acquisition. Such activity is not dependent on learners' ability to interact socially, although, doubtlessly this is one way in which it can be stimulated. Input that has been carefully chosen or suitably premodified to facilitate processing constitutes an effective stimulus for the kinds of mental work that promotes acquisition. Furthermore, as Chapter Six demonstrated, learners can be trained to handle such input in ways that are beneficial for vocabulary learning.

Future research, then, can be more profitably directed at investigating (1) the kinds of intrapsychological interaction that promote acquisition, (2) ways of inducing learners to engage in appropriate intrapsychological interaction and (3) the specific properties of premodified and interactionally modified input that induce effective intrapsychological interaction. In other words, what is required is not just research that plots the degree of correlation between properties of the input and learning outcomes (as occurred in Study 3 in Chapter Three) but more especially research that examines the relationship between input/social interaction and intrapsychological interaction and between intrapyschological interaction and learning outcomes. In this respect, research based on the depth-of-processing model is promising, although further work is needed to delineate the various levels of mental processing that L2 learners engage in. As we noted in Chapter One, this model is beginning to attract the attention of SLA researchers but remains somewhat underspecified at the present time.

The relative effects of modified input and modified output

The taste for dichotomous constructs in SLA, evident in the juxtaposition of pre-modified and interactionally modified input, also emerges in the contrast between modified input and modified output. In part, this dichotomy reflects the evolution of SLA theory. Initially, a strong case was made for comprehensible input as a causative factor in L2 acquisition; subsequently, beginning with Swain's seminal article published in 1985, the case was made for output, in particular 'pushed output', playing a significant role. Not surprisingly these claims have come to be seen as rivalling each other, although Swain has been at pains to emphasise that she sees output playing a complementary not a replacement role to that of input. Krashen has fostered this conflictual perspective in a number of articles (e.g. Krashen 1989, 1994 and 1998) that specifically pit claims made for input against those made for output. However, this disputatious approach to input and output and their roles in L2 acquisition may be missing the mark.

Nevertheless, it was such an approach that informed the study reported in Chapter Four. This study attempted to investigate the relative effects of modified input and output on L2 learner's acquisition of new lexis. Modified output was operationalized as giving learners the opportunity to produce their own sentences containing the target items and then to negotiate understanding of these in pairs. In other words, the learners in the modified output group had the opportunity to both produce their own modified output and to listen to the modified output produced by another learner. Thus, the modified output group experienced both modified output and modified input. This was an inevitable consequence of the attempt to construct opportunities for learners to modify output in the context of negotiation sequences. It is not surprising, perhaps, that this group outperformed the other two groups, both of which only experienced modified input. Moreover, as we pointed out in Chapter Three, the interactions between the learners in the modified output condition seemed to be qualitatively different from those between the teacher and the learners in the modified input conditions, the former displaying much greater sensitivity to the processing difficulties the learners experienced.

It is not clear to me that much is to be gained by continuing to investigate modified input and modified output as separate phenomena. It is possible to operationalize modified output in a way that more clearly distinguishes it from modified input. This can be achieved through the use of focussed communication tasks performed between an individual learner and a native speaker/teacher, as in Nobuyoshi and Ellis (1993). In this study, the researcher requested clarification every time the individual learner produced an utterance containing a deviant past tense form thus creating a discourse context for the learner to produce modified output. There is a degree of artificiality in such a procedure, however. For example, the researcher was not allowed to respond to the learner's attempt to reformulate in order to prevent any chance of modified input occurring. Also, such an operationalization is not possible in a setting where there is the opportunity to overhear what others say — the prototypical condition of L2 classrooms.[6] Thus, if the goal of the research is to examine the interactional conditions that can promote acquisition in a classroom setting, little mileage is to be gained from studying modified output in isolation. Nor is it likely that learners experience many opportunities for modified output separate from modified input in most natural settings. In short, the atomistic approach to the study of interaction that has been the mainstay of SLA and which Van Lier (1996) has criticized (see Chapter One) appears increasingly dubious.

It would follow from these arguments that it may be more useful to explore how modified input and output jointly contribute to L2 acquisition in a holistic approach that examines how learner's participation in discourse shapes opportunities to acquire. As I have suggested elsewhere, this might be effectively achieved by examining interactions microgenetically over time and by incorporating tailor-made tests to ascertain whether what learners manage to do in interaction results in the internalisation of new language. Such an approach calls for a sociocultural orientation to research — one that emphasizes how participants jointly construct discourse in accordance with their personally determined goals and their socio-historically determined values. This is the approach that Swain has recently opted for (see, for example, Swain and Lapkin 1998; Swain forthcoming) in her own efforts to explore the roles that modified output plays in acquisition.

The role of learner participation

The constructs of 'input' and 'interaction' can be most easily distinguished with reference to a third construct, 'participation'. The term 'input' suggests the provision of data for language learning that does not involve learners in active participation in the sense of their having to produce the L2 themselves. In contrast, the term 'interaction' presupposes that learners engage not just in listening or reading L2 texts but in speaking or writing them. Interaction supplies the learners with data to which they have actively contributed through their own participation.

The classroom setting provides an opportunity to investigate whether learners participation in interaction is an important factor in creating opportunities for acquisition or whether input is sufficient. This is because what is 'interaction' for one learner is potential 'input' for other learners who are involved in the discourse only as 'hearers'. A question of obvious interest is whether learners benefit from actively participating in classroom interaction or whether they can successfully acquire from the input that is afforded them when their classmates interact. This is an interesting question not least because there is a general assumption in language pedagogy that active participation is desirable and perhaps even necessary for acquisition to take place. In fact, however, research into the effects of participation on language learning have produced very mixed results with some studies showing a positive relationship, others a zero relationship and still others a negative relationship (see Ellis 1988 for a review of some of the earlier research).

In this book, the role of participation has been considered in studies reported in Chapter Three and in Chapter Seven. In each case the question addressed was 'Does participation in sequences involving the negotiation of meaning result in higher levels of acquisition than simply listening to others engage in such sequences?' The results that were obtained from the various studies were quite uniform; no advantage arose out of actually participating in negotiation. Thus, in the input studies of Chapter Three, learners who listened to the interactionally modified input comprehended as well and acquired as many words as learners who took part in the meaning negotiation. In the pushed output study of Chapter Seven, learners who listened in to exchanges where other learners were pushed to modify their output in the context of an oral narrative task demonstrated similar gains in accuracy in the use of the past tense. Thus, where the classroom setting is concerned, there does not appear to be any obvious advantage for either the acquisition of vocabulary or grammar of actively participating in interaction.[7] This accords with the earlier conclusions and with Krashen's general position, namely that the interaction that occurs during meaning negotiation is neither essential for nor especially facilitative of language acquisition. It challenges the claims that have been made regarding the role of interaction in L2 acquisition for as Long (1996: 447) points out 'the claim that conversation facilitates the emergence of at least some types of grammatical devices is essentially one about learner production'. However, at least some learners need to be prepared to engage in conversation in the classroom for otherwise there would be no input for the rest of the learners to listen in to.

The question arises as to why participating in negotiating meaning does not appear to convey any special advantage in the studies reported in this book. One might expect learners to be motivationally primed to attend carefully to the modified input that they obtain through their own efforts to signal a comprehension problem. Such learners, one would think, would be more likely to notice features in the input than learners who functioned only as observers. It is possible, however, that for some learners at least the act of trying to produce the L2 in the public forum of the classroom is so stressful as to detract from their ability to process input. Such might be the case with the Japanese subjects of the modified input and output studies reported in Chapters Three and Seven. Japanese students are well known for their reluctance to participate actively during English lessons. In contrast, the learners who maintain silence may experience less anxiety and so be better able to 'let in' the input their fellow students have secured for them. If this explanation is right, it would follow that in a different instructional context where participation is not viewed as stressful, active participation might prove more beneficial for acquisition.

It is clearly premature to conclude that participation does not facilitate acquisition. The limitations referred to above pertain to just one type of interaction, that associated with the repair of communication problems, and to just one acquisitional setting, classrooms in Japan. Sociocultural theory suggests that social interaction is not just facilitative of acquisition but is the actual site where acquisition takes place. However, the kinds of interaction that sociocultural theory deems important are very different from those the IH claims will assist acquisition. Whereas the IH is concerned narrowly with participation in the negotiation for meaning, sociocultural theory views interaction more broadly as a matrix in which participants can co-construct goals and scaffold each other's attempts to achieve them. In a Vygotskyan framework, interaction may not be necessary for acquisition but it serves as the primary means of mediating learning. In this respect, the construct of 'scaffolding' is of particular importance because, as we saw in Chapter One, it addresses not just the cognitive help a learner might need but the affective help also. Modified input can be made available without interaction but scaffolding can only take place through interaction. One interpretation of the positive results obtained for the modified output condition in the study described in Chapter Four (the only study to show a clear advantage for learners engaging in production) is that this condition was successful in promoting acquisition because it involved effective scaffolding.

Clearly, our understanding of the role of learner production in L2 acquisition is still very limited. Very different positions are currently held. Whereas nobody would probably wish to claim that participation in interaction is necessary for acquisition many believe that it is helpful. However, whereas some see learner production as contributing to acquisition directly, others consider it important because it elicits negative input and facilitates noticing. Furthermore, where some researchers focus their attention on learners' involvement in repair sequences, others examine their participation in interaction more broadly. The case for a broader perspective than has figured in mainstream SLA is strengthening. It would seem foolishly blinkered to continue to invest so much effort in studying the role of learner production in terms of a single type of interaction, especially as the research reported in the previous chapters has not been able to show any clear advantage for learner participation in this particular domain.

Creating an acquisition-rich classroom

Studying the effects of input/interaction on L2 acquisition provides a way of appoaching teaching from an internal as opposed to an external perspective — to see teaching not just as a matter of method or techniques but as the provision of opportunities for learning through the interactions that occur in the classroom. In this respect, research that has actually taken place inside the classroom, as opposed to research that is merely classroom-oriented (Seliger and Long 1983), is of special value.[8] All the studies reported in this book were carried out in real classroom settings. I would like to conclude this chapter, therefore, by drawing generally on this research to consider a number of aspects of teaching that can help to build an 'acquisition-rich' classroom. I shall consider four aspects;

1. Providing acquisition-rich input
2. Building acquisition-rich interaction
3. Fostering intrapersonal interaction for acquisition
4. Teaching grammar

There are, of course many other aspects of an acquisition-rich classroom but these four have all been addressed directly by the research we have previously examined.

The relationship between research, even research that is conducted within the classroom, and language pedagogy is a complex one (see Ellis 1997 for a general discussion). The position that I have adopted is that research findings cannot be used to prescribe, proscribe or even advise teachers about what or how to teach. Research findings are best treated as 'provisional specifications' (Stenhouse 1975), which teachers can choose to act on or ignore, in accordance with the exigencies of their own teaching situation. In cases where they decide to act, the specifications should be treated as hypotheses about teaching and thus subjected to critical scrutiny through teaching, accompanied ideally by some form of action research. The following discussion should be seen in the light of this general position.

Providing acquisition-rich input

One of the conclusions based on the research reported in previous chapters is that learners do not need to engage in social interaction in order to acquire the L2; they can benefit equally, and perhaps in some cases, to a greater extent by simply attending to non-interactive input. Two provisional specifications follow. The first is that teachers should be prepared to allocate ample time to non-interactive activities that expose learners to input. The second is that they should consider the nature of the input to which they expose learners in order to ensure that it is maximally effective for acquisition.

The first proposal is controversial. An implication of communicative language teaching, particularly as this is manifested through task-based language teaching, is that teachers should engage learners in interaction in the classroom and that the more interaction there is the better it is for learning. The idea that teachers should spend more time in non-reciprocal activities that provide learners with plentiful input would appear to be in opposition to this. However, this is not entirely the case. First, task-based language teaching potentially involves the use of non-reciprocal as well as reciprocal tasks even though definitions of 'task' and of task-based research frequently assume learner production is required. The studies reported in Chapters Three and Four demonstrate the pedagogic viability of non-reciprocal, listen-and-do tasks. Second, an instructional language programme needs to provide activities that learners can undertake outside as well as inside the classroom. Whereas there are obvious practical problems in engaging learners in out-of-class activities that involve interaction, it is a relatively easier matter to provide out-of-class input activities. One obvious way in which this can be achieved is through an extensive reading programme of the kind Krashen

(1989) advocates.[9] Creating an input-rich language programme, therefore, need not be seen as antithetical to the principles of communicative language teaching. Arguably, it constitutes the single most important feature of successful teaching.

It is, of course, not sufficient just to create an input-rich instructional programme; what is needed is a programme that supplies input that is acquisition-rich. In other words, of crucial importance is the nature of the input learners are exposed to. It is here that the notion of 'modification' is crucial; learners need input that is adjusted to their level. There would seem little sense in exposing learners to unmodified input in the name of 'authenticity'. What matters for acquisition is not whether the input contains the kind of language that native speakers use when communicating with each other (the usual definition of 'authenticity') but whether the learners are able to process the input both for comprehension and for acquisition (i.e. whether they are able to 'authenticate' the input, as Widdowson (1979b) puts it). There is plenty of evidence that premodified input aids comprehension (see Chapter One) and rather less that it aids acquisition. However, Study One in Chapter Three demonstrated that learners receiving premodified input were able to learn and subsequently remember more new words than learners exposed to unmodified, 'authentic' input.

What is the nature of the input modifications that will promote acquisition? Here little is yet known as most of the research to date has focussed on modifications that assist comprehension. Clearly, the modified input needs to incorporate features that have not yet been acquired by the learners. The studies reported in this book achieved this by pre-testing learners in order to establish a set of lexical items that were unknown to most of the learners. Such a procedure is not practical in the context of everyday teaching but perhaps this is less of a problem than it appears. The problem teachers face is less that of ensuring that learners are exposed to input that is sufficiently complex to provide data for language acquisition as that of offering input that is sufficiently simple for learners to be capable of authenticating it. As Krashen has argued, 'rough tuning' is likely to achieve both goals. It would be helpful, however, if the research could provide some general guidance. Study Three in Chapter Three makes a start in this direction. It found the following modifications related to vocabulary acquisition: range, frequency and length of direction. Range, in particular, emerged as an important factor; learners need the opportunity to experience a new item in a number of different contexts. Clearly, though, we cannot generalize from the results of this study. It is likely that different variables will emerge as important for different learners, depending in particular on their level of proficiency in the L2. Thus the variables found to be significant in the case of Japanese high school students may not prove to be the same as those for other groups of learners. Input modification is necessarily a dynamic process so we can expect somewhat different factors to be important for learners at different levels of L2 development.

The question as to what constitutes acquisition-rich input can be approached from another angle; the manner in which learners are led to process the input they are exposed to. We have noted that learners have a limited processing capacity and, as a result, frequently experience difficulty in processing input simultaneously for form and meaning, allocating their scarce resources to one or the other, depending on the task they are being asked to perform and their own goals. However, without attention to form, acquisition is not possible. It follows, therefore, that teachers need to engage learners in attending to form. One way in which this might be achieved is by designing separate input activities for comprehension and for acquisition. First, learners might be invited to process input in order to understand it. Second, they could be asked to return to the input in order to notice specific formal features. Materials developed by Ellis and Gaies (1998) illustrate how this can be done.

Building acquisition-rich interaction

In emphasizing the importance that teachers should attach to acquisition-rich input, I do not wish to suggest that this should be at the expense of building acquisition-rich interaction in the classroom. We have seen in a number of studies reported in this book that interaction serves as an effective means of promoting acquisition. For many language learners the classroom constitutes the primary and perhaps only opportunity to engage in face-to-face interaction in the L2.

One of the problems many teachers face is how to involve learners with limited L2 proficiency and/or an inherent reluctance to risk taking part in interaction. The listen-and-do tasks used in the various studies would seem to provide one solution to this problem. This is because they limit and structure the extent of the learners' participation. By providing a set of formulas for performing clarification requests the burden of production on learners is minimized while still affording them the opportunity to exert some control over the way the interaction unfolds. These tasks worked remarkably well with learners noted for their inability or unwillingness to participate in English discourse. They provide a means of engaging learners in interaction in a whole-class context (as in the studies in Chapter Three) and also in pairs (as in the study in Chapter Four), where, of course the learners have responsibility for building the interaction by themselves.

Listen-and-do tasks of the kind used in Chapter Three require considerable communication skills on the part of the teacher. When learners request clarification the teacher needs to be able to provide responses that deal adequately with the problem. Frequently this will involve teachers in defining lexical items that students have not understood. As we have seen, this can easily result in teachers providing more information in their definitions than learners can process, with a negative impact on acquisition. Definitions work best when they are relatively short and frugal, identifying one of two key features of the referent of the item. Building acquisition-rich interactions out of such tasks, then, requires teachers to be skilled interactors. A question of some interest is whether teachers will develop the necessary communication skills experientially through the practice of teaching or whether training in these skills is needed or is helpful.

The listen-and-do tasks were designed to lead to one particular type of interaction — the negotiation for meaning. However, in this chapter, I have voiced my doubts regarding the centrality afforded to discourse repair in mainstream SLA, suggesting that its importance for L2 acquisition may have been overestimated. I have even graver doubts regarding the proposal that arises implicitly, and sometimes explicitly, from researchers working in this paradigm, namely that classroom discourse needs to be organized in such a way that it affords plentiful opportunities for learners to experience and repair communication problems. I have suggested that researchers adopt a broader view of interaction such as that afforded by sociocultural theory. From this perspective, the key construct is that of scaffolding. How can teachers use interaction to help learners construct utterances using linguistic resources the learners have not yet developed? In Chapter Nine I attempted to answer this question by arguing the need for learner topic-control. When learners are in control of the topic or, at least, of the development of a teacher-nominated topic, more opportunities arise for teachers to build on what the learners say by means of topic-continuation devices such as repetitions, expansions, extensions and prompts. These enable the teacher to scaffold the learner's utterances in very similar ways to those used by caretakers talking to young children (see Gaies 1979). Chapter Nine suggested a number of ways in which learners can be given control of a topic in the classroom. I see topic control as a far more important construct than meaning negotiation where language teaching is concerned.

Finally, there are obvious implications for teaching to be drawn from the conclusion that active learner participation in classroom discourse (or, at least, in sequences involving meaning negotiation) does not result in higher levels of acquisition than simply listening to the input generated by others. Teachers have traditionally emphasized learner participation, sometimes even assigning grades on the basis of individual learners' contributions in the classroom. In such ways teachers put learners under pressure to participate. Krashen (1982) has suggested that this can result in learners experiencing anxiety which can impact negatively on acquisition. An alternative approach, the one that I favour and that is compatible with the results of the research in Chapters Three and Seven, is to allow learners to self-nominate, thus giving them the option of participating if they so wish or of adopting a listening role. Such an approach assumes that there will always be some learners who are prepared to participate, an assumption again supported by the research results.

In Allwright's terms, interaction is the 'fundamental fact of language pedagogy' (Allwright 1984a: 156) because it entails the joint management of learning and is the means by which learners obtain samples of the language. This is a view with which I have long been in sympathy. However, I have come to be less certain of the fundamental importance of *social* interaction (for its is this kind that Allwright is referring to). Interpersonal interaction clearly has an important role to play in language teaching/learning and I have tried to suggest ways in which this role might be accomplished. However, I now see it as somewhat less than 'fundamental'. More fundamental, perhaps, is the other type of interaction, intrapersonal interaction.

Fostering intrapersonal interaction

It is not unreasonable to assume that when learners take part in a language lesson there is as much if not more 'conversation' going on inside their heads as there is in the classroom itself. Learners 'talk' to themselves, sometimes stimulated by the language they hear or read, and sometimes, of course, by other entirely personal matters. This 'private speech', sociocultural theory suggests, is especially likely to arise when learners are confronted with a task that is cognitively challenging; it serves as a means by which learners try to achieve self-control. It is also, potentially, a mechanism by which learners can acquire the L2. Teachers, of course, have no direct control over when learners engage in private talk nor over what they choose to 'talk' about. Nevertheless, there are various procedures that teachers can employ to encourage learners to engage in private talk and to make use of it to focus on language matters.

In Chapter Six we looked at one such procedure, one that involves what Allwright (1984a) refers to as 'interacting with a text'. The procedure consists of the following steps:

1. Demonstration of the self-questioning strategy.
2. Presentation of generic question stems to promote self-questioning.

3. Opportunity for students to practice using the question stems on a written passage.
4. Discussion of general metacognitive strategies (e.g. monitoring understanding while reading).
5. Further opportunity for students to practise asking and answering their own questions in writing.

The study reported in Chapter Six showed that students who received training in this procedure were better able to construct 'generative' questions, comprehended the test passage better, and acquired more words from it than students who simply read the test passage and formulated questions without training. In short, this study suggests that where one strategy for engaging in 'interaction with a text' is concerned learners can improve their performance as a result of training. It also indicates the value of encouraging learners to externalize the mental processing (in this case, posing and answering questions) that is involved in intrapersonal interaction.

I have suggested that the notion of intrapsychological interaction can profitably be explored with reference to the depth-of-processing model. This claims that learning is enhanced when learners process material deeply, for example by forming interconnections between propositions and elaborate on the input they are exposed to. Depth of processing theory suggests that language acquisition is enhanced when the mental activity learners engage in causes them to go *beyond* the input. Good teachers, I suspect, have always been adept at finding ways of helping learners achieve this. One way is the kind of direct training described above. Another way, of course, is through social interaction. Teachers can stimulate thinking by the way they talk to students, for example by the kinds of questions they ask.[10] However, as I have already pointed out, we know very little about the relationship between social and intrapyshcological interaction and even less about intrapsychological interaction and L2 learning.

Language learning is not just a matter of processing input and output but of engaging in the kinds of thinking processes that language serves and that can serve language development. Language teaching needs to be conceptualized in terms of how learners can be engaged at these deeper psychological levels, not just in terms of dishing out input and providing opportunities for output. It is perhaps this aspect that has been most neglected in current theories of language teaching (e.g. task-based language teaching).

Teaching grammar

One of the profoundest questions facing language teachers is how to integrate a focus on language as a system (by teaching grammar, for example) with the kind of focus on meaning-making that is required by a pedagogy that emphasizes incidental language acquisition through interaction. Two chapters in this book have addressed this issue.

One way of integrating a focus on grammatical form and on meaning-making is through output enhancement. This involves the use of a focussed communication task (i.e. a task designed to stimulate the use of a specific grammatical form in the context of message-oriented communication). The focussed communication task in Chapter Seven involved students using a picture story to produce an oral narrative which created obligatory occasions for the past tense. Output enhancement was achieved by the teacher requesting clarification every time a student narrator produced an utterance containing a deviant past tense form. This created an opportunity for the student to reformulate his/her utterance by correcting the past tense form. Focussed communication tasks may or may not result in learners becoming aware of the grammatical focus. However, they are premised on the assumption that students' primary attention will be on meaning-making not on the correct production of the target form. Chapter Seven showed that the learners studied did treat the task as primarily requiring them to tell a story but that it also created opportunities for them to modify their output by correcting past tense errors. It suggests that focussed communication tasks can be effective in integrating form and meaning. However, it is not clear to what extent such tasks can be designed for a wide range of grammatical structures, for, as Loschky and Bley Vroman (1993) have pointed out, it is difficult to construct tasks that make the use of particular structures essential.

The second way of inducing a focus on form while communicating is through what I have called consciousness-raising tasks (Ellis 1991 and 1993). A consciousness-raising task is a task that makes grammar the topic to be communicated about. This was the approach adopted in Chapter Eight. Learners were given cards on which were written sentences with verbs that take dative forms. They were asked to first share their sentences and classify them into three groups and then to formulate rules to describe the sentence patterns in the three groups. Such tasks embody a discovery-based approach to the teaching of grammar; learners are given data and guided to discovering grammatical rules for themselves. They also involve the students in communicating, including, potentially, negotiating for meaning when a comprehension problem arises. Chapter Nine showed that the conciousness-raising task was successful on both fronts. The students who completed the task scored as highly in a grammaticality judgement test as students who received a direct explanation and they engaged in a number of negotiation sequences, although these appeared to be somewhat mechanical in nature. Other consciousness-raising tasks, such as dictogloss[11] (Wajnryb 1990), have also been successful in encouraging learners to communicate about grammar, producing much richer interactions than those reported in Chapter Seven (see Swain 1995).

Conciousness-raising tasks are premised on the assumption that learners benefit from explicit knowledge of a grammatical structure. Elsewhere, I have argued that explicit knowledge has a role to play not only in language use (i.e. through monitoring, as proposed by Krashen (1981), but also in facilitating the processes of noticing and noticing-the-gap, which in a computational model of L2 acquisition, are viewed as necessary steps in the development of implicit L2 knowledge (see Ellis 1990 and 1993). I would now add that consciousness-raising tasks can also assist acquisition by promoting the depth of processing, which in intrapsychological terms, I have claimed can promote acquisition. Requiring learners to think and talk about grammar potentially involves greater intellectual effort than simply listening to a teacher's explanation and, if this takes place in the target language may foster both the process of acquiring new knowledge and that of analyzing and restructuring existing knowledge.

Conclusion

At the theoretical level, the role of social interaction remains controversial in SLA. On the one hand there are innatist models of acquisition that emphasize the learner's rather than the environment's contribution to learning, while, as we have seen in this book, there are interactionist models that view interaction as more fundamental to learning. As Long (1996) has wisely pointed out, little is to be gained from pitting innatist and interactionist theories against each other. He comments 'a reasonable working hypothesis ... would be that neither the environment nor innate knowledge suffice' (p. 414). It follows from such a hypothesis that there is a need to explore the contribution of the linguistic environment and inevitably this will involve the study of how social interaction contributes to acquisition. There has been, however, a marked paucity of research that has actually studied how interaction affects L2 acquisition, most of the previous research having focussed on how it affects comprehension or task performance. One the purposes of this book has been to remedy this by reporting a number of empirical studies of the language that is actually acquired from input and interaction.

The book has also tried to place the research that has taken place to date, including that reported in the various chapters, in a wide theoretical context. In particular, it has drawn attention to the limitations of the theoretical framework that has informed much of research, namely the Interaction Hypothesis. These limitations relate both to the restrictive nature of the kind of discourse that has been addressed (i.e. to sequences involving the repair of a communication problem) and to the failure to acknowledge the importance of the intrapyschological interactions that occur as learners struggle to make and to learn the L2. In this respect, it has been suggested that the research net be widened to encompass both sociocultural theory and the depth-of-processing model. So far, there have been few studies that have examined the role of interaction in L2 acquisition from these theoretical perspectives, which have also been insufficiently represented in this book. The future will hopefully witness both an increased interest in the role of social interaction, broadly defined, and in the intrapyschological talk that learners engage in and that mediates between social interaction and language acquisition.

Notes

1. A distinction needs to be drawn between implicit/explicit learning and implicit/explicit knowledge. Whereas the first of these is controversial the second is not. There is general acceptance that language learners, especially adult ones, develop both implicit and explicit knowledge. However, as we have seen, there is less agreement regarding the nature of learning itself.

2. Long, Inagaki and Ortega (1998) report a study designed to investigate the effects of 'models' (that supply positive evidence) and 'recasts' (that supply negative evidence) on the acquisition of grammatical structures. The study failed to provide convincing evidence that the latter was more effective than the former. The interactions which were experimentally manipulated to ensure that the participants experienced either models or recasts were very artificial in nature.

3. A number of recent studies, however, have made a start on investigating intake. Alanen (1995) studied L2 learners' intake of a number of features of semi-artificial Finnish, showing a relationship between what learners reported noticing and what they 'acquired' as measured by discrete item post tests. Leow (1997) used think aloud protocols to measure noticing of grammatical forms in Spanish during a crossword task, also finding a relationship between reported noticing and performance on a post-test. Both of these studies involved written input however. Philp (1999) examined whether learners notice feedback in conversations, demonstrating that they were able to recall a recast immediately following it in most cases.

4. There is of course a problem with such longitudinal studies. It most cases it will be impossible to obtain a record of all the interactions that learners participate in and therefore to document the effects of specific interactional features on long-term acquisition. Nevertheless, much is to be gained by exploring how learners perform the same kind of interactional task from one time to the next.

5. Krashen could argue that the relatively weak correlations between comprehension and acquisition obtained in some of the studies are the result of learners' affective orientations; that is, they sometimes comprehended but because they were lacking in motivation failed to 'let in' the new linguistic material.

6. Chapter Seven reports a study where an attempt to create opportunities for modified output in a classroom setting was made. However, as in the study in Chapter Four, one learner's pushed output inevitably became another learner's modified input.

7. It should be noted, however, that other studies have found that participating in meaning negotiation is more effective than simply listening in to interactionally modified input. As we noted in Chapter One, Mackey (1995) found that participation in interaction led to higher levels of WH question acquisition that simply observing interaction.

8. Nunan (1991), in a review of 50 classroom-oriented studies, found that only 15 drew their data directly from the language classroom. The majority obtained data outside in laboratory-like settings.

9. Learners can also be provided with extensive listening materials to use outside the classroom. Beebe (1992) found that one of the characteristics of Japanese high school students who were successful in developing oral fluency in English was the extent to which they engaged in listening activities outside the classroom.

10. There is a fairly rich literature that has addressed the relationship between the kinds of questions teachers ask (in particular, whether they are display or referential questions) and various aspects of classroom discourse and learner production (see Ellis 1994 for a review). However, in L2 classroom research there has been no attempt to investigate how teacher's questions influence the mental activity that language learners engage in. In the context of the L1 classroom, however, there has been some (e.g. Barnes 1969 and 1976).

11. Dictogloss is based on texts that have been specially written to model a particular grammatical construction. The teacher reads out the text twice at normal speed and the students take written notes. The speed of delivery prevents them writing down the text verbatim. They then work in small groups to reconstruct the text, pooling the information they have in their notes. Kowal and Swain (1994) found that such tasks generate a considerable number of 'language related episodes', although these were often not focussed on the specific grammatical feature that the text was modelling.

References

Ahmed, M. 1988. Speaking as Cognitive Regulation: A Study of L1 and L2 Dyadic Problem-solving Activity. Ph. D. dissertation. Newark: University of Delaware.

Aitcheson, J. 1987. *Words in the Mind: An Introduction to the Mental Lexicon.* Oxford: Blackwell.

Alanen, R. 1995. "Input Enhancement and Rule Presentation in Second Language Acquisition". In R. Schmidt (ed.).

Aljaafreh, A. and J. Lantolf. 1994. "Negative Feedback as Regulation and Second Language Learning in the Zone of Proximal Development". *Modern Language Journal* 78: 465–83.

Allen, P., M. Swain, B. Harley, and J. Cummins. 1990. "Aspects of Classroom Treatment: Toward a More Comprehensive View of Second Language Education". In B. Harley, P. Allen, J. Cummins, and M. Swain (eds).

Allwright, R. 1984a. "The Importance of Interaction in Classroom Language Learning". *Applied Linguistics* 5: 156–171.

Allwright, B. 1984b. Why Don't Learners Learn What Teachers Teach? — The Interaction Hypothesis. In D. Singleton and D. Little (eds), *Language Learning in Formal and Informal Contexts.* Dublin: IRAAL.

Anderson, A. and T. Lynch. 1988. *Listening.* Oxford: Oxford University Press.

Appel, G. and J. Lantolf. 1994. "Speaking as Mediation: A Study of L1 and L2 Text Recall Tasks". *The Modern Language Journal* 78: 437–452.

Arnaud, P and H. Bejoint (eds). *Vocabulary and Applied Linguistics.* Basingstoke: MacMillan.

Artigal, J. 1992. Some Considerations on Why a New Language is Acquired by Being Used". *International Journal of Applied Linguistics* 2: 221–240.

Asher, J. 1977. *Learning Another Language Through Actions: The Complete Teacher's Guidebook.* Los Gatos, CA.: Sky Oak Publications.

Aston, G. 1986. "Trouble-shooting in Interaction with Learners: The More the Merrier?" *Applied Linguistics* 7: 128–43.

Bardovi-Harlig, K. and D. Reynolds. 1995. "The Role of Lexical Aspect in the Acquisition of Tense and Aspect". *TESOL Quarterly* 29: 55–84.

Barnard, H. 1961. "A Test of P. U. C. Students: Vocabulary in Chotanagpur". *Bulletin of the Central Institute of English* 1: 90–110 (cited in Nation 1990).

Barnes, D. 1969. Language in the Secondary Classroom. In D. Barnes, J. Britton and M. Torbe (eds), *Language, the Learner and the School*. Harmondsworth: Penguin.

Barnes, D. 1976. *From Communication to Curriculum*. Harmondsworth: Penguin.

Beck, I., McKeown, M. and Omanson, R. 1987. "The Effects of Diverse Vocabulary Instructional Techniques". In M. McKeown and M. Curtis (eds).

Beebe, J. 1992. "'To Speak English With my Voice': A Study of Seven Successful English Conversationalists". Unpublished paper. Tokyo: Temple University Japan.

Benoussan, M. and B. Laufer. 1984. "Lexical Guessing in Context in EFL Reading Comprehension". *Journal of Research in Reading* 7: 15–32.

Bialystok, E. 1978. A Theoretical Model of Second Language Learning. *Language Learning* 28: 69–84.

Bialystok, E. 1981. "The Role of Linguistic Knowledge in Second Language Use". *Studies in Second Language Acquisition* 4: 31–45.

Bialystok, E. and M. Sharwood Smith. 1985. "Interlanguage is not a State of Mind: An Evaluation of the Construct for Second Language Acquisition. *Applied Linguistics* 6: 101–17.

Bloom, B. 1956. *Taxonomy of Educational Objectives: The Classification of Educational Goals. Handbook 1: Cognitive Domain*. New York: McKay.

Braidi, S. 1995. "Reconsidering the Role of Interaction and Input in Second Language Acquisition". *Language Learning* 45: 141–175.

Brown, C. 1993. "Factors Affecting the Acquisition of Vocabulary: Frequency and Saliency of Words. In T. Huckin, M. Haynes and J. Coady (eds).

Brown, G. 1995. *Speakers, Listeners and Communication*. Cambridge: Cambridge University Press.

Brown, G. and G. Yule. 1993. *Discourse Analysis*. Cambridge: Cambridge University Press.

Brown, R. 1973. *A First Language: The Early Stages*. Cambridge, Mass.: Harvard University Press.

Brown, T. and F. Perry. 1991. "A Comparison of Three Learning Strategies for ESL Vocabulary Acquisition. *TESOL Quarterly* 25: 665–670.

Brumfit, C. 1984. *Communicative Methodology in Language Teaching*. Cambridge: Cambridge University Press.

Bygate, M. 1988. "Units of Oral Expression and Language Learning in Small Group Interaction. *Applied Linguistics* 9: 59–82.

Carpay, J. 1975. "Onderwijsleerpsychologie en Leergangontwikkeling in het Moderne Vreemde Talen-onderwijs". Groningen: Wolters-Noordhoff (cited in Palmberg 1987).

Carroll, J. 1981. "Twenty-five Years of Research on Foreign Language Aptitude". In K. Diller (ed.).

Carroll, J. 1987. "New Perspectives in the Analysis of Abilities". In R. Ronning, J. Glover, J. Conoley and J. Witts (eds), *The Influence of Cognitive Psychology on Testing* (pp. 267–284). Hillsdale, NJ: Lawrence Erlbaum.

Carroll, J. 1990. "Cognitive Abilities in Foreign Language Aptitude: Then and Now". In T. Parry and C. Stansfield (eds).

Carroll, J. and S. Sapon. 1959. *Modern Language Aptitude Test — Form A*. New York: The Psychological Corporation.

Clark, H. and E. Clark. 1977. *Psychology and Language: An Introduction to Psycholinguistics*. New York: Harcourt Brace Jovanovich.

Chaudron, C. 1982. Vocabulary Elaboration in Teachers' Speech to L2 Learners. *Studies in Second Language Acquisition* 4: 170–80.

Chaudron, C. 1988. *Second Language Classroom Research*. Cambridge: Cambridge University Press.

Clark, E. 1993. *The Lexicon in Acquisition*. Cambridge: Cambridge University Press.

Coady, J. 1993. "Research on ESL/EFL Vocabulary Acquisition: Putting it in Context". In T. Huckin, M. Haynes, and J. Coady (eds).

Coady, J. 1997. "L2 Vocabulary Acquisition through Extensive Reading. In J. Coady and T. Huckin (eds).

Coady, J. and T. Huckin (eds) 1997. *Second Language Vocabulary Acquisition*. Cambridge: Cambridge University Press.

Cohen, A. 1998. "Strategies in Learning and Using a Second Language". London: Longman.

Cohen, J. and P. Cohen. 1975. "Applied Multiple Regression/Correlation Analysis for the Behavioural Sciences". Hillsdale, NJ.: Lawrence Erlbaum.

Coughlan, P. and P. Duff. 1994. "Same Task, Different Activities: Analysis of SLA from an Activity Theory Perspective". In J. Lantolf and G. Appel (eds).

Curtis, M. 1987. "Vocabulary Testing and Vocabulary Instruction". In M. McKeown and M. Curtis (eds).

Craik, F. and E. Tulving. 1972. Levels of Processing: A Framework for Memory Research. *Journal of Verbal Learning and Verbal Behavior* 11: 671–684.

Craik, F. and E. Tulving. 1975. "Depth of Processing and the Retention of Words in Episodic Memory". *Journal of Experimental Psychology* 104: 268–294.

Crookes, G. and R. Schmidt. 1990. "Motivation: Reopening the Research Agenda". *University of Hawaii Working Papers in ESL* 8: 217–256.

Crookes, G. and S. Gass (eds). 1993. "Tasks and Language Learning: Integrating Theory and Practice". Clevedon: Multilingual Matters.

Crow, J. and J. Quigley. 1985. "A Semantic Field Approach to Passive Vocabulary Acquisition for Reading Comprehension". *TESOL Quarterly* 19: 497–513.

Cummins, J. 1981. "Bilingualism and Minority Children". Ontario: Ontario Institute for Studies in Education.

Cummins, J. 1983. "Language Proficiency and Academic Achievement". In J. Oller (ed.), *Issues in Language Testing Research*. Rowley, Mass: Newbury House.

Davey, B. and S. McBride. "Effects of Question Generation Training on Reading Comprehension". *Journal of Educational Psychology* 78: 256–262.

Day, R. 1994. "Student Participation in the ESL Classroom, or Some Imperfections of Practice". *Language Learning* 34: 69–102.

Day, R. (ed.). 1986. *Talking to Learn*. Rowley, MA.: Newbury House.

Day, R., C. Omura and M. Hiramatsu. 1991. "Incidental Vocabulary Learning and Reading". *Reading in a Foreign Language* 7: 541–551.

De Bot, K. "The Psycholinguistics of the Output Hypothesis". *Language Learning* 46: 529–555.

DeKeyser, R. 1995. "Learning Second Language Grammar Rules: An Experiment with a Miniature Linguistic System". *Studies in Second Language Acquisition* 17: 379–410.

DeKeyser, R. 1998. "Beyond Focus on Form: Cognitive Perspectives on Learning and Practicing Second Language Grammar". In C. Doughty and J. Williams (eds).

DiCamilla, J. and Anton, M. 1997. "Repetition in the Collaborative Discourse of L2 learners: A Vygotskyan Perspective". *Canadian Modern language Journal* 53: 609–633.

Dickens, P. and E. Woods. 1988. "Some Criteria for the Development of Communicative Grammar Tasks". *TESOL Quarterly* 22: 621–646.

Di Pietro, R. 1987. *Strategic Interaction*. Cambridge: Cambridge University Press.

Doctorow, M., M. Wittrock and C. Marks. 1978. "Generative Processes in Reading Comprehension". *Journal of Educational Psychology* 70: 109–118.

Donato, R. 1994. "Collective Scaffolding in Second Language Learning". In J. Lantolf and G. Appel (eds).

Donato, R. 2000. "Sociocultural Contributions to Understanding the Foreign and Second Language Classroom". In J. Lantolf (ed.).

Doughty, C. and T. Pica. 1986. "'Information Gap' Tasks: Do they Facilitate Second Language Acquisition?" *TESOL Quarterly* 20: 305–325.

Doughty, C. and E. Varela. 1998. "Communicative Focus on Form". In C. Doughty and J. Williams (eds).

Doughty, C. and J. Williams (eds). 1998. *Focus on Form in Classroom Second Language Acquisition*. Cambridge: Cambridge University Press.

Drum, P. 1983. "Vocabulary Knowledge". In J. Niles and L. Harris (eds.), *Searches for Meaning in Reading: Language Processes and Instruction*. Rochester, NY: National Reading Conference.

Drum, P. and B. Konopak. 1987. "Learning Word Meanings from Written Context". In M. McKeown and M. Curtis (eds).

Duff, P. 1986. "Another Look at Interlanguage Talk: Taking Task to Task. In R. Day (ed.).

Duncan, S. and de E. Avila. 1981. *Peabody Picture Vocabulary Test — Revised*. Circle Pines, MN: American Guidance Service.

Dupuy, B. and S. Krashen. 1993. Incidental Vocabulary Acquisition in French as a Foreign Language". *Applied Language Learning* 4: 55–63.

Edwards, P. (ed.) 1967. *The Encyclopedia of Philosophy, Vol. 1*. New York and London: MacMillan.

Ehrlich, S. P. Avery, and C. Yorio. 1989. "Discourse Structure and the Negotiation of Comprehensible Input". *Studies in Second Language Acquisition* 11: 397–414.

Ehrman, M. and R. Oxford. 1995. "Cognition Plus: Correlates of Language Learning Success". *The Modern Language Journal* 79: 67–89.

Eller, R., Pappas, C. and E. Brown. 1988. "The Lexical Development of Kindergarteners: Learning from Written Context. *Journal of Reading Behavior* 20: 5–24.

Elley, W. 1989. "Vocabulary Acquisition from Listening to Stories". *Reading Research Quarterly* 24: 174–187.

Ellis, N. 1996. "Sequencing in SLA: Phonological Memory, Chunking, and Points of Order". *Studies in Second Language Acquisition* 18: 91–126.

Ellis, N. 1997. "Vocabulary Acquisition: Word Structure, Collocation, Word-class, and Meaning". In N. Schmitt and M. McCarthy (eds).

Ellis, N. and A. Beaton. 1993a. "Factors Affecting the Learning of Foreign Language Vocabulary Learning: Imagery Keyword Mediators and Phonological Short-term Memory". *Quarterly Journal of Experimental Psychology* 46: 533–58.

Ellis, N. and A. Beaton. 1993b. "Psycholinguistic Determinants of Foreign Language Vocabulary Learning". *Language Learning* 43: 559–617.

Ellis, R. 1984a. "Can Syntax be Taught? A Study of the Effects of Formal Instruction on the Acquisition of WH Questions by Children". *Applied Linguistics* 5: 138–55.

Ellis, R. 1984b. *Classroom Second Language Development*. Oxford: Pergamon.

Ellis, R. 1985. "Teacher-pupil Interaction in Second Language Development". In S. Gass and C. Madden (eds).

Ellis, R. 1988. "The Role of Practice in Classroom Language Learning". *Teanga* 8: 1–28.

Ellis, R. *Instructed Second Language Acquisition*. Oxford: Blackwell.

Ellis, R. 1991. *Second Language Acquisition and Language Pedagogy*. Clevedon: Multilingual Matters.

Ellis, R. 1992. "Learning to Communicate in the Classroom". *Studies in Second Language Acquisition* 14: 1–23.

Ellis, R. 1993. "Second Language Acquisition and the Structural Syllabus". *TESOL Quarterly* 27: 91–113.

Ellis, R. 1994. *The Study of Second language Acquisition*. Oxford: Oxford University Press.

Ellis, R. 1995. "Uptake as Language Awareness". *Language Awareness* 4: 147–160.

Ellis, R. 1997. *SLA Research and Language Teaching*. Oxford: Oxford University Press.

Ellis, R. and R. Heimbach. 1997. "Bugs and Birds: Children's Acquisition of Second Language Vocabulary through Interaction". *System* 25: 247–259.

Ellis, R., Y. Tanaka and A. Yamazaki. 1994. "Classroom Interaction, Comprehension, and L2 Vocabulary Acquisition. *Language Learning* 44: 449–491.

Ellman, J. and J. McClelland. 1982. "Exploiting the Lawful Variability of the Speech Wave". In J. Perkell and D. Klatt (eds), *Invariance and Variability in the Speech Wave*. Hillsdale, NJ: Lawrence Erlbaum.

Ernst, S. 1994. "'Talking Circle': Conversation, Negotiation in the ESL Classroom". *TESOL Quarterly* 28: 293–322.

Eskey, D. 1989. "Holding in the Bottom: An Interactive Approach to the Language Problems of Second Language Readers". In P. Carrell, J. Devine and D. Eskey (eds), *Interactive Approaches to Second Language Reading.* Cambridge: Cambridge University Press.

Faerch, C. and G. Kasper. 1985. "Procedural Knowledge as a Component of Foreign Language Learners' Communicative Competence". In H. Bolte and W. Herrlitz (eds), *Kommunikation im Sprachunterricht.* Utrecht: Instituut 'Franzen', University of Utrecht.

Faerch, C., and G. Kasper. 1986. "The Role of Comprehension in Second-language Learning". *Applied Linguistics* 7: 257–74.

Faerch, C., K. Haastrup and R. Phillips. 1984. *Learner Language and Language Learning.* Copenhagen: Gyldendals Sprogbibliotek.

Feitelson, D., Z. Goldstein, J. Iraqi and D. Share. 1993. "Effects of Listening to Story Reading on Aspects of Literacy Acquisition in a Diglossic Situation". *Reading Research Quarterly* 28: 70–79.

Felix, S. 1978. "Some Differences between First and Second Language Acquisition". In N. Waterson and C. Snow (eds).

Firth, A. and J. Wagner. 1997. "On Discourse, Communication, and (Some) Fundamental Concepts in SLA Research". *The Modern Language Journal* 81: 285–300.

Flowerdew, J. 1992a. "Definitions in Science Lectures". *Applied Linguistics* 13: 202–21.

Flowerdew, J. 1992b. "Salience in the Performance of one Speech Act: The Case of Definitions". *Discourse Processes* 15: 165–81.

Foley, J. 1991. "A Psycholinguistic Framework for Task-based Approaches to Language Teaching". *Applied Linguistics* 12: 62–75.

Foster, P. 1998. "A Classroom Perspective on the Negotiation of Meaning". *Applied Linguistics* 19: 1–23.

Francis, W. and H. Kucera. 1982. "Frequency Analysis of English Usage: Lexicon and Grammar". In T. Huckin, M. Haynes, and J. Coady (eds).

Frawley, W. and J. Lantolf. 1985. "Second Language Discourse: A Vygotskyan Perspective". *Applied Linguistics* 6: 19–44.

Frawley, W. and J. Lantolf. 1986. "Private Speech and Self-regulation: A Commentary on Frauenglass and Diaz". *Developmental Psychology* 22: 706–708.

Gaies, S. 1977. "The Nature of Linguistic Input in Formal Second Language Learning: Linguistic and Communicative Strategies". In H. Brown, C. Yorio, and R. Crymes (eds), *On TESOL '77.* Washington, D. C.: TESOL.

Gaies, S. 1979. "Linguistic Input in First and Second Language Learning". In F. Eckman and A. Hastings (eds), *Studies in First and Second Language Acquisition*. Rowley, MA: Newbury House.

Gardner, R. 1980. "On the Validity of Affective Variables in Second Language Acquisition: Conceptual, Contextual, and Statistical Considerations". *Language Learning* 30: 255–270.

Gardner, R. 1985. *Social Psychology and Second Language Learning: The Role of Attitude and Motivation*. London: Edward Arnold.

Gardner, R and P. MacIntyre. 1992. "A Student's Contributions to Second Language Learning. Part 1: Cognitive Variables". *Language Teaching* 25: 211–220.

Gass, S. 1988. "Integrating Research Areas: A Framework for Second Language Studies". *Applied Linguistics* 9: 198–217.

Gass, S. 1997. *Input, Interaction and the Second Language Learner*. Mahwah, NJ: Lawrence Erlbaum.

Gass, S., A. Mackey and T. Pica. 1998. "The Role of Input and Interaction in Second Language Acquisition: Introduction to the Special Issue". *The Modern Language Journal* 82: 299–305.

Gass, S. and C. Madden (eds). 1985. *Input and Second Language Acquisition*. Rowley, MA.: Newbury House.

Gass, S. and E. Varonis. 1984. "The Effect of Familiarity on the Comprehension of Nonnative Speech". *Language Learning* 34: 65–89.

Gass, S. and E. Varonis. 1994. "Input, Interaction, and Second Language Production". *Studies in Second Language Acquisition* 16: 283–302.

Gathercole, S. and A. Baddeley. 1990. "The Role of Phonological Memory in Vocabulary Acquisition: A Study of Young Children Learning New Names". *British Psychology* 81: 439–454.

Genesee, F. 1976. "The Role of Intelligence in Second Language Learning". *Language Learning* 26: 267–80.

Harris, M. 1992. *Language Experience and Early Language Development: From Input to Uptake*. Hove: Lawrence Erlbaum.

Goodman, K. 1967. "Reading: A Psycholinguistic Guessing Game". *Journal of the Reading Specialist* 6: 126–135.

Goulden, R., P. Nation and J. Read. 1990. "How Large Can Receptive Vocabulary Be?" *Applied Linguistics* 11: 341–363.

Grabe, W. 1991. "Current Developments in Second Language Reading Research". *TESOL Quarterly* 25: 375–397.

Grice, H. 1975. "Logic and Conversation". In P. Cole and J. Morgan (eds), *Syntax and Semantics Vol. 3: Speech Acts*. New York: Academic Press.

Graves, M. 1987. "The Role of Instruction in Fostering Vocabulary Development". In M. McKeown and M. Curtis (eds).

Haastrup, K. 1991. *Lexical Inferencing Procedures or Talking About Words.* Tübingen: Gunter Narr.

Haastrup, K. 1992. "Approaching Learning Theory from a Different Angle: A Comprehension Perspective on the Integrated Theory of Instructed Learning". *Die Neueren Sprachen* 91: 148–165.

Hall, J. 1995. "(Re)creating our Worlds with Words: A Sociohistorical Perspective of Face-to-face Interaction". *Applied Linguistics* 16: 206–32.

Hammerley, H. 1987. "The Immersion Approach: Litmus Test of Second Language Acquisition through Classroom Communication". *Modern Language Journal* 71: 395–401.

Harley, B., P. Allen, J. Cummins, and M. Swain. 1990. *The Development of Second Language Proficiency.* Cambridge: Cambridge University Press.

Harmer, J. *The Practice of English Language Teaching.* London: Longman.

Harrison, C. *Readability in the Classroom.* Cambridge: Cambridge University Press.

Hatch, E. (ed.). 1978a. *Second Language Acquisition.* Rowley, MA.: Newbury House.

Hatch, E. 1978b. "Discourse Analysis and Second Language Acquisition. In E. Hatch (ed.).

Hatch, E. and C. Brown. 1997. *Vocabulary, Semantics, and Language Education.* Cambridge: Cambridge University Press.

Hatch, E. and H. Farhady. 1982. *Research Design and Statistics for Applied Linguistics.* Rowley, MA: Newbury House.

Henning, G. 1973. "Remembering Foreign Language Vocabulary: Acoustic and Semantic Parameters". *Language Learning* 23: 185–196.

Holley, F. 1973. "A Study of Vocabulary Learning in Context: The Effect of New-word Density in German Reading Materials". *Foreign Language Annals* 6: 339–347.

Holmes, J. and R. Ramos. 1993. "False Friends and Reckless Guessers: Observing Cognate Recognition Strategies. In T. Huckin, M. Haynes, and J. Coady (eds).

Hopkins, D and M. Nettle. 1994. "Second Language Acquisition Research: A Response to Rod Ellis". *ELTJ* 48: 157–161.

Horst, M., T. Cobb and P. Meara. 1998. "Beyond a Clockwork Orange: Acquiring Second Language Vocabulary through Reading". *Reading in a Foreign Language* 11: 207–223.

Horwitz, E. 1987b. "Linguistic and Communicative Competence: Reassessing Foreign Language Aptitude". In B. VanPatten, T. Dvorak and J. Lee (eds).

Huckin, T. and J. Bloch. 1993. Strategies for Inferring Word Meaning in Context: A Cognitive Model". In T. Huckin, M. Haynes, and J. Coady (eds).

Huckin, T., M. Haynes and J. Coady (eds). 1983. *Second Language Reading and Vocabulary Learning*. Norwood, N. J.: Ablex.

Hulstijn, J. 1992. "Retention of Inferred and Given Word Meanings: Experiments in Incidental Vocabulary Learning". In P. Arnaud and H. Bejoint (eds), *Vocabulary and Applied Linguistics*. Basingstoke: MacMillan.

Jamieson, P. The Acquisition of English as a Second Language by Young Tokelau Children Living in New Zealand. Unpublished Ph.D. thesis. Wellington: Victoria University (cited in Nation 1990).

Joe, A. 1998. "What Effects do Text-based Tasks Promoting Generation Have on Incidental Vocabulary Acquisition?" *Applied Linguistics* 19: 357–377.

Johnson, K. 1995. *Understanding Communication in Second Language Classrooms*. Cambridge: Cambridge University Press.

Johnson, K. 1996. *Language Teaching and Skill Learning*. Oxford: Blackwell.

Kachru, J. 1962. "Report on an Investigation into the Teaching of Vocabulary in the First Year of English. *Bulletin of the Central Institute of English* 2: 67–72.

Kadia, K. 1987. "The Effect of Formal Instruction on Monitored and Spontaneous Naturalistic Interlanguage Performance". *TESOL Quarterly* 22: 509–515.

Keenan, E. and B. Schieffelin. 1976. "Topic as a Discourse Notion: A Study of Topic in Conversations of Children and Adults". In C. Li (ed.), *Subject and Topic*. New York: Academic Press.

King, A. 1989. "Effects of Self-questioning Training on College Students' Comprehension of Lectures". *Contemporary Educational Psychology* 14: 4 1–6.

King, A. 1992. "Facilitating Elaborative Learning through Guided Student-generated Questioning". *Educational Psychologist* 27: 111–126.

Kowal, M. and M. Swain. 1994. "Using Collaborative Production Tasks to Promote Students' Language Awareness". *Language Awareness* 3: 73–93.

Krashen, S. 1981. *Second Language Acquisition and Second Language Learning*. Oxford: Pergamon.

Krashen, S. 1982. *Principles and Practice in Second Language Acquisition*. Oxford: Pergamon.

Krashen, S. 1985. *The Input Hypothesis*. London: Longman.

Krashen, S. 1989. "We Acquire Vocabulary and Spelling by Reading: Additional Evidence for the Input Hypothesis". *Modern Language Journal* 73: 440–464.

Krashen, S. 1994. "The Input Hypothesis and its Rivals". In N. Ellis (ed.), *Implicit and Explicit Learning of Languages*. London: Academic Press.

Krashen, S. 1998. "Comprehensible Output?" *System* 26: 175–182.

Lantolf, J. 1996. "Second Language Acquisition Theory-building: 'Letting all the Flowers Bloom!'" *Language Learning* 46: 713–749.

Lantolf, J. 2000a. "Introducing Sociocultural Theory". In J. Lantolf (ed).

Lantolf, J. 2000b. *Sociocultural Theory and Second Language Learning*. Oxford: Oxford University Press.

Lantolf, J. and A. Aljaafreh. 1995. "Second Language Learning in the Zone of Proximal Development: A Revolutionary Experience". *International Journal of Educational Research* 23: 619–632.

Lantolf, J. and G. Appel. 1994. *Vygotskian Approaches to Second Language Research*. Norwood, NJ: Ablex.

Lantolf, P. and A. Pavlenko. 1995. "Sociocultural Theory and Second Language Acquisition". *Annual Review of Applied Linguistics* 15: 108–124.

LaPierre, D. 1994. Language Output in a Cooperative Learning Setting: Determining its Effects on Second Language Learning. MA Thesis. Toronto: University of Toronto (OISE).

Larsen-Freeman, D. and M. Long. 1991. *An Introduction to Second Language Acquisition Research*. London: Longman.

Laufer, B. 1997. "The Lexical Plight in Second Language Reading: Words you Don't Know, Words you Think you Know, and Words you can't Guess". In J. Coady and T. Huckin (eds).

Leow, R. 1997. "Attention, Awareness, and Foreign Language Behavior". *Language Learning* 47: 467–506.

Li, D. 1998. "'It's Always More Difficult Than You Plan and Imagine'": Teachers' Perceived Difficulties in Introducing the Communicative Approach in South Korea. *TESOL Quarterly* 32: 677–703.

Li, X. 1989. "Effects of Contextual Cues on Inferring and Remembering Meanings of New Words". *Applied Linguistics* 10: 402–413.

Lightbown, P. and N. Spada. 1990. "Focus-on-form and Corrective Feedback in Communicative Language Teaching: Effects on Second Language Learning". *Studies in Second Language Acquisition* 12: 429–448.

Lightbown, P., N. Spada, and R. Wallace. 1980. "Some Effects of Instruction on Child and Adolescent ESL learners". In R. Scarcella and S. Krashen (eds).

Linnell, J. 1995. "Can Negotiation Provide a Context for Learning Syntax in a Second Language? *Working Papers in Educational Linguistics* 11: 83–103.

Long, M. 1980. Input, Interaction and Second Language Acquisition. Unpublished Ph. D. dissertation: University of California at Los Angeles.

Long, M. 1981. "Input, Interaction and Second Language Acquisition". In H. Winitz (ed), *Native Language and Foreign Language Acquisition*. Annals of the New York Academy of Sciences 379.

Long, M. 1983b. "Native Speaker/non-native Speaker Conversation in the Second Language Classroom". In M. Clarke and J. Handscombe (eds), *On TESOL '82: Pacific Perspectives on Language and Teaching*. Washington DC.: TESOL.

Long, M. 1983a. "Native Speaker/Non-native Speaker Conversation and the Negotiation of Comprehensible Input". *Applied Linguistics* 4: 126–41.

Long, M. 1985. "Input and Second Language Acquisition Theory". In S. Gass and C. Madden (eds).

Long, M. 1988. "Instructed Interlanguage Development". In L. Beebe (ed.), *Issues in Second Language Acquisition*. Rowley, Mass: Newbury House.

Long, M. 1991. "Focus on Form: A Design Feature in Language Teaching Methodology". In K. de Bot, R. Ginsberg, and C. Kramsch (eds), *Foreign Language Research in Cross-Cultural Perspective* (pp. 39–52). Amsterdam: John Benjamins.

Long, M. 1996. "The Role of the Linguistic Environment in Second Language Acquisition". In W. Ritchie and T. Bhatia (eds), *Handbook of Second Language Acquisition*. San Diego: Academic Press.

Long, M., S. Inagaki and L. Ortega. 1998. "The Role of Implicit Negative Feedback in SLA: Models and Recasts in Japanese and Spanish". *The Modern Language Journal* 82: 357–371.

Long, M. and P. Porter. 1985. "Group Work, Interlanguage Talk, and Second Language Acquisition". *TESOL Quarterly* 19: 207–228.

Long, M. and C. Sato. 1983. "Classroom Foreigner Talk Discourse: Forms and Functions of Teachers' Questions". In H. Seliger and M. Long (eds).

Loschky, L. 1994. "Comprehensible Input and Second Language Acquisition: What is the Relationship?" *Studies in Second Language Acquisition* 16: 303–23.

Loschky, L. and R. Bley-Vroman. 1993. "Grammar and Task-based Methodology". In Crookes, G. and S. Gass (eds).

Lyster, R. and L. Ranta. 1997. Corrective Feedback and Learner Uptake: Negotiation of Form in Communicative Classrooms. *Studies in Second Language Acquisition* 19: 37–66.

MacIntyre, P. and R. Gardner. 1991a. Methods and Results in the Study of Foreign Language Anxiety: A Review of the Literature. *Language Learning* 41: 25–57.

MacIntyre, P. and R. Gardner. 1991b. "Language Anxiety: Its Relationship to Other Anxieties and to Processing in Native and Second Languages". *Language Learning* 41: 513–534.

McLaughlin, B. 1990. "Restructuring". *Applied Linguistics* 11: 113–28.

Mackey, A. 1995. Stepping up the Pace: Input, Interaction and Interlanguage Development. Unpublished Ph.D. dissertation. Sydney: University of Sydney.

Mackey, A. and J. Philp. 1998. "Conversational Interaction and Second Language Development: Recasts, Responses and Red Herrings?" *The Modern Language Journal* 82: 338–356.

Mackey, W. 1962. *Language Teaching Analysis*. London: Longman.

Markee, N. 1994. "Toward an Ethnomethodological Specification of Second-language Acquisition Studies". In S. Gass and J. Schachter (eds), *Issues in Conducting Second Language Classroom Research*. Hillsdale, NJ: Lawrence Erlbaum.

Mayer, R. 1984. "Aids to Prose Comprehension". *Educational Psychologist* 19: 30–42.

McArthur, T. "Where do YOU Stand in the Classroom? A Consideration of Roles, Rules and Priorities in the Language Classroom". In J. Handscombe, R. Orem, and B. Taylor (eds), *On TESOL '83: The Question of Control*. Washington, DC.: TESOL.

McCafferty, S. 1994a. "Adult Second Language Learners' Use of Private Speech: A Review of Studies". *The Modern Language Journal* 78: 421–436.

McCafferty, S. 1994b. "The Use of Private Speech by Adult ESL Learners at Different Levels of Proficiency". In J. Lantolf and G. Appel (eds).

McCarthy, M. 1991. *Discourse Analysis for Language Teachers*. Cambridge: Cambridge University Press.

McCarthy, M. and R. Carter. 1997. "Written and Spoken Vocabulary". In N. Schmitt and M. McCarthy (eds).

McKeown, M. and M. Curtis (eds). 1987. *The Nature of Vocabulary Acquisition*. Hillsdale, NJ: Lawrence Erlbaum.

Meara, P. 1982. "Word Associations in a Foreign Language: A Report on the Birkbeck Vocabulary Project". *Nottingham Linguistic Circular* 11: 29–37.

Meara, P. 1984. "The Study of Lexis in Interlanguage". In A. Davies, C. Criper and A. Howatt (eds), *Interlanguage*. Edinburgh: Edinburgh University Press.

Meara, P. 1992. "Network Structures and Vocabulary Acquisition". In P. Arnaud and H. Bejoint (eds).

Meara, P. 1997. "Towards a New Approach to Modelling Vocabulary Acquisition". In N. Schmitt and M McCarthy (eds).

Mitchell, R. 1988. *Communicative Language Teaching*. London: Centre for English Language Teaching.

Mito, K. 1993. The Effects of Modelling and Recasting on the Acquisition of L2 Grammar Rules. Unpublished manuscript, Hawaii: University of Hawaii at Manoa.

Nagy, W. 1997. "On the Role of Context in First- and Second-language Vocabulary Learning". In R. Schmitt and M. McCarthy (eds).

Nagy, W., R. Anderson and P. Herman. 1987. "Learning Word Meanings from Context During Normal Reading". *American Educational Research Journal* 24: 237–270.

Nagy, W., G. Garcia, A. Durgunoglu. and B. Hancin-Bhatt. 1993. "Spanish-English Bilingual Students' Use of Cognates in English Reading". *Journal of Reading Behavior* 25: 241–259.

Nagy, W. and D. Gentner 1990. "Semantic Constraints on Lexical Categories". *Language and Cognitive Processes* 5: 169–201.

Nagy, W., P. Herman and R. Anderson. 1985. "Learning Words from Context. Reading". *Research Quarterly* 20: 233–253.

Nagy, W. and J. Scott. 1990. "Word Schemas: Expectations About the Form and Meaning of New Words". *Cognition and Instruction* 7: 105–127.

Nation, P. 1990. *Teaching and Learning Vocabulary*. New York: Newbury House/Harper Row.

Nobuyoshi, J. and R. Ellis. 1993. "Focussed Communication Tasks". *English Language Teaching Journal* 47:203–210.

Nunan, D. 1989. *Designing Tasks for the Communicative Classroom*. Cambridge: Cambridge University Press.

Nunan, D. 1991. "Methods in Second Language Classroom-oriented Research: A Critical Review". *Studies in Second Language Acquisition* 13: 249–274.

Ohta, A. 1995. "Applying Socio-cultural Theory to an Analysis of Learner Discourse: Learner-learner Collaborative Interaction in the Zone of Proximal Development". *Issues in Applied Linguistics* 6: 93–122.

Ohta, A. 2000. "Rethinking Interaction in SLA: Developmentally Appropriate Assistance in the Zone of Proximal Development and the Acquisition of L2 Grammar". In J. Lantolf (ed).

O'Malley. J. 1987. "The Effects of Training on the Use of Learning Strategies on Acquiring English as a Second Language". In A. Wenden and J. Rubin (eds), *Learner Strategies for Language Learning*. Englewood Cliffs, NJ: Prentice Hall.

O'Malley, J. and A. Chamot. 1990. *Learning Strategies in Second Language Acquisition*. Cambridge: Cambridge University Press.

Oxford, R. 1990. *Language Learning Strategies: What Every Teacher Should Know*. Rowley, Mass: Newbury House.

Oxford, R. 1992. "Who are our Students? A Synthesis of Foreign and Second Language Research on Individual Differences with Implications for Instructional Practice". *TESL Canada Journal* 9: 30–49.

Palmberg, R. 1987. "Patterns of Vocabulary Development in Foreign Language Learners". *Studies in Second Language Acquisition* 9: 201–219.

Paribakht, T. and M. Wesche. 1997. "Vocabulary Enhancement Activities and Reading for Meaning in Second Language Vocabulary Acquisition". In J. Coady and T. Huckin (eds).

Parker, K. and C. Chaudron. 1987. "The Effects of Linguistic Simplifications and Elaborative Modifications of L2 Comprehension". *University of Hawaii Working Papers in ESL* 6: 107–133.

Patterson, C. and M. Kister. 1981. "The Development of Listener Skills for Referential Communication". In W. Dickson (ed.), *Children's Oral Communication Skills*. New York: Academic Press.

Philp, J. 1999. Interaction, Noticing and Second Language Acquisition: An Examination of Learners' Noticing Recasts in Task-based Interaction. Unpublished Ph. D. dissertation. University of Tasmania.

Pica, T. 1983. "Adult Acquisition of English as a Second Language under Different Conditions of Exposure". *Language Learning* 33: 465–97.

Pica, T. 1987. "Second Language Acquisition, Social Interaction in the Classroom". *Applied Linguistics* 7: 1–25.

Pica, T. 1988. "Interlanguage Adjustments as an Outcome of NS-NNS Negotiated Interaction". *Language Learning* 38: 45–73.

Pica, T. 1991. "Classroom Interaction, Participation, and Comprehension: Redefining Relationships". *System* 19: 437–452.

Pica, T. 1992. "The Textual Outcomes of Native Speaker-non-native Speaker Negotiation: What do They Reveal about Second Language Learning". In C. Kramsch and S. McConnell-Ginet (eds), *Text and Context: Cross-Disciplinary Perspectives on Language Study*. Lexington, Mass.: D. C. Heath and Company.

Pica, T. 1994. "Research on Negotiation: What does it Reveal about Second-language Learning Conditions, Processes, and Outcomes?" *Language Learning* 44: 493–527.

Pica, T. 1996a. "Second Language Learning through Interaction: Multiple Perspectives". *Working Papers in Educational Linguistics* 12: 1–22.

Pica, T. 1996b. "The Essential Role of Negotiation in the Communicative Classroom". *JALT Journal* 78: 241–268.

Pica, T. and C. Doughty. 1985b. "The Role of Group Work in Classroom Second Language Acquisition". *Studies in Second language Acquisition* 7: 233–48.

Pica, T., L. Holliday, N. Lewis and L. Morgenthaler. 1989. "Comprehensible Output as an Outcome of Linguistic Demands on the Learner". *Studies in Second Language Acquisition* 11: 63–90.

Pica, T., R. Young, and C. Doughty. 1987. "The Impact of Interaction on Comprehension". *TESOL Quarterly* 21: 737–58.

Pienemann, M. 1984. "Psychological Constraints on the Teachability of Languages". *Studies in Second Language Acquisition* 6: 186–214.

Pimsleur, P. 1966. *The Pimsleur Language Aptitude Battery*. New York: Harcourt Brace Jovanovich.

Pitts, M., H. White and S. Krashen. 1989. "Acquiring Second Language Vocabulary through Reading: A Replication of the 'Clockwork Orange' Study Using Second Language Acquirers". *Reading in a Foreign Language* 5: 271–275.

Polio, C. and S. Gass. 1998. "The Role of Interaction in Native Speaker Comprehension of Nonnative Speaker Speech". *The Modern Language Journal* 82: 308–319.

Porter, P. 1986. "How Learners Talk to Each Other: Input and Interaction in Task-centred Discussions. In R. Day (ed.).

Prabhu, N. S. 1987. *Second Language Pedagogy*. Oxford: Oxford University Press.

Pressley, M., J. Levin and M. McDaniel. 1987. "Remembering Versus Inferring What a Word Means: Mnemonic and Contextual Approaches". In M. McKeown and M. Curtis (eds).

Pressley, M., M. McDaniel, J. Turnure, E. Wood and M. Ahmad. 1987. "Generation and Precision of Elaboration: Effects on Intentional and Incidental Learning". *Journal of Experimental Psychology: Learning, Memory and Cognition* 13: 191–300.

Quinn, G. 1968. The English Vocabulary of Some Indonesian University Students. *IKIP Kristen Satya Watjana, Salatiga* (cited in Nation 1990).

Reid, J. 1987. "The Learning Style Preferences of ESL Students". *TESOL Quarterly* 21: 87–111.

Richards, J. 1976. "The Role of Vocabulary Teaching". *TESOL Quarterly* 10: 77–89.

Richardson, M. 1993. *Negative Evidence and Grammatical Morpheme Acquisition: Implications for SLA*. Graduate School of Education, Perth: University of Western Australia.

Robinson, P. 1993. "Procedural and Declarative Knowledge in Vocabulary Learning: Communication and the Learner's Lexicon. In T. Huckin, M. Haynes, and J. Coady (eds).

Robinson, P. 1995. "Attention, Memory, and the 'Noticing' Hypothesis". *Language Learning* 45: 283–331.

Rodgers, T. 1969. "On Measuring Vocabulary Difficulty: An Analysis of Item Variables in Learning Russian-English Vocabulary Pairs". *IRAL* 7: 327–342.

Rosch, E. 1975. "Cognitive Representations of Semantic Categories". *Journal of Experimental Psychology: General* 104: 192–233.

Rost, M. 1990. *Listening in Language Learning*. London: Longman.

Rulon, K. and J. McCreary. 1986. "Negotiation of Content: Teacher-fronted and Small Group Interaction". In R. Day (ed.).

Saragi, T., L. Nation, and G. Master. 1978. "Vocabulary Learning and Reading". *System* 6: 72–88.

Sasaki, M. 1993. "Relationships among Second Language Proficiency, Foreign Language Aptitude, and Intelligence: A Structural Equation Modelling Approach. *Language Learning* 43: 313–344.

Sato, C. 1996. "Conversation and Interlanguage Development: Rethinking the Connection". In R. Day (ed).

Sawyer, M. 1993. The Modern Language Aptitude Test: A Rasch Analysis of its Behavior with Native and Non-native Populations. Unpublished paper. Hawaii: University of Hawaii at Manoa.

Scarcella, R. and C. Higa. 1981. "Input, Negotiation and Age Differences in Second Language Acquisition". *Language Learning* 31: 409–307.

Scarcella, R. and S. Krashen (eds). 1980. *Research in Second Language Acquisition*. Rowley, MA.: Newbury House.

Schegloff, E., G. Jefferson and H. Sacks. 1977. "The Preference for Self-correction in the Organization of Repair in Conversation". *Language* 53: 361–92.

Schmidt, R. 1990. "The Role of Consciousness in Second Language Learning". *Applied Linguistics* 11: 129–58.

Schmidt, R. 1994. "Deconstructing Consciousness in Search of Useful Definitions for Applied Linguistics". *AILA Review* 11: 11–26.

Schmidt, R. 1995. "Consciousness and Foreign Language Learning: A Tutorial on the Role of Attention and Awareness in Learning". In R. Schmidt (ed.).

Schmidt, R. (ed). 1995. *Attention, Awareness in Foreign Language Learning.* Honolulu: University of Hawaii Press.

Schmidt, E. and S. Frota. 1986. "Developing Basic Conversational Ability in a Second Language: A Case-study of an Adult Learner". In R. Day (ed.).

Schmitt, N. and M. McCarthy (eds). 1997. *Vocabulary: Description, Acquisition and Pedagogy.* Cambridge: Cambridge University Press.

Schumann, J. 1978. *The Pidginization Process: A Model for Second Language Acquisition.* Rowley, Mass.: Newbury House.

Seliger, H. and M. Long (eds). 1983. *Classroom-Oriented Research in Second Language Acquisition.* Rowley, MA: Newbury House.

Sfard, A.1998. "On Two Metaphors for Learning and the Dangers of Choosing Just One". *Educational Researcher* 27: 4–13.

Sharwood Smith, M. 1981. "Consciousness-raising and the Second Language Learner". *Applied Linguistics* 2: 159–69.

Sharwood Smith M. 1986. "Comprehension vs. Acquisition: Two Ways of Processing Input". *Applied Linguistics* 7: 239–56.

Skehan, P. 1982. Memory and Motivation in Language Aptitude Testing. Unpublished Ph. D. thesis. University of London.

Skehan, P. 1986. "Where Does Language Aptitude Come From?" In P. Meara (ed.), *Spoken Language.* London: Centre for Information on Language Teaching.

Skehan, P. 1989. *Individual Differences in Second Language Learning.* London: Edward Arnold.

Skehan, P. 1990. "The Relationship between Native and Foreign Language Learning Ability: Educational and Linguistic Factors". In H. Dechert (ed.), *Current Trends in European Second language Acquisition Research.* Clevedon, Avon: Multilingual Matters.

Skehan, P. 1991. "Individual Differences in Second Language Learning". *Studies in Second Language Acquisition* 13: 275–298.

Skehan, P. 1996. "Second Language Acquisition Research and Task-based Instruction". In J. Willis and D. Willis (eds), *Challenge and Change in Language Teaching.* Oxford: Heinemann.

Skehan, P. 1998. *A Cognitive Approach to Language Learning.* Oxford: Oxford University Press.

Skehan, P. and P. Foster. 1997. "Task Type and Task Processing Conditions as Influences on Foreign Language Performance". *Language Teaching Research* 1: 185–211.

Slimani, A. 1989. "The Role of Topicalization in Classroom Language Learning". *System* 17: 223–234.

Smith, F. 1978. *Understanding Reading*, 2nd Edition. New York: Holt, Rinehart and Winston.

Snow, C., R. van Eeden and P. Muysken. 1981. "The Interactional Origins of Foreigner Talk". *Interactional Journal of Sociology of Language* 28: 81–92.

Spada, N. 1997. "Form-focused Instruction and Second Language Acquisition: A Review of Classroom and Laboratory Research". *Language Teacher* 30: 73–87.

Sparks, R., L. Ganschow and J. Patton. 1995. "Prediction of Performance in First-year Foreign Language Courses: Connections between Native and Foreign Language Learning". *Journal of Educational Psychology* 87: 638–655.

Stanovich, K. 1980. "Toward an Interactive-compensatory Model of Individual Differences in the Development of Reading Fluency". *Reading Research Quarterly* 15: 10–29.

Stansfield, C. and L. Hansen. 1983. "Field-dependence-independence as a Variable in Second Language Cloze Test Performance". *TESOL Quarterly* 17: 29–38.

Stein, M. 1993. "The Healthy Inadequacy of Contextual Definition". In T. Huckin, M. Haynes, and J. Coady (eds).

Stenhouse. 1975. *An Introduction to Curriculum Research and Development*. London: Heinemann.

Sternberg, R. 1967. "Most Vocabulary is Learned from Context". In M. McKeown and M. Curtis (eds).

Stoller, F. and W. Grabe. 1993. "Implications for L2 Vocabulary Acquisition and Instruction from L1 Vocabulary Research". In T. Huckin, M. Haynes, and J. Coady (eds).

Stevick, E. 1993. "Social Meanings for How we Teach". In J. Alatis (ed.), *Georgetown University Round table on Language and Linguistics 1992: Language, Communications and Social Meaning*. Washington, DC: Georgetown University Press.

Swain, M. 1985. "Communicative Competence: Some Roles of Comprehensible Input and Comprehensible Output in its Development". In S. Gass and C. Madden (eds.).

Swain, M. 1995. "Three Functions of Output in Second Language Learning". In G. Cook and B. Seidlhofer (eds), *For H. G. Widdowson: Principles and Practice in the Study of Language*. Oxford: Oxford University Press.

Swain, M. 2000. "The Output Hypothesis and Beyond: Mediating Acquisition through Collaboration". In J. Lantolf (ed.).

Swain, M. and S. Lapkin. 1998. "Interaction and Second Language Learning: Two Adolescent French Immersion Students Working Together". *The Modern Language Journal* 82: 320–337.

Takashima, H. 1995. A Study of Focused Feedback, or Output Enhancement, in Promoting Accuracy in Communication Activities. Unpublished doctoral dissertation. Tokyo: Temple University Japan.

Tharp, R. and R. Gallimore. 1988. *Rousing Minds to Life: Teaching, Learning, and Schooling in Social Context*. New York: Cambridge University Press.

Tsui, A. 1996. "Reticence and Anxiety in Second Language Learning". In K. Bailey and D. Nunan (eds), *Voices from the Classroom*. Cambridge: Cambridge University Press.

Tudor, L. and F. Hafiz. 1989. "Extensive Reading as a Means of Input to L2 Learning". *Journal of Research in Reading* 12: 164–178.

Twadell, F. 1973. "Vocabulary Expansion in the TESOL Classroom". *TESOL Quarterly* 7: 61–78.

Ur, P. 1988. *Grammar Practice Activities*. Cambridge: Cambridge University Press.

Ur, P. 1996. *A Course in Language Teaching*. Cambridge: Cambridge University Press.

Van den Branden, K. 1997. "Effects of Negotiation on Language Learners' Output". *Language Learning* 47: 589–636.

Van Lier, L. 1988. *The Classroom and the Language Learner*. London: Longman.

Van Lier, L. 1991. "Inside the Classroom: Learning Processes and Teaching Procedures". *Applied Language Learning* 2: 29–69.

Van Lier, L. 1996. *Interaction in the Language Curriculum*. London: Longman.

VanPatten, B. 1990. "Attending to Content and Form in the Input: An Experiment in Consciousness". *Studies in Second Language Acquisition* 12: 287–301.

VanPatten, B. 1993. "Grammar Teaching for the Acquisition-rich Classroom". *Foreign Language Annals* 26: 435–450.

VanPatten, B., T. Dvorak and J. Lee (eds) 1987. *Foreign Language Learning: a Research Perspective*. Rowley, MA: Newbury House.

VanPatten, B. and C. Sanz 1995. "From Input to Output: Processing Instruction and Communicative Tasks". In F. Eckman, D. Highland, P. Lee, J. Mileham, and R. Weber (eds.), *Second Language Acquisition Theory and Pedagogy*. Mahwah, NJ.: Lawrence Erlbaum.

Varonis, E. and S. Gass. 1985. "Non-native/Non-native Conversations: A Model for Negotiation of Meaning". *Applied Linguistics* 6: 71–90.

Vygotsky, L. 1978. *Mind and Society: The Development of Higher Psychological Processes*. Cambridge, Mass: Harvard University Press.

Vygotsky, L. 1981. "The Genesis of Higher Mental Functions". In J. Wertsch (ed), *The Concept of Activity in Soviet Psychology*. Armonk, NY: M. E. Sharpe.

Wagner-Gough, J. 1975. "Comparative Studies in Second Language Learning". *CAL-ERIC/CLL Series on Language and Linguistics* 26.

Wajnryb, R. 1990. *Grammar Dictation*. Oxford: Oxford University Press.

Watanabe, Y. 1997. "Input, Intake, and Retention: Effects of Increased Processing on Incidental Learning of Foreign Language Vocabulary". *Studies in Second Language Acquisition* 19: 287–307.

Wells, G. 1985. *Language Development in the Pre-school* Years. Cambridge: Cambridge University Press.

Wells, G. 1986. *The Meaning Makers: Children Learning Language and Using Language to Learn*. London: Hodder and Stoughton.

Wells, G. 1998. "Using L1 to Master L2: A Response to Anton and DiCamilla's Socio-cognitive Functions of L1 Collaborative Interaction in the L2 Classroom". *The Canadian Modern Language Review* 54: 343–353.

Wells, G. and M. Montgomery. 1981. "Adult-child Interaction at Home and at School". In P. French and M. McLure (eds), *Adult-child Conversation*. New York: St Martin's Press.

Wesche, M. 1981. "Language Aptitude Measures in Streaming, Matching Students with Methods, and Diagnosis of Learning Problems". In K. Diller (ed.).

West, M. 1955. *Learning to Read in a Foreign Language*. London: Longman.

White, L. 1987. "Against Comprehensible Input: The Input Hypothesis and the Development of Second Language Competence". *Applied Linguistics* 8: 95–110.

White, L. 1989. *Universal Grammar and Second Language Acquisition*. Amsterdam: John Benjamins.

Widdowson, H. 1978. *Teaching Language as Communication*. Oxford: Oxford University Press.

Widdowson, H. 1979a. "The Process and Purpose of Reading". In H. Widdowson. *Explorations in Applied Linguistics*. Oxford: Oxford University Press.

Widdowson, H. 1979b. "The Authenticity of Language Data". In H. Widdowson, *Explorations in Applied Linguistics*. Oxford: Oxford University Press.

Widdowson, H. 1984. "Reading and Communication". In H. Widdowson, *Explorations in Applied Linguistics 2*. Oxford: Oxfxord University Press.

Willing, K. 1987. *Learning Styles and Adult Migrant Education*. Adelaide: National Curriculum Resource Centre.

Willis, J. 1992. "Inner and Outer: Spoken Discourse in the Language Classroom". In R. Coulthard (ed.), *Advances in Spoken Discourse*. London: Routledge.

Wittrock, M. 1974. "Learning as a Generative Process". *Educational Pyschologist* 11: 87–95.

Wittrock, M. 1990. "Generative Processes in Comprehension". *Educational Pyschologist* 24: 345–376.

Wittrock, M. and J. Carter. 1975. "Generative Processing of Hierarchically Organized Words". *American Journal of Psychology* 88: 489–501.

Wittrock, M., C. Marks and M. Docotrow. 1975. "Reading as a Generative Process". *Journal of Educational Psychology* 67: 484–489.

Wode, H., A. Rohde, F. Gassen, B. Weiss, M. Jekat, and P. Young. 1992. "L1, L2, L3: Continuity vs. Discontinuity in Lexical Acquisition". In P. Arnaud and H. Bejoint (eds).

Wong, B. 1985. "Self-questioning Instructional Research: A Review". *Review of Educational Research* 55: 227–268.

Wood, D., J. Bruner and G. Ross. 1976. "The Role of Tutoring in Problem Solving". *Journal of Child Psychology and Psychiatry* 17: 89–100.

Yoshida, M. 1978. "The Acquisition of English Vocabulary by a Japanese-speaking Child". In E. Hatch (ed).

Yule, G. and D. McDonald. 1990. "Resolving Referential Conflicts in L2 Interaction: The Effect of Proficiency and Interactive Role". *Language Learning* 40: 539–556.

Zobl, H. 1985. "Grammars in Search of Input and Intake". In S. Gass and C. Madden (eds), *Input in Second Language Acquisition*. Rowley, Mass: Newbury House.

Index

A

Academic task structures   220, 222
Acquisition, definition of   233–5
Acquisition-rich classroom   Chapter
   9, 247–254
Activity vs. task   129–30, 131 (n. 1),
   132 (n. 6), 236
Affective filter   240
Attention   35–6, 154, 155, 166, 167,
   175, 221, 241, 250, 254
Authenticity   249
Auto-input   176, 181

B

Background knowledge   53, 59
Basic interpersonal communication
   skills (BICS)   137, 138, 147
Bottom-up processing   152, 153, 154,
   155

C

Child L2 learners   15, 83–5, 91–95
Clarification requests   11, 12, 51, 70,
   73, 98, 104, 110, 116, 121,
   172–4, 175, 176, 177, 179, 185,
   186, 187, 188 (n. 1, n. 9), 193,
   197, 215, 218, 223, 250, 254,
Classroom language   200–2, 211–19,
   247–53
Cognates   57, 59
Cognitive academic language
   proficiency (CALP)   137, 138, 147

Collaborative problem solving   31
   (n. 6)
Communicative language teaching
   193–4, 248
Complexity (*see* input complexity)
Comprehensible input   5, 80, 83,
   109–8, 112, 171, 189, 193, 223,
   235, 240, 243
Comprehensible output (*see* Output
   and Output Hypothesis)
Comprehension   5–6, 60, 66, 72–5,
   77–8, 79–80, 89–90, 93–5,
   101–2, 105, 107–8, 111, 112,
   122, 123, 127–8, 142, 143, 144,
   146, 148, 154, 160, 164, 167,
   240–1, 257 (n. 5)
Comprehension checks   73, 98, 197,
   201
Computational metaphor/model
   16–17, 19, 234, 235, 255
Confirmation requests   4, 6, 11, 12,
   73, 98, 174, 197, 204, 215
Consciousness-raising   192, 194–5,
   206, 254
Contextual clues   48–50, 59, 155
Conversational adjustments   (*see*
   input and interactional
   modifications)
Cooperative principle   152

D

Dative verbs   195, 196, 208, 254

Declarative knowledge   234
Definitions   52, 98–100, 104, 105,
   107, 111, 121, 130, 251
Density of unknown words   50–1
Depth of processing theory   2, 26–29,
   156, 236, 243, 253, 255, 256
Developmental sequence   190, 191
Dictogloss   22, 255, 257 (n. 11)
Discourse control   210, 211, 214–29,
   251
Discourse topic   211

E
Elaboration of input   7, 51–2, 59,
   98–99, 109–110, 112, 242
Elaborative interrogation   28
Ethnomethodology   3, 17
Explicit L2 knowledge   172, 190,
   191–3, 195, 196, 203, 205, 234,
   237, 255, 256 (n. 7)
Explicit learning (see Implicit vs.
   explicit learning)
External view of teaching   209–10,
   225, 247

F
Fast-mapping   84–5
Fluency vs. accuracy   184
Focus-on-form   187
Focussed negotiation   177, 183–4,
   187, 188 (n. 8), 254
Foreignizing   57
Frequency (see word frequency)

G
Generative model of learning   27–8,
   152–3, 253
Grammar learning   Chapters 7 and 8,
Grammar teaching   254–5
Grammaticality judgement test   196,
   208
Grammaticalization   13
Group work   92, 194, 204, 205, 226

Guided generative output   156, 160,
   164

H
Hidden curriculum   210
Hierarchical model of text content
   160–1

I
Imageability   45, 58
Immediate phonological memory   56,
   59
Implicit L2 knowledge   190, 191–2,
   206, 234, 235, 237, 255, 256
   (n. 1)
Implicit vs. explicit learning   233,
   235, 256 (n. 1)
Improvisation in teaching   228, 229
Incidental acquisition   4, 33, 25–6,
   45, 49, 58, 60, 106, 117, 145,
   146, 147, 155, 165, 168, 233,
   235, 254
Inferencing   37, 49, 55, 155, 167
Information gap (see Tasks)
Information processing models   8,
   147–8, 154, 233, 250
Inner speech   20
Input
   Baseline (unmodified)   66, 72
   Comprehensible (see
      Comprehensible input)
   Complexity   50, 59, 72, 78, 100
   Elaborated (see elaboration of
      input)
Input-interaction variables   97–100,
   102
Input-output model   ix, 16
   Interactionally modified   4, 6, 7,
      51, 66, 71–2, 78, 79, 81, 83,
      96, 98, 101–5, 110-11, 112,
      121, 123–130, 171, 195, 206,
      241–43

(pre)Modified   4, 5, 6, 7, 8, 50,
    66, 71–2, 78, 99, 107–8,
    110–1, 112, 120, 123–30, 142,
    146, 167, 171, 176, 241–44,
    249
  Oral vs. written   37
Input Hypothesis   5, 13, 108, 115,
    130, 186, 239–40, 241
Input processing instruction   147, 250
Instruction   48, 156, 159–60, 164–5,
    190–3, 225–229, 247–55
Instructional conversation   19, 22
Intake   234, 235, 236, 239, 256 (n. 3)
Intelligence   53, 138
Intentional acquisition   4, 35–6, 45,
    49, 60, 106, 117, 145, 165, 233,
    235
Interactional modifications (see Input,
    interactionally modified)
Interaction, definition of   1, 3
Interaction Hypothesis   2, 3–16, 73,
    111, 112–3, 115, 130, 171, 172,
    190, 193, 206, 223, 224, 235,
    239, 241, 246, 256
Interactionist perspective   30
Internal view of teaching   209–10,
    247
IRF exchanges   216–7, 220, 226

K
Knowledge vs. control   234, 235

L
Language aptitude   34, 133, 134–9,
    149 (n. 4)
Language-related episode   116, 257
    (n. 11)
Language transfer   56–7, 59
Learner-centred approach   133
Learner factors   53–57, Chapter 5,
    238
Lexical density   50, 98, 104, 107, 111
Lexical domain   54

Linguistic coding deficit hypothesis
    148 (n. 1)
Listening   38, 147, 148, 185

M
Metacognitive strategy   153, 159, 253
Mediation   17–18, 25, 29, 239, 246
Memory   95, 135, 140–1, 147, 148,
    154
Microgenesis/microgentic method   17,
    24, 25, 172, 238, 244
Modern Language Aptitude Test   134,
    135
Monitoring   192, 255
Mother-child talk   214–6

N
Negative evidence/feedback   9–10,
    11, 171–2, 236–7
Negotiation of meaning   3–4, 5, 6, 7,
    8, 12, 14, 15, 29, 37, 51, 52, 55,
    56, 66, 77, 78–9, 80, 82, 84,
    88–95, 115–6, 121, 122, 167–8,
    172, 177, 193, 194, 195–6,
    200–2, 203–5, 223, 226, 239,
    245-6, 251, 257 (n. 7)
negotiation styles   16
non-reciprocal tasks (see tasks)
noticing   8, 9, 35, 37, 81, 154, 155,
    166, 185, 191, 234, 236, 241,
    246, 255, 256 (n. 3)

O
object regulation 20, 25
optimal conditions for L2 acquisition
    221
outer vs. inner classroom language
    213–4, 227
output
    comprehensible   1,12, 115–132,
    175
    enhancement of   173–4, 175,
    184–6, 187, 254

frequency of forms in 166–7
modified 9, 11–13, 116, 122,
123–30, 132 (n. 7), 172,
173–4, 186, 193, 204, 243–4,
245
Output Hypothesis 13, 115, 130,
172, 174–5, 186, 193
Overgeneralization error 174, 175,
176, 177

P

Participation, role in acquisition of
(*see also* Practice) 245–7, 257
(n. 7)
Part of speech 43, 58
Past tense, acquisition of 176–7, 254
Phatic communication 212
Pimsleur Language Aptitude Battery
134, 135
Polysemy 45, 58
Positive evidence/feedback 8, 236–7
Practice 191, 192, 206
Principle of Continuous Access 21
Private speech 1, 20, 23–4, 25, 29,
239, 252
Procedural knowledge 55–6, 31
(n. 7), 234
Pronounceability of words 42–3, 58
Pseudo vs. free classroom language
214, 216, 217
Psycholinguistic guessing game 151

Q

Question types (*see* Teacher questions)

R

Range (*see* word form)
Rate of acquisition 101, 107, 165
Reading 36, 60, 151–4, 160–1,
248–9
Recasts 9–11, 12, 171–2, 175, 188,
256 (n. 2)
Reciprocal tasks (*see* tasks)

Redundancy 71, 78, 79, 113, 177
Referential communication paradigm
84
Repetitions 197, 251
Restructuring 175, 234

S

Scaffolding 19, 21–23, 115, 116,
129, 130, 224–5, 226, 246, 251
Self-corrections (*see also* Monitoring)
184–5
Self-questioning strategy 28, 29, 151,
153, 154, 155, 156, 159–60,
164–7, 252–3
Self-regulation 20, 25, 252
Skill-building theory 186
Social participation structures 220
Social perspective in SLA 16–17
Sociocultural theory ix, 2, 15, 16–26,
115, 116, 129–30, 131, 172,
224–5, 234-5, 236, 244, 246,
251, 256
Socio-historical theory 229, 237
Synforms 44

T

Talking circle 218, 227
Tasks
Bugs and Birds Task 87
Closed vs. open 194
Consciousness-raising (*see*
Consciousness-raising)
Convergent vs. divergent 194
Grammar 188–90, 194–5, 202–8
Furniture Task 120
Kitchen Task 65, 69, 142
Information transfer 65
Interactivity of 67
Non-reciprocal (one-way) 63–67,
82, 87–8, 113 (n. 5), 120, 139,
225, 226–7, 228, 235, 248,
250–1
Planned vs. unplanned 194, 227

Reciprocal (two-way)   193, 225,
    248
Response manner   67
Time on   116–7, 128
Task-based approach   193–4, 225–7,
    248
Teacher questions   153, 162, 216,
    218, 257 (n. 10)
Teacher talk   216–9
Tests   69–70, 87, 108, 118, 119–20,
    134–6, 140–2, 145, 148-9 (n. 2),
    157–9, 178–9, 195–6, 197, 208,
    237
Top-down processing   151–2, 153,
    154, 155
Topic control (*see* Discourse control)
Topicalization   217, 220, 222
Topic vs. activity   212–3, 215, 225
Transcription conventions   114 (n. 8)
Transitional constructions   175

U
Unequal encounters   214
Universal Grammar   ix, 30, 236
Uptake   97, 100, 104, 109, 110, 174,
    222, 237
Use vs. acquisition   237

V
Vertical constructions   18

Vocabulary
    Breadth   38–39
    Depth   39–42, 47, 58, 98, 114
        (n. 10), 165
    Implicit vs. explicit   41
    Knowledge vs. control   40–1
    Prototypicality and   114 (n. 11)
    Receptive vs. productive   40, 90,
        93, 113 (n. 4), 122, 124–7
Vocabulary acquisition (*see* Chapters
    2, 3, 4, 5 and 6), 249
Vygotsky   1

W
Word association   41–2, 44–5
Word form
    Distinctiveness   43, 58
    Frequency   46–7, 59, 96, 97–8,
        104, 105, 108, 111, 114
        (n. 12), 155,   249
    Length   44, 58, 97, 104, 105
    Range   98, 103, 104, 105, 108,
        111, 112, 249
    Saliency   47–8, 59, 168 (n. 1)
Word schemas   54

Z
Zone of proximal development
    19–20, 25, 130, 224

In the series STUDIES IN BILINGUALISM (SiBil) ISSN 0298-1533 the following titles have been published thus far or are scheduled for publication:

1. FASE, Willem, Koen JASPAERT and Sjaak KROON (eds): *Maintenance and Loss of Minority Languages.* 1992.
2. BOT, Kees de, Ralph B. GINSBERG and Claire KRAMSCH (eds): *Foreign Language Research in Cross-Cultural Perspective.* 1991.
3. DÖPKE, Susanne: *One Parent - One Language. An interactional approach.* 1992.
4. PAULSTON, Christina Bratt: *Linguistic Minorities in Multilingual Settings. Implications for language policies.*1994.
5. KLEIN, Wolfgang and Clive PERDUE: *Utterance Structure. Developing grammars again.*
6. SCHREUDER, Robert and Bert WELTENS (eds): *The Bilingual Lexicon.* 1993.
7. DIETRICH, Rainer, Wolfgang KLEIN and Colette NOYAU: *The Acquisition of Temporality in a Second Language.* 1995.
8. DAVIS, Kathryn Anne: *Language Planning in Multilingual Contexts. Policies, communities, and schools in Luxembourg.* Amsterdam/Philadelphia, 1994.
9. FREED, Barbara F. (ed.) *Second Language Acquisition in a Study Abroad Context.* 1995.
10. BAYLEY, Robert and Dennis R. PRESTON (eds): *Second Language Acquisition and Linguistic Variation.* 1996.
11. BECKER, Angelika and Mary CARROLL: *The Acquisition of Spatial Relations in a Second Language.* 1997.
12. HALMARI, Helena: *Government and Codeswitching. Explaining American Finnish.* 1997.
13. HOLLOWAY, Charles E.: *Dialect Death. The case of Brule Spanish.* 1997.
14. YOUNG, Richard and Agnes WEIYUN HE (eds): *Talking and Testing. Discourse approaches to the assessment of oral proficiency.* 1998.
15. PIENEMANN, Manfred: *Language Processing and Second Language Development. Processability theory.* 1998.
16. HUEBNER, Thom and Kathryn A. DAVIS (eds.): *Sociopolitical Perspectives on Language Policy and Planning in the USA.* 1999.
17. ELLIS, Rod: *Learning a Second Language through Interaction.* 1999.
18. PARADIS, Michel: *Neurolinguistic Aspects of Bilingualism.* n.y.p.
19. AMARA, Muhammad Hasan: *Politics and Sociolinguistic Reflexes. Palestinian border villages.* 1999.
20. POULISSE, Nanda: *Slips of the Tongue. Speech errors in first and second language production.* 1999.